Illustrators:
Kathy Bruce
Wendy Chang

Editor:
Evan D. Forbes, M.S. Ed.

Editor-in-Chief:
Sharon Coan, M.S. Ed.

Art Director:
Elayne Roberts

Cover Artist:
Keith Vasconcelles

Imaging:
David Bennett
Hillary Merriman

Product Manager:
Phil Garcia

Publishers:
Rachelle Cracchiolo, M.S. Ed.
Mary Dupuy Smith, M.S. Ed.

Explore Our World
Geography of the Continents

(This book combines seven books in one. A book for each of the seven continents can be purchased separately.)

Author:

Julia Jasmine, M.A.

Teacher Created Materials, Inc.
P.O. Box 1040
Huntington Beach, CA 92647
ISBN-1-55734-664-X

©1995 Teacher Created Materials, Inc.   Made in U.S.A.

Table of Contents

Introduction

What Has Happened to Geography?

Studies made during the last couple of decades show geography as a neglected science, even physical geography, its most traditional form. One of the suspected causes has been the higher priority of teaching subjects like math and science in the classroom. There have been many well-publicized surveys showing that people in the United States are not very well informed about the Earth they live on. Large numbers of people—including students on campuses of important universities where some of the best-publicized surveys have been conducted—were unable to identify the three largest countries on the North American continent, find Florida on a United States map, or name the oceans that border the United States on a world map. (Elementary school students love to hear about these surveys because if they are studying geography, they will be able to answer all of the questions that these college students cannot.)

During the years that the study of geography was being set aside in many of our schools in favor of other priorities, the whole focus of geography changed. Geography was once divided into two major categories: physical geography and human geography. Physical geography is concerned with the natural features of the earth (land, water, and climate), how they relate to each other, and the living organisms, including people, on the Earth. Physical geography has been divided into several categories: biogeography, climatology, geomorphology, oceanography, and soil geography. Human geography studies the patterns of human activity and how it relates to the environment around them. Human geography has been divided into several categories: cultural, economic, historical, political, population, social, and urban.

It was easy to compare and contrast geography with other sciences such as astronomy, which describes the Earth in relation to its position in space, and geology, which studies the Earth's structure and composition.

Today, however, geography is crossing into other sciences, as well. We are seeing it in cultural anthropology, demographics, ecology, economics, meteorology, sociology, and zoology. Although these remain separate sciences, the lines separating them are more blurry than ever before, and many new approaches to the study of geography are being advocated.

GENIP—A National Project

In 1984, the Association of American Geographers (AAG) together with the National Council for Geographic Education (NCGE) published *Guidelines for Geographic Education: Elementary and Secondary Schools* in which they identified five fundamental themes of geography. These five themes were specifically designed and written to be used by teachers. (Crossland, 1994) In 1987, these two groups were joined by the American Geographical Society (AGS) and the National Geographic Society (NGS) to form the Geographic Education National Implementation Project (GENIP) for the purpose of implementing the aforementioned guidelines and improving the status and quality of geographic education in the United States.

Introduction *(cont.)*

What Has Happened to Geography? *(cont.)*

The Five Themes

The first theme is called *Location: Position on the Earth's Surface.* There are two kinds of locations: absolute and relative. The absolute, or exact, location of any place on Earth can be specified by giving its latitude and longitude. The relative location of a place is given by describing its relationship to other places. Absolute location is like a street address. ("I live at 2100 Oak Lane, Smalltown, CA 98765.") Relative location is a more qualitative set of directions. ("I live in the white two-story house on the corner across from the tennis courts in the park.")

The second theme is *Place: Physical and Human Characteristics.* These are the characteristics that differentiate one place from another. They include physical characteristics like landforms, bodies of water, climate, and plant and animal life, as well as land use, architecture, language, religion, type of government, and even communication and transportation if they are unique.

The third theme is *Relationships Within Places: Humans and Their Environment.* Here we ask students to take a look at the ways in which people react with their environments. This is important in this age of ecological awareness when we are trying to make good choices about the Earth.

The fourth theme is *Movement: Humans Interacting on the Earth.* This theme focuses on human interdependence. This is where a more general and comprehensive look is taken at transportation and communication.

The fifth and last theme is entitled *Regions: How They Form and Change.* GENIP defines a region as an area with one or more common characteristics or features which give it a measure of unity and make it different from the surrounding areas. The geography of the United States is often divided into a consideration of its regions—Northeast, Southeast, Midwest, Southwest, Rocky Mountain, and Pacific.

A New Mix

These themes are really a new mix of the old physical/human divisions. The first and fifth themes are more "physical" and the second and fourth more "human," while the third theme contains much of the material connected with our concern for the safety of the environment. The chief benefit of this approach may be the freshness it brings to one of the oldest of the academic disciplines. The themes themselves can be taught and discussed in any order or combination.

North America

Table of Contents

Introduction *(cont.)*

North America

This book was designed to present an overview of the geography of the continent of North America. It is divided into five sections to match the themes of the Geographic Education National Implementation Project (GENIP), an educational project backed by some of the nation's most prestigious geographers.

Each section contains a selection of teaching pages, maps, activities, interesting facts, review questions, and puzzles or games. A plan for using the material to construct a geography center is also included, as well as ideas for putting together a book as a culminating activity.

You will also find a glossary of specialized vocabulary used by geographers. This will make it easier for your students to talk about the world in which they live.

A Word or Two About Maps

Projections

The landforms shown on maps and globes do not look exactly alike. This is because it is just as hard to "peel" a globe and flatten the Earth's "skin" out into a map as it is to peel an orange and flatten out its skin to make a smooth, even surface. Even if you can get the skin off the orange in one piece, the top and bottom edges must be broken and spread out.

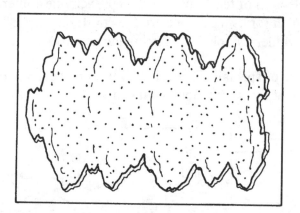

Different map makers (cartographers) have had different ideas about how to do this and have made different "projections." A projection is the way in which the map maker has chosen to flatten out the Earth's surface to make a flat map. Sometimes the map maker allows the breaks in Earth's surface to show.

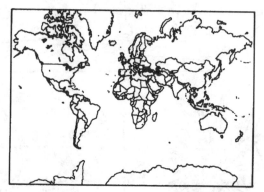

Sometimes the map maker stretches the Earth's "skin." This makes the countries near the poles look much bigger than they really are.

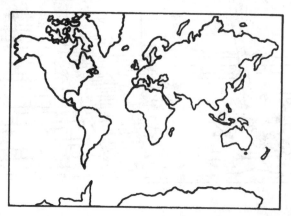

A Word or Two About Maps (cont.)

Projections (cont.)

Use your reference materials to find out the names of other common map projections and list them below. Research the advantages and disadvantages of each map projection you list and write them down below.

Map Projection	Advantages	Disadvantages

A Word or Two About Maps *(cont.)*

The Compass Rose

The compass rose is a small drawing that shows direction on a map. Most maps show north at the top and south at the bottom, west on the left and east on the right.

Look at maps to find some different styles of compass roses and then design your own. You can shrink your drawing and make multiple copies to use on the maps you make, color, or label.

Where on Earth Is North America?

- North America extends from the cold Arctic Ocean to the warm Caribbean Sea.

- North America stretches from the Atlantic to the Pacific Oceans.

- North America is the third largest of the seven continents.

- North America contains the world's largest island.

Use these clues to find North America on this map. Color it blue.

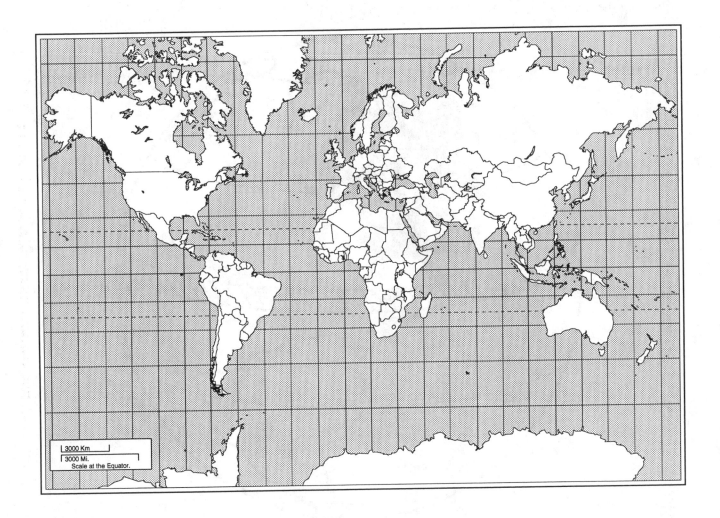

Where on Earth Is North America? *(cont.)*

If you think of the Earth as a ball (a sphere or globe), you can draw a line around the middle (the equator) and separate the two halves into the top half (Northern Hemisphere) and the bottom half (Southern Hemisphere). Now you can talk about something as being in the Northern or Southern Hemisphere.

More lines are drawn around the Earth parallel to the equator and evenly spaced from the equator to the North and South Poles. They are called parallels or lines of latitude. They are numbered in degrees, starting with 0° at the equator and usually spaced at 15° intervals, ending with 90 ° N at the North Pole and 90° S at the South Pole.

(Geographers further divide their degrees into minutes and seconds so they can be very precise in locating the position of anything on the Earth's surface.)

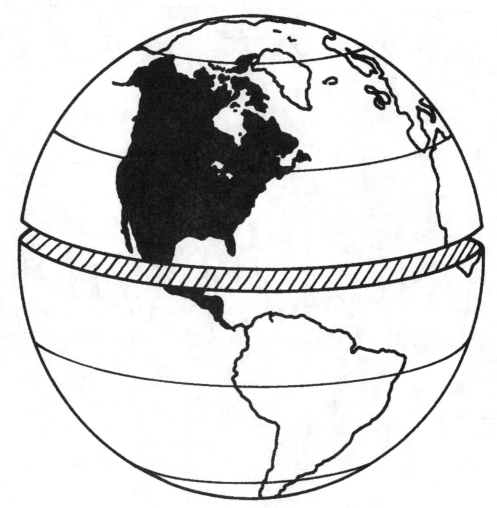

If you divide the Earth into its Northern and Southern Hemispheres, North America lies almost entirely in the_____Hemisphere.

Where on Earth Is North America? *(cont.)*

You can also draw lines north and south around the Earth. These lines are called meridians or lines of longitude. They are usually shown 15° apart at the equator, but they all come together at the North and South Poles. (They also can be further divided into minutes and seconds just like the parallels.)

The line that runs through Greenwich, England, is called the prime meridian (0°). Longitude is the distance east or west of the prime meridian. The line directly opposite the prime meridian is at 180° and is called the date line. If you are still thinking of the Earth as a ball (a sphere or globe), you can separate the two halves into the Western Hemisphere and the Eastern Hemisphere. (This is usually done along the meridians of 20° W and 160° E so all of Africa is in one hemisphere.)

If you divide the Earth into its Western and Eastern Hemispheres, North America is in the_____Hemisphere.

Where on Earth Is North America? *(cont.)*

You can tell where things on the Earth are in two ways:

- You can give their exact or absolute location using latitude and longitude expressed in degrees (minutes and seconds).

- You can tell where they are in relation to other things.

Fill out the missing information to give the exact location of where you live:

house number	street name	apartment number
city	state/country	zip code

Now, use information from a map or globe to complete this description of the exact location of North America.

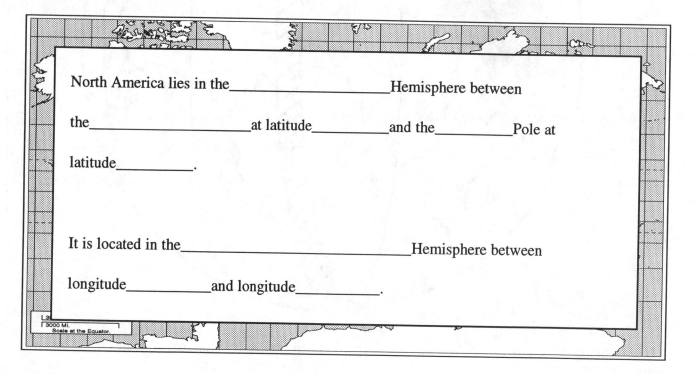

North America lies in the_____Hemisphere between

the_____at latitude_____and the_____Pole at

latitude_____.

It is located in the_____Hemisphere between

longitude_____and longitude_____.

Where on Earth Is North America? *(cont.)*

You can tell where things on the Earth are in two ways:

- You can give their exact or absolute location using latitude and longitude expressed in degrees (minutes and seconds).

- You can tell where they are in relation to other things.

Fill out the missing information to give the location of where you live in relation to other things:

I live
between_____and_____

near_____

and across
from_____.

Now, use the information from a map or globe to complete this description of the relative location of North America.

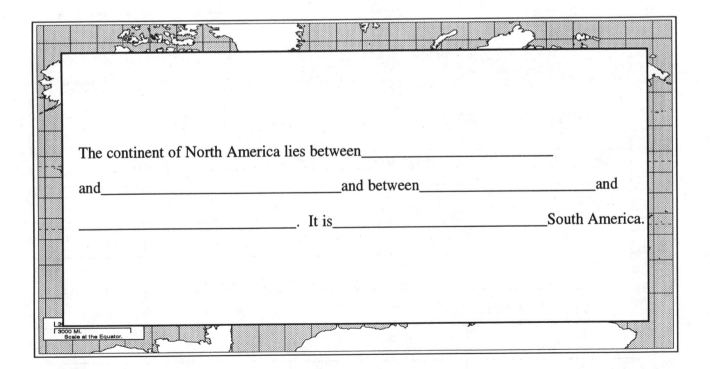

The continent of North America lies between_____

and_____and between_____and

_____. It is_____South America.

Where in North America Is_____?

Use information from a globe or map, an atlas, an encyclopedia, and your geography book to write both the exact and relative locations of five of the countries on the North American continent. See the next page for the names of countries to choose from.

1. _____
   _____
   _____
   _____
   _____

2. _____
   _____
   _____
   _____

3. _____
   _____
   _____
   _____

4. _____
   _____
   _____
   _____

5. _____
   _____
   _____
   _____

Countries, Departments, Dependencies, and Territories of North America

There are 36 countries, departments, dependencies, and territories of North America listed below. Find them forwards, backwards, and diagonally in the word search below.

```
G Q W F R E N C H O V E R S E A S D E P A R T M E N T S
R R E R T Y U A C O S T A R I C A I O P A S D F G H T T
E Z E X C V B N N M N Q T W E R T Y U I O P L K J P O V
N Z X E C V C A B N M D M R L K J H G F D S G A I A B I
A B P O N U U D T R E W U Q I Q A S D B F R G E H N A N
D A Z X C L B A A S Q W E R R N T Y A A E S R M D A G C
I R M N G U A T E M A L A V A C I H X N Z R A I S M O E
N B N Z X C V N B N M P O I U S A D A R E W M Q Q A A N
E A S E A S D F D G H S F D S M A D A W E R T U Y U J T
S D T P V O I U Y T E R E W A Q A A Z D X C V E D R T Y
N O K Q W I E R T T R E W S Q D O M I N I C A L A A S E
I S I Z X C S J A M A I C A C V B N M K J H G O W E R L
C W T E R N E T H E R L A N D S D E P E N D E N C I E S
A S T D F G S R B R I T I S H D E P E N D E N C I E S A
R R S M T D Y U I P U E R T O R I C O M N B V C X Z A L
A Q A Z E X S W E R T Y U L M N B V C X Z E B W E R T V
G R T T Y X O I U B A R B U D A M N B V C X Z E A S D A
U W I C H A I T I R E W Q C P O I U Y T R E W Q L K K D
A N P O I U Y C Y T D O M I N I C A N R E P U B L I C O
U F G H J K J H O G F D S A N T I G U A Q W E R T Y Z R
U N I T E D S T A T E S V I R G I N I S L A N D S G H E
```

Cross off the countries, departments, dependencies, and territories as you find them: Greenland, Canada, St. Pierre, Miquelon, Tobago, Mexico, Guatemala, Belize, El Salvador, Honduras, Nicaragua, Costa Rica, Panama, Bermuda, Bahamas, Cuba, Jamaica, Haiti, Puerto Rico, St. Lucia, St. Kitts, Nevis, Antigua, Barbuda, Dominica, St. Vincent, Grenadines, Barbados, Grenada, Trinidad, Dominican Republic, French Overseas Departments, British Dependencies, United States, Netherlands Dependencies, United States Virgin Islands

Countries of North America

Use information from an atlas, encyclopedia, your geography book, or any other reference book to write two interesting facts about each North American country.

1. Antigua

_____

_____

2. Bahamas

_____

_____

3. Barbados

_____

_____

4. Barbuda

_____

_____

5. Belize

_____

_____

6. Bermuda

_____

_____

7. British Dependencies

_____

_____

8. Canada

_____

_____

9. Costa Rica

_____

_____

10. Cuba

_____

_____

11. Dominica

_____

_____

12. Dominican Republic

_____

_____

Countries of North America *(cont.)*

13. El Salvador

_____

_____

14. French Overseas Departments

_____

_____

15. Greenland

_____

_____

16. Grenada

_____

_____

17. Grenadines

_____

_____

18. Guatemala

_____

_____

19. Haiti

_____

_____

20. Honduras

_____

_____

21. Jamaica

_____

_____

22. Mexico

_____

_____

23. Miquelon

_____

_____

24. Nevis

_____

_____

25. Netherlands Dependencies

_____

_____

Countries of North America *(cont.)*

26. Nicaragua

_____

_____

27. Panama

_____

_____

28. Puerto Rico

_____

_____

29. St. Kitts

_____

_____

30. St. Lucia

_____

_____

31. St. Pierre

_____

_____

32. St. Vincent

_____

_____

33. Tobago

_____

_____

34. Trinidad

_____

_____

35. United States

_____

_____

36. United States Virgin Islands

_____

_____

Bonus Question!

Which of these countries make up the area called Central America?

_____

_____

Look at the Map

Use the numbered list of North American countries on pages 18–20 to label the map below. Write the number of each country on the map and use the list for a key.

Physical Characteristics of North America

Major Bodies of Water

North America is surrounded by the *Atlantic Ocean* to the east, the *Pacific Ocean* to the west, the *Arctic Ocean* and the *Bering Sea* to the north, and the *Caribbean Sea* and *Gulf of Mexico* to the south.

Use reference sources to label these major bodies of water on the map of North America.

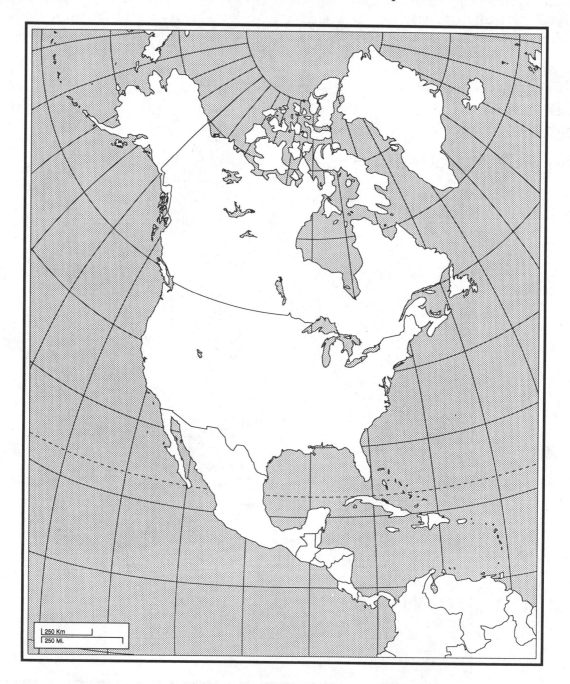

250 Km
250 MI.

Physical Characteristics of North America *(cont.)*

Mountains and Plains

The three largest countries on the North American continent—the United States, Canada, and Mexico—share many physical characteristics. The *Coast Range* runs along the Pacific coast, stretching from Northern Canada all the way through Mexico to the southern tip of Baja California. The *Rocky Mountains* run from northern Alaska almost all the way to Mexico where another range, the *Sierra Madre Occidental*, continues until it surrounds a high plateau in the heart of that country. The *Appalachian Mountains* start in Newfoundland and continue into the southern United States.

The *Great Basin* lies between the Coast Range and the Rocky Mountains in the United States. The *Great Plains* are the prairie lands that lie between the Rocky Mountains and the Appalachians in the center of the continent. The fertile *Coastal Plain* runs along the Atlantic coast and around the Gulf of Mexico.

Use reference books to label these physical characteristics on the map of North America.

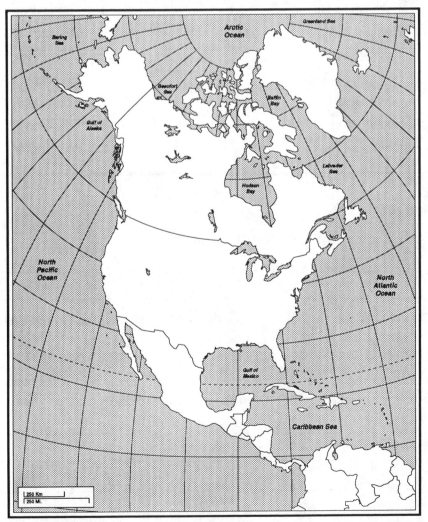

Physical Characteristics of North America *(cont.)*

Lakes and Rivers

Both Canada and the United States have many lakes and rivers. Four of the five *Great Lakes* form part of the border between these two countries. Only one of Mexico's major rivers is listed below. It forms part of that country's border with the United States. Also, a small stretch of the *Colorado River* flows through Mexico, dividing the Baja California peninsula from the rest of that country.

Using reference sources and the map on page 25, draw the lakes and rivers listed below. Then label those rivers and the other bodies of water with their numbers and use the list for a key.

1. Lake Superior	12. Yukon River
2. Lake Huron	13. Mackenzie River
3. Lake Erie	14. Nelson River
4. Lake Ontario	15. St. Lawrence River
5. Lake Michigan	16. Mississippi River
6. Hudson Bay	17. Missouri River
7. Lake Winnipeg	18. Ohio River
8. Great Slave Lake	19. Tennessee River
9. Great Bear Lake	20. Arkansas River
10. Snake River	21. Colorado River
11. Columbia River	22. Rio Grande

Bonus Questions!

Into what body of water does the Colorado River empty?

_____

_____

Which of the Great Lakes does not form part of the border between the United States and Canada?

_____

_____

The Great Lakes can be reached by ship from the Atlantic Ocean by way of which river?

_____

_____

Physical Characteristics of
North America *(cont.)*

Lakes and Rivers

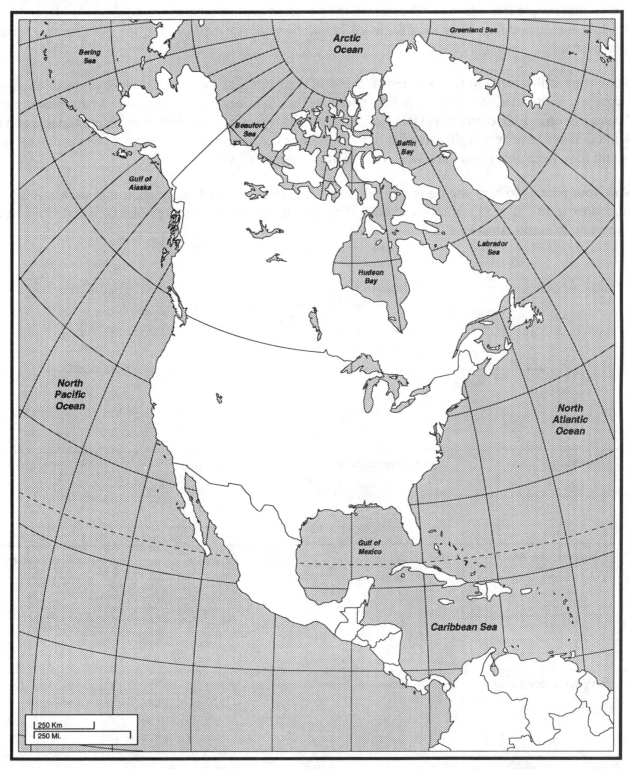

People in North America

Everyone who lives in North America is either an immigrant or the descendant of an immigrant. Even the people who are called Native Americans are thought to have come to the Americas from Asia. Scientists think that the ocean levels were low enough during the Ice Ages to have exposed a land bridge across the Bering Strait between the areas that are now known as Russia and Alaska.

These first people had already built civilizations when the explorers came from Europe to claim the land for their countries. They were followed in turn by settlers, first from Europe and then from other continents.

People are still coming to North America. Most of them come as the result of wars, persecution, and economic hard times. Some of them come because their families are already here. Many people come because people all over the world think of North America as a good place to live. Both Canada and the United States have very high standards of living. Since the invention of television, people all over the world have been able to see how well some North Americans live.

Ask your parents to help you make a family tree. A family tree is a kind of chart that shows who your ancestors were. Try to find out where each of the people on your family tree was born and when he or she came to North America.

_____

your name

_____   _____
mother   father

_____   _____   _____   _____
grandmother (mother)   grandfather (mother)   grandmother (father)   grandfather (father)

_____   _____   _____   _____
great grandmother (mother)   great grandfather (mother)   great grandmother (father)   great grandfather (father)

_____   _____   _____   _____
great grandmother (mother)   great grandfather (mother)   great grandmother (father)   great grandfather (father)

People in North America *(cont.)*

Three groups of Indians built great civilizations in the Americas before European explorers came. Two of these civilizations were located in North America. Do some research to find out something about the Aztec and the Maya civilizations.

The Aztecs

_____

_____

_____

_____

_____

_____

_____

The Maya

_____

_____

_____

_____

_____

_____

_____

_____

Animals in North America

Read the clues and unscramble the names of the North American animals.

1. _____ a large, horned, grazing mammal that lives in the northern part of North America (somoe)

2. _____ a small animal with mask-like markings on its face (aconor)

3. _____ a large, white, furry mammal that lives in the frozen Arctic (proal rabe)

4. _____ small rodents that dig their burrows in the grassy plains (pirerai sodg)

5. _____ a poisonous snake that warns of its approach by making a noise with its tail (altterskane)

6. _____ a reptile that has been hunted for its skin (gaillarot)

7. _____ an animal that is covered with sharp quills (ciepuporn)

8. _____ the correct name for the animal that used to roam the prairies in large herds (snoib)

9. _____ the common name for the animal that used to roam the prairies in large herds (falubof)

10. _____ a woodland animal that has antlers (rede)

11. _____ a sure-footed horned animal that romps around in the Canadian Rockies (nutonaim toga)

12. _____ a large ferocious bear that lives in the American northwest (zigryzl raeb)

13. _____ the original dam builder (raveeb)

14. _____ a small animal that hides nuts in trees and in holes in the ground (rilsquer)

15. _____ a four-footed meat eater that runs in packs (flow)

16. _____ a poisonous insect found in the deserts (pircoons)

17. _____ a poisonous lizard (gali stormen)

18. _____ a large hairy spider (alatuntar)

19. _____ a bird that is famous as the symbol of the United States (dabl glaee)

20. _____ an aquatic mammal (ase onli)

People Depend on the Environment

Make a list of North America's natural resources.

_____

_____

_____

_____

_____

Then create a symbol to go with each natural resource and make a key. Using your newly created symbols, show these resources on the map of North America on the next page.

Resource Key

People Depend on the Environment *(cont.)*

Resource Map

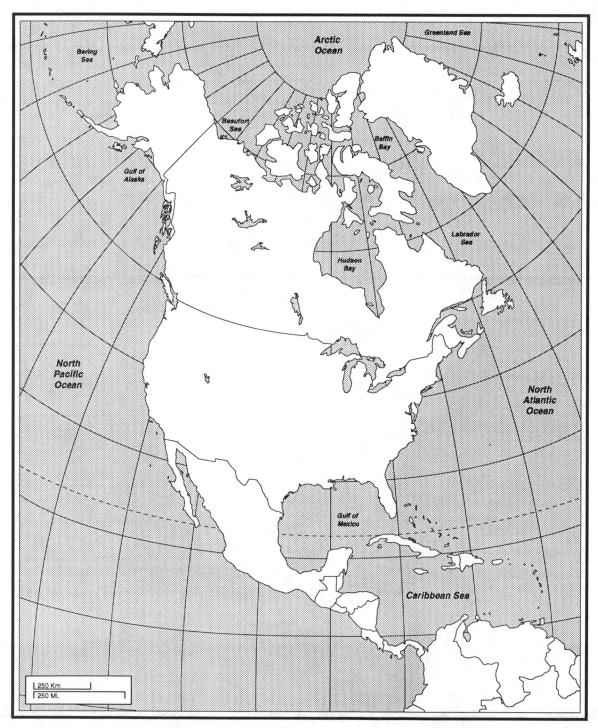

People Adapt to and Change the Environment

People adapt to and change the environment in many ways. Think of some possible solutions that may solve these environmental problems:

Very dry conditions for farming:

_____

_____

_____

_____

Hills too steep for crops:

_____

_____

_____

_____

Areas that flood:

_____

_____

_____

_____

Housing in hot climates:

_____

_____

_____

_____

People Adapt to and Change the Environment *(cont.)*

People adapt to and change the environment in many ways. Think of some possible solutions that may solve these environmental problems:

Housing in cold climates:

_____

_____

_____

Clothing in hot climates:

_____

_____

_____

Clothing in cold climates:

_____

_____

_____

Transportation in mountainous or hilly areas:

_____

_____

_____

Technology Impacts the Environment

Resources are things valued and used by people. Natural resources are resources that occur in nature, such as minerals in the Earth, trees, water, and air.

The way people feel about and use natural resources changes as new technologies are developed.

Research the use of natural resources and how they have changed society in North America. How may natural resources change society in the future?

Type of Resource	Past	Present	Future
Fuel for heating			
Fuel for ships			
Fuel for trains			
Fuel for cars			

Technology Impacts the Environment *(cont.)*

Type of Resource	Past	Present	Future
Materials for building			
Materials for containers			
Propellant for spray cans			
Material for paper			
Treatment of the air			
Use of water			

34

Movement Demonstrates Interdependence

Why do human activities require movement? _____

_____

_____

Do the people in your family go places?_____Choose two people and answer the following questions:

	Person #1	Person #2
Who?		
When?		
Where?		
How far?		
How often?		
Why?		
Mode of transportation?		

Movement Demonstrates
Interdependence *(cont.)*

Use reference sources to figure the distances between these North American cities.

Los Angeles/New York _____

San Francisco/Quebec _____

Vancouver/Detroit _____

Seattle/San Diego _____

Edmonton/Calgary _____

Washington, D.C./Miami _____

Houston/Denver _____

Miami/Nassau _____

Dallas/Mexico City _____

Atlanta/Philadelphia _____

New York/Puerto Rico _____

Portland, Oregon/Portland, Maine _____

New York 1750 km.

Denver 890 km.

Quebec 2030 km.

Mexico City 2200 km.

Movement Involves Linkages

List several different ways people traveled in years past from place to place in North America.

_____

_____

_____

_____

_____

_____

List several different ways people travel today from place to place in North America.

_____

_____

_____

_____

_____

_____

Bonus Question!

Why do you think methods of transportation changed?

_____

_____

_____

_____

_____

Movement Involves Linkages *(cont.)*

How will people travel around North America in the future?

_____

_____

_____

_____

Design your own future method of transportation. Explain it and then draw a picture of it below.

_____

_____

_____

_____

This Is How My Future Transportation Will Work:

_____

_____

_____

_____

This Is How My Future Transportation Will Look:

Movement Includes People, Ideas, and Products

People go places for business and for pleasure. Going somewhere for pleasure is called touring.

Where have you gone for pleasure?

_____

_____

_____

_____

Where would you like to go?

_____

_____

_____

_____

Ideas can travel too. List some of the different ways ideas travel from place to place.

_____

_____

_____

_____

Products also travel. What are some of the ways products travel?

_____

_____

_____

_____

_____

Movement Includes People, Ideas, and Products *(cont.)*

Think about one of the places you would like to spend your vacation. Design a cover for a travel brochure about that place. Sketch your design below. Write a description of the place that will make other people want to travel there too.

_____

_____

_____

_____

The Far North

Arctic Plants

A region is a portion of the Earth's surface that has characteristics unlike any other. The far north is considered its own region. You may think it is similar to Antarctica at the South Pole because of the cold, ice and snow, and the auroras, which look like dazzling light shows in the sky. However, it is quite different.

The far north is mostly ocean. This makes it less cold than the Antarctic and friendlier to animal and plant life. During the short summer of the northern region, some of the land that borders the Arctic Ocean becomes warm and thaws. This thawing allows a variety of different kinds of plants to grow; these plants include: mosses, lichen, algae, and hundreds of kinds of flowering plants. However, only the top few inches (cm) of this land thaws out, and the roots of these plants cannot penetrate below the permafrost which is the permanently frozen ground.

Several of these Arctic plants are very beautiful. Find a picture of one in a reference book and sketch it below. Be sure to write the plant's name below your sketch.

The Far North *(cont.)*

Animals Across the Curriculum

Many animals live in the Arctic. The *walrus*, *polar bear*, and *narwhal* are true animals of the ice floes and the icy ocean. Still more animals live on the tundra, the huge land mass that circles the North Pole, extending from the edge of the northern forests to the shores of the Arctic Ocean. The *barren-ground grizzly*, *snowy owl*, *ptarmigan*, and *lemming* share their tundra home with the *musk ox*, *caribou*, and such waterfowl as the *Canada goose*.

1. The Walrus

Be ready to report on the walrus. Find out what this animal eats, if it migrates, and if its territory has become smaller. Write down any other facts that you think are interesting.

_____

_____

_____

_____

_____

_____

_____

_____

2. The Polar Bear

Write a poem about the polar bear. This is an animal with no natural enemies. It is hunted only by people. It may live its whole life without setting foot on land. Try to see a video tape or read an illustrated book about this bear before you write your poem.

_____

_____

_____

_____

_____

_____

_____

The Far North (cont.)

Animals Across the Curriculum (cont.)

3. Put the names of the italicized animals on page 42 in ABC order and tell how many are syllables in each of the names.

_____   _____

_____   _____

_____   _____

_____   _____

_____   _____

4. **The Lemming**

    What story is told about the habits of lemmings? Do scientists still think it is true? What facts are known about lemmings?

_____

_____

_____

_____

_____

_____

_____

_____

_____

_____

The Far North *(cont.)*

Animals Across the Curriculum *(cont.)*

5. **The Narwhal**
   The Narwhal is a very strange animal. Find out about it. What legend is associated with it?
   Write your own legend about the narwhal. Call your legend "Why The Narwhal
   Has_____."

_____

_____

_____

_____

_____

_____

_____

_____

_____

_____

_____

_____

_____

_____

The Far North *(cont.)*

Animals Across the Curriculum *(cont.)*

6. **The Penguin**

   This cold-weather animal is often associated with the far north in stories. Where does it really live? Is it an Arctic animal? It is a bird, but can it fly? How does it get around? Find five more facts about the penguin.

   _____

   _____

   _____

   _____

7. A Bar Graph

   Make a bar graph comparing the features of the Arctic with the features of the Antarctic. Keep track of your facts here as you do your research.

Features	Arctic	Antarctica
High temperatures		
Low temperatures		
Thickness of ice		
Varieties of plant life		
Varieties of animal life		

Central America

Central America is the name given to the tapering isthmus that connects Mexico with South America. It is divided into seven countries. Six of them share a Spanish and Native Indian background. One of them is believed to have been founded by shipwrecked British sailors and has connections with the English-speaking island nations in the Caribbean Sea.

Find these nations in reference books and answer these questions.

1. What is the largest city in Central America?

   _____

2. In which country will you find the Maya ruin of Tikal?

   _____

3. Which country is supposed to have been founded by shipwrecked British sailors?

   _____

4. What is El Salvador's chief crop?

   _____

5. What is the poorest and least developed country in Central America?

   _____

6. What name is given to the Caribbean shore of Nicaragua?

   _____

7. Which country has the canal that links the Atlantic and Pacific Oceans?

   _____

Central America *(cont.)*

8. Which Central American country has done away with its armed forces?

   _____

9. With which country are the Sandinista rebels associated?

   _____

10. Which Central American country has the smallest population?

    _____

11. Which country was founded because of the discovery of silver?

    _____

12. Which country has the highest literacy rate in Central America?

    _____

13. What is the capital city of each Central American Country?

    Guatemala _____

    Belize _____

    El Salvador_____

    Honduras _____

    Nicaragua_____

    Costa Rica _____

    Panama_____

Central America (cont.)

Do some research on the building of the Panama Canal and write a short report about it. Find out who built it, why it was built in Panama, how long it took to build, how much it cost, and the dangers and problems that were overcome in building it.

The Panama Canal

_____

_____

_____

_____

_____

_____

_____

_____

_____

_____

_____

_____

_____

_____

_____

_____

_____

_____

North American Fact Game

This game can be played in different ways:

Game 1—You can use a *Jeopardy* format. Students love this and they can set it up all by themselves or with just a little help. Run the answer cards on one color of paper and the question cards on another color for easy sorting.

Game 2—You can make a card game like *rummy*. All the cards should be run on one color for this. Shuffle the cards and deal five to each player. Put the leftovers facedown or in the middle of the table. Players draw from the stack and discard in another stack. The object of the game is to lay down pairs by matching questions and answers. You can make it more complicated by allowing students to challenge one another's matched pairs if they think the matches are incorrect. Have students keep track of the rules they make and write game directions.

Fact Game Cards

It is the area where the North Pole is located.	What is the Arctic?
These falls are between New York, USA, and Ontario, Canada.	What is Niagara Falls?
The soil is permanently frozen in these Arctic plains.	What is tundra?

North American Fact Game (cont.)

Fact Game Cards (cont.)

These mountains extend through the western United States and Canada.	What are the Rockies?
These five lakes lie between the United States and Canada.	What are the Great Lakes?
Hawaiians wear these wreaths of flowers.	What is a lei?
Ottawa is the capital of this country.	What is Canada?
This abbreviation stands for the United States of America.	What is USA?
This huge canyon was formed by the Colorado River.	What is the Grand Canyon?

North American Fact Game (cont.)

Fact Game Cards (cont.)

This is the northernmost state in the USA.	What is Alaska?
This is a name commonly give to the countries that lie between Mexico and South America.	What is Central America?
This state belongs to the United States, but it lies in the middle of the Pacific Ocean.	What is Hawaii?
This is the highest point in North America.	What is Mt. McKinley?
This is the lowest point in North America.	What is Death Valley, California?
This canal connects the Atlantic and Pacific Oceans.	What is the Panama Canal?

North American Fact Game *(cont.)*

Fact Game Cards *(cont.)*

This North American capital city is one mile above sea level.	What is Denver, Colorado?
These two states in the U.S. are not connected to the other 48 states.	What are Alaska and Hawaii?
This North American country is the largest in land area.	What is Canada?
This city is the capital of the United States of America.	What is Washington, D.C.?
This is the capital city of Nicaragua.	What is Managua?
This river forms part of the border between Mexico and the U.S.	What is the Rio Grande?

North American Fact Game (cont.)

Fact Game Cards (cont.)

Let your students make their own question-and-answer fact cards. Students usually like to make extra hard ones in hopes of stumping each other, so have them write the book and page number where the information can be found for each card.

	Book:_____ Page: _____
	Book:_____ Page: _____
	Book:_____ Page: _____
	Book:_____ Page: _____
	Book:_____ Page: _____

The Geography Center

Putting the Center Together

You can set up your Geography Center in a corner of your classroom and make it as simple or as elaborate as you want. The center should have a map, a globe, and an atlas. (Several maps, a couple of globes, and multiple copies of the atlas would be even better.) A table and chairs will facilitate group activities and discussions. A supply of writing and drawing materials will also come in handy. A bookcase, shelf, or window sill can be utilized for storing reference books. The more reference books you can provide, the better the assigned projects will be. If you have access to a TV, VCR, and tapes, you can show movies about the places you are studying. There are many tapes of this variety available, and the visual learners in your class will really appreciate this. Cushions for sitting on the floor to read or view tapes add a cozy touch.

Making the Center Work

You can make the Geography Center part of your instructional day by scheduling groups to do center work. Change the materials daily or weekly or provide a set of task cards at the beginning of the unit and expect each student to work through them individually or as part of a group. (See pages 55–57.)

Use Portfolios

Have students make portfolios and store them in containers in an accessible area of your center. Try using the inexpensive but sturdy plastic crates that are available at local hardware stores. Make students responsible for their own progress by having them file their own work, both completed work and work in progress. Have students create attractive covers for their portfolios so the accumulated work can be attractively displayed at your school's open house.

Deck the Walls

Encourage artwork, creative writing, and exploratory math to go along with your geography unit and spread it throughout the curriculum. Display these products on a bulletin board in your Geography Center. Have students mount and post their own work. They can cut out letters and create colorful captions for the board.

Have another bulletin board reserved for posting newspaper and magazine articles dealing with the continent you are studying. Encourage your students to bring in these articles, share them, and discuss their meaning and importance.

The Geography Center *(cont.)*

Task Cards

Task Card #3

What is the highest mountain peak on the continent?

How tall is it?

In which country is it found?

Task Card #4

What is the largest country on the continent?

What countries or bodies of water border it?

What is its capital city?

Task Card #1

What is the longest river on the continent?

How long is it?

Through which country or countries does it flow?

Task Card #2

What is the most important mountain range on the continent?

How long is it?

In which country or countries are these mountains found?

The Geography Center (cont.)

Task Cards (cont.)

Task Card #5

What is the smallest country on the continent?

What countries or bodies of water border it?

What is its capital city?

Task Card #7

What animals are associated with the continent?

In what country or countries do they live?

Are they in any danger in today's civilization?

Task Card #6

What is the largest lake on the continent?

In which country or countries is it found?

Which river is associated with it?

Task Card #8

What variations in climate are found on the continent?

What variations in weather are found on the continent?

Can people live in all parts of the continent?

The Geography Center *(cont.)*

Task Card Response

Leave a stack of these task card response forms in the geography center for students to use.

Name _____ Date _____

Task Card # _____

Question #1

_____

_____

_____

_____

Question #2

_____

_____

_____

_____

Question #3

_____

_____

_____

_____

Bonus

I also learned _____

_____

_____

_____

The Culminating Activity: Making a Book

Method

You and your students can go about bookmaking in many different ways. Here are some suggestions:

- The book can be your students' showcase portfolios.

- Students can review and reflect upon the work they have accumulated in their portfolios, select the most representative samples or the pieces they like best, and put these things together in book form.

- The book can be a showcase portfolio based on the teacher's criteria.

- Have students select work from their portfolios, based on a list you develop.

- The book can be comprised of new material that sums up the unit.

- Have students complete various assignments meant specifically for inclusion in their books, showing their grasp of the material. (See pages 59–69.)

Contents

In most cases you will probably want your students to include maps, facts about both physical and political geography, research about animals, people, and resources. They can review or report on any books they have read about the continent, and they can write about what they have learned and how it has affected the way they view the world.

Cover

You can specify and provide the design for the cover so that all of the books will be uniform, or you can encourage your students to design a cover that is representative of the continent. A collage of pictures cut from magazines and travel brochures is an option that works well.

Be sure to laminate the finished covers so the books can be used as part of your classroom library or Geography Center reference shelf. Your students may also want to share their books with students in other classes.

Exciting ideas for binding and publishing follow on pages 70–72.

The Culminating Activity:
Making a Book *(cont.)*

Trace an outline map of North America. Transfer information about its physical features from all of the maps you have made. You might want to use different colors to create a key.

Name _____ Date_____

Map of Physical Features

The Culminating Activity: Making a Book *(cont.)*

Use the information you have already gathered or do some new research to complete this page.

Name _____Date_____

Facts About Physical Features

Area: _____

_____

Highest Point: _____

_____

Lowest Point: _____

_____

Largest Island: _____

_____

Longest River: _____

_____

Largest Lake: _____

_____

Tallest Waterfall: _____

_____

Largest Desert: _____

_____

Longest Reef: _____

_____

The Culminating Activity: Making a Book *(cont.)*

Trace an outline map of North America. Transfer the information about its political features from all of the maps you have made. You might want to use a numbered list to create a key.

Name _____ Date_____

Map of Political Features

The Culminating Activity: Making a Book *(cont.)*

Use the information you have already gathered or do some new research to complete this page.

Name _____ Date_____

Facts About Political Features

Population: _____

Largest Country (by area): _____

Largest Country (by population): _____

Smallest Country (by area): _____

Smallest Country (by population): _____

Largest Metropolitan Area (by population):_____

_____

_____

_____

_____

_____

Newest Countries:_____

_____

_____

_____

_____

_____

The Culminating Activity: Making a Book (cont.)

Use the information you have already gathered or do some new research to complete this page.

Name _____ Date_____

The People

The people of this continent belong to these ethnic groups:

_____

_____

_____

They speak these languages:

_____

_____

_____

They live in these different environments:

_____

_____

_____

_____

Their ways of life have changed or are changing:

_____

_____

_____

_____

_____

The Culminating Activity: Making a Book *(cont.)*

Pick the city on the continent that is most interesting to you. Use the information you have already gathered or do some new research to complete this page.

Name _____ Date_____

The city of_____.

This city is in _____

Area: _____

Population: _____

_____

Language(s): _____

_____

Ethnic Groups: _____

_____

Religious Groups: _____

_____

Famous Natural Features: _____

_____

_____

Famous Constructed Features: _____

_____

_____

_____

_____

The Culminating Activity: Making a Book *(cont.)*

Use the information you have already gathered or do some new research to complete this page.

Name _____ Date_____

The Animals

The best known animals of this continent are _____

_____

_____

The animals of this continent are important because _____

_____

_____

The animals that still live in their natural habitats are _____

_____

_____

The animals that are on the endangered list are _____

_____

_____

_____

They are on the endangered list because _____

_____

_____

_____

_____

The Culminating Activity:
Making a Book *(cont.)*

Keep track of the books you read about the continent on this log.

Name _____ Date_____

Book Log

Title: _____   Fiction: _____

Author: _____   Nonfiction: _____

Illustrator: _____   Rating:_____

Title: _____   Fiction: _____

Author: _____   Nonfiction: _____

Illustrator: _____   Rating:_____

Title: _____   Fiction: _____

Author: _____   Nonfiction: _____

Illustrator: _____   Rating:_____

Title: _____   Fiction: _____

Author: _____   Nonfiction: _____

Illustrator: _____   Rating:_____

The Culminating Activity: Making a Book *(cont.)*

Use copies of this form to review your favorite nonfiction books about the continent you have been studying.

Name _____ Date_____

Book Review/Nonfiction

Title: _____

Author: _____

Illustrator: _____

Summary: _____

_____

_____

_____

_____

Reasons I liked or did not like this book:_____

_____

_____

_____

_____

_____

_____

Bonus!

If you liked this book and think other people should read it, you can do one of two things. (1) Write a paragraph or two telling how a nonfiction book can help you understand a continent or a country and post it on the bulletin board in the Geography Center. (2) Make a poster advertising the book and post it on the bulletin board in the Geography Center.

The Culminating Activity: Making a Book (cont.)

Use copies of this form to review your favorite fiction books about the continent you have been studying.

Name _____ Date_____

Book Review/Fiction

Title: _____

Author: _____

Illustrator: _____

Summary: _____

_____

_____

_____

_____

_____

Reasons I liked or did not like this book:_____

_____

_____

_____

_____

_____

_____

Bonus!

If you liked this book and think other people should read it, you can do one of two things. (1) Write a paragraph or two telling how a fiction book can help you understand a continent or a country and post it on the bulletin board in the Geography Center. (2) Make a poster advertising the book and post it on the bulletin board in the Geography Center.

The Culminating Activity:
Making a Book *(cont.)*

Write a reflective essay in which you discuss the ways that studying geography has given you a better understanding of the world and the people in it.

Name _____ Date_____

Title:_____

_____

_____

_____

_____

_____

_____

_____

_____

_____

_____

_____

_____

_____

_____

_____

_____

_____

_____

_____

The Culminating Activity: Making a Book *(cont.)*

Book Binding Ideas

1. Stack all the pages of the book in a neat pile.

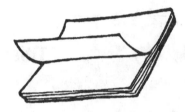

2. Place a blank sheet of paper on the top and bottom of the pages.

3. Leaving approximately 1/2" (1.25 cm) border, staple or sew all of the pages together on the left side.

4. Place two pieces of lightweight cardboard side by side. (Cereal boxes work well.) Each piece should be 1/2 to 1" (1.25 to 2.5 cm) larger than the size of the pages in the book.

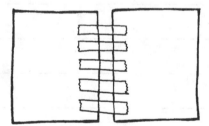

5. Leaving approximately 1" (2.5 cm) between them, tape the cardboard pieces together.

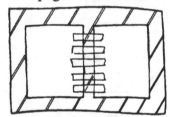

6. Put the cardboard on top of your covering material (e.g., fabric, wallpaper, contact paper, or wrapping paper). Glue the cardboard and covering material together, leaving a 1 to 1 1/2" (2.5 to 3.25 cm) material border.

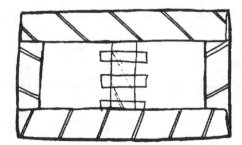

7. Fold up the edges of material over the cardboard and glue in place.

8. Glue the blank pages to the inside of the cardboard covers. Your book is ready to read and share.

70

The Culminating Activity: Making a Book *(cont.)*

Pop-Up Books

1. Fold a 8 1/2" x 11" (22 cm x 28 cm) piece of paper in half crosswise.

2. Measure and mark 2 3/4" (7 cm) from each side along the fold. Cut 2 3/4" (7 cm) slits at the marks.

3. Push cut area inside-out and crease to form the pop-up section.

4. Draw, color, and cut out the object to get "popped-up."

5. Glue it onto the pop-up section.

6. Glue two pages back to back, making sure the pop-up section is free.

7. Glue additional pages together, making as many pages (including pop-up pages) as you like. Be sure to include a free sheet on both the front and back so that those pages can be glued to a cover.

8. Glue a cover over the entire book.

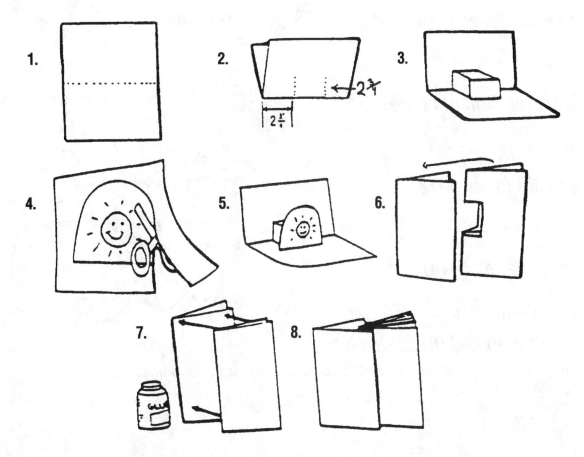

The Culminating Activity: Making a Book *(cont.)*

Real Markets for Student Writing

Student writing can be sent to the following addresses. Check your professional journals for more sources.

Children's Playmate (ages 5–8)

P.O. Box 567B
Indianapolis, Indiana 46206

Cricket (ages 6–12)

Cricket League
P.O. Box 300
Peru, Illinois 61354

Ebony Jr! (ages 6–12)

820 S. Michigan Avenue
Chicago, Illinois 60605

Flying Pencil Press (ages 8–14)

P.O. Box 7667
Elgin, Illinois 60121

Highlights for Children (ages 2–11)

803 Church Street
Honesdale, Pennsylvania 18431

Jack and Jill (ages 8–12)

P.O. Box 567B
Indianapolis, Indiana 46206

Stone Soup (ages 5–14)

P.O. Box 83
Santa Cruz, California 95063

National Written and Illustrated by...

(This is an awards contest for students in all grade levels. Write for rules and guidelines.)
Landmark Editions, Inc.
P.O. Box 4469
Kansas City, Missouri 64127

Software Review

Software: *The Oregon Trail* (MECC)

Hardware: CD-ROM player, Macintosh or IBM/Windows compatible computer (4MB)

Grade Level: Intermediate

Summary: *The Oregon Trail* is a program that simulates one of America's early pioneer movements. Your students will become the pioneers who crossed the American West by wagon train along the Oregon Trail. The Oregon Trail stretched 2,000 miles (3,200 km), starting in Independence, Missouri and ending in the Willamette Valley of the Oregon Region. Some obstacles of the trip will be to cross wild rivers, trek dangerous mountain passes, experience disease and possible starvation, cope with inclement weather, among a number of other things that can go wrong. Just like the pioneers did, your students will have to prepare for their trip, making sure they have enough food, ammunition, clothes, spare wagon parts, etc. This simulation challenges students to make difficult decisions in difficult places. Should you trade food for fresh drinking water? What kind of trade can be made for a spare wagon wheel? Should you wait for the river to subside or cross it to save time? This is a simulation of trial and error and each time your students go through it they will become better pioneers.

Bibliography

Aylesworth, Thomas G. and Virginia L. Aylesworth. *Eastern Great Lakes: Indiana, Michigan, Ohio.* Chelsea, 1991.

Aylesworth, Thomas G. and Virginia L. Aylesworth. *Territories and Possessions: Guam, Puerto Rico, U.S. Virgin Islands, American Samoa, North Marina Islands.* Chelsea, 1992.

Berger, Gilda. *The Southeast States.* Watts, 1984.

Brickenden, Jack. *Canada.* Watts, 1989.

Bulmer, Thomas. *Journey Through Mexico.* Troll, 1990.

Canada in Pictures. Lerner, 1989.

Carpenter, Allan. *Far Flung America.* Childrens, 1979.

Crossland, Bert. *Where On Earth Are We?* Book Links, 1994.

Department of Geography, Lerner Publications Company Staff. *Mexico in Pictures.* Lerner, 1988.

Dickinson, Mary B. (Ed.). *National Geographic Picture Atlas of Our World.* National Geographic Society, 1993.

Geographic Education National Implementation Project. Guidelines, 1987.

Gilfond, Henry. *The Northeast States.* Watts, 1984.

Harrison, Ted. *O Canada.* Tickner, 1993.

Herda, D.J. *Ethnic America: The North Central States.* Millbrook, 1991.

Hicks, Peter. *The Aztecs.* Thomson, 1993.

Jacobson, Daniel. *The North Central States.* Watts, 1984.

Lawson, Don. *The Pacific States.* Watts, 1984.

LeVert, Suzanne. *Canada: Facts and Figures.* Chelsea, 1992.

LeVert, Suzanne. *Dominion of Canada.* Chelsea, 1992.

LeVert, Suzanne. *Ontario.* Chelsea, 1990.

Lourie, Peter. *Yukon River: An Adventure to the Gold Fields of the Klondike.* Boyds Mills, 1992.

McCarry, Charles. *The Great Southwest.* National Geographic, 1980.

Moran, Tom. *A Family in Mexico.* Lerner, 1987.

Bibliography (cont.)

Meyerricks, William and Frank Ronan. *All About Our 50 States.* Random, 1978.

Reilly, Mary J. *Mexico.* Marshall Cavendish, 1991.

Smith, Eileen Latell. *Mexico: Giant of the South.* Dillon, 1983.

Stein, R. Conrad. *Mexico.* Childrens, 1984.

St. George, Judith. *The Mount Rushmore Story.* Putnam, 1985.

The Story of America: A National Geographic Picture Atlas. National Geographic, 1984.

Technology

Broderbund. *MacGlobe & PC Globe and MacUSA & PC USA.* Available from Learning Services, (800) 877-9378. disk

Broderbund. *Where in the USA Is Carmen Sandiego? and Where in America's Past is Carmen Sandiego?* Available from Troll (800)526-5289. CD-ROM and disk

DeLorme Publishing. *Global Explorer.* Available from DeLorme Publishing, 1995. CD-ROM

Didatech. *Crosscountry USA.* Available from Learning Services, (800)877-9378. disk

Discis. *Great Cities of the World, Volumes 1 & 2.* Available from Learning Services, (800)877-9378. CD-ROM

Macmillan/McGraw-Hill. *U.S. Atlas Action and World Atlas Action.* Available from Learning Services, (800)877-9378. disk

MECC. *Canada Geograph II, The Oregon Trail, The Yukon Trail, and USA Geograph II.* Available from MECC, (800)685-MECC; in Canada call (800)663-7731. CD-ROM and disk

National Geographic. *Rain Forest.* Available from Educational Resources, (800)624-2936. laserdisc

Orange Cherry. *Talking U.S.A. Map.* Available from Learning Services, (800)877-9378. disk

Orange Cherry. *Time Traveler.* Available from Educational Resources, (800)624-2936. CD-ROM

Software Toolworks. *U.S. Atlas and World Atlas.* Available from Learning Services, (800)877-9378. CD-ROM and disk

SVE. *Geography on Laserdisc.* Available from Learning Services, (800)877-9378. laserdisc

Troll. *All About America, America Coast to Coast, Crosscountry Canada, Game of the States, The States Game, Time Tunnel: Early America, and U.S. Map.* Available from Troll, (800)526-5289. disk

Answer Key

Page 17

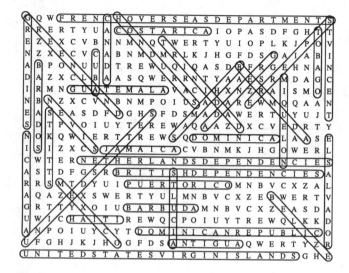

Page 28

1. moose
2. racoon
3. polar bear
4. prairie dogs
5. rattlesnake
6. alligator
7. porcupine
8. bison
9. buffalo
10. deer
11. mountain goat
12. grizzly bear
13. beaver
14. squirrel
15. wolf
16. scorpion
17. gila monster
18. tarantula
19. bald eagle
20. sea lion

Pages 46–47

1. Guatemala City
2. Guatemala
3. Belize
4. coffee
5. Honduras
6. The Mosquito Coast
7. Panama
8. Costa Rica
9. Nicaragua
10. Belize
11. Honduras
12. Costa Rica
13. Guatemala City

 Belmopan

 San Salvador

 Tegucigalpa

 Managua

 San Jose

 Panama City

South America

Table of Contents

Introduction *(cont.)*

South America

This book was designed to present an overview of the geography of the continent of South America. It is divided into five sections to match the themes of the Geographic Education National Implementation Project (GENIP), an educational project backed by the nation's most prestigious geographers.

Each section contains a selection of teaching pages, maps, activities, interesting facts, review questions, and puzzles or games. A plan for using the material to construct a geography center is also included, as well as ideas for putting together a book as a culminating activity.

You will also find a glossary of the specialized vocabulary used by geographers. This will make it easier for your students to talk about the world in which they live.

A Word or Two About Maps

Projections

The landforms shown on maps and globes do not look exactly alike. This is because it is just as hard to "peel" a globe and flatten the Earth's "skin" out into a map as it is to peel an orange and flatten out its skin to make a smooth, even surface. Even if you can get the skin off the orange in one piece, the top and bottom edges must be broken and spread out.

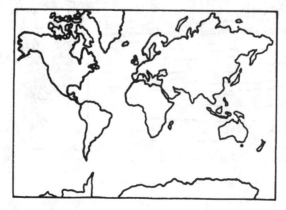

Different mapmakers (cartographers) have had different ideas about how to do this and have made different "projections." A projection is the way in which the map maker has chosen to flatten out the Earth's surface to make a flat map. Sometimes the map maker allows the breaks in the Earth's surface to show.

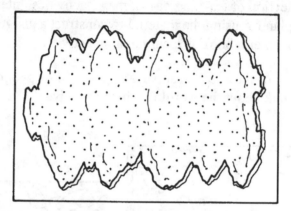

Sometimes the map maker stretches the Earth's "skin." This makes the countries near the poles look much bigger than they really are.

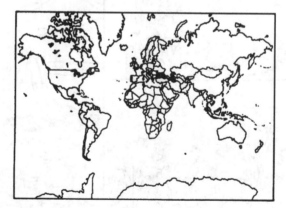

A Word or Two About Maps *(cont.)*

Projections *(cont.)*

Use your reference materials to find out the names of other common map projections and list them below. Research the advantages and disadvantages of each map projection you list and write them down below.

Map Projection	Advantages	Disadvantages

A Word or Two About Maps *(cont.)*

The Compass Rose

The compass rose is a small drawing that shows direction on a map. Most maps show north at the top and south at the bottom, west on the left and east on the right.

Look at maps to find some different styles of compass roses and then design your own. You can shrink your drawing and make multiple copies to use on the maps you make, color, or label.

Where on Earth Is South America?

- South America reaches from about 10 degrees N, above the equator in the warm Caribbean Sea, to about 55 degrees S, about 10 degrees away from the Antarctic Peninsula.

- South America extends from the Atlantic Ocean to the Pacific Ocean.

- South America is smaller than Asia, Africa, and North America and larger than Antarctica, Europe, and Australia.

- South America is attached to the North American continent by the slender string of countries known as Central America.

Use these clues to find South America on this map. Color it blue.

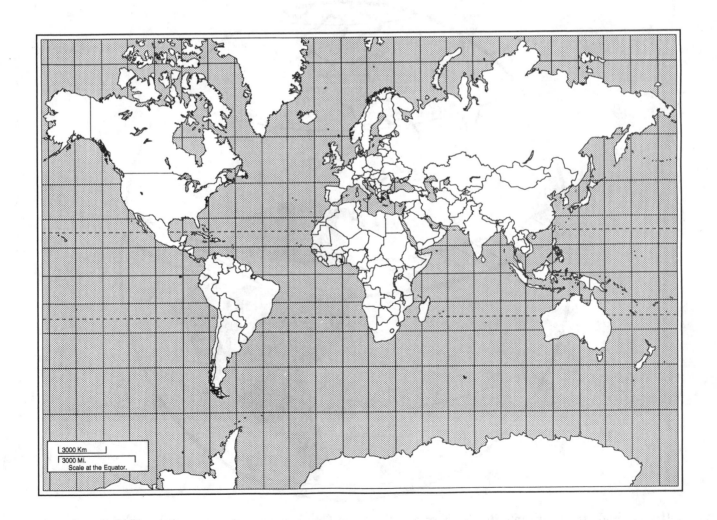

Where on Earth Is South America? *(cont.)*

If you think of the Earth as a ball (a sphere or globe), you can draw a line around the middle (the equator) and separate the two halves into the top half (Northern Hemisphere) and the bottom half (Southern Hemisphere). Now you can talk about something as being in the Northern or Southern Hemisphere.

More lines are drawn around the Earth parallel to the equator and evenly spaced from the equator to the North and South Poles. They are called parallels or lines of latitude. They are numbered in degrees, starting with 0° at the equator and usually spaced at 15° intervals, ending with 90° N at the North Pole and 90° S at the South Pole.

(Geographers further divide their degrees into minutes and seconds so they can be very precise in locating the position of anything on the Earth's surface.)

If you divide the Earth into its Northern and Southern Hemispheres, most of South America is in the_____Hemisphere.

Where on Earth Is South America? *(cont.)*

You can also draw lines north and south around the Earth. These lines are called meridians or lines of longitude. They are usually shown 15° apart at the equator, but they all come together at the North and South Poles. (They also can be further divided into minutes and seconds just like the parallels.)

The line that runs through Greenwich, England, is called the prime meridian (0°). Longitude is the distance east or west of the prime meridian. The line directly opposite the prime meridian is at 180° and is called the date line. If you are still thinking of the Earth as a ball (a sphere or globe), you can separate the two halves into the Western Hemisphere and the Eastern Hemisphere. (This is usually done along the meridians of 20° W and 160° E so all of Africa is in one hemisphere.)

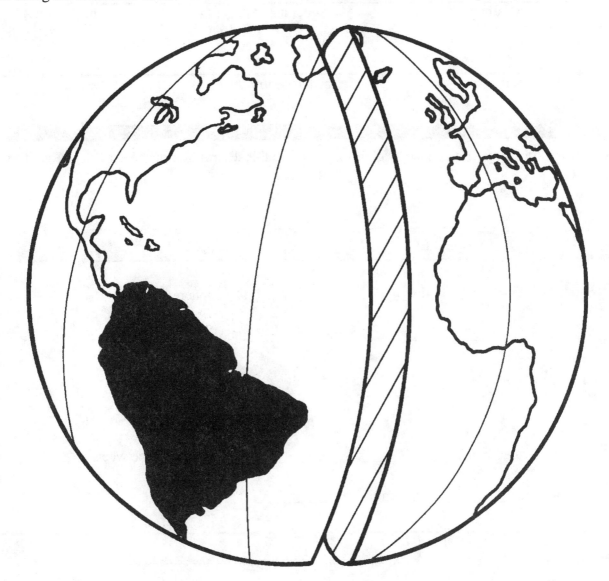

If you divide the Earth into its Western and Eastern Hemispheres, South America is in the_____Hemisphere.

Where on Earth Is South America? *(cont.)*

You can tell where things on the Earth are in two ways:

- You can give their exact or absolute location using latitude and longitude expressed in degrees (minutes and seconds).

- You can tell where they are in relation to other things.

Fill out the missing information to give the exact location of where you live:

house number	street name	apartment number
city	state/country	zip code

Now, use information from a map or globe to complete this description of the exact location of South America.

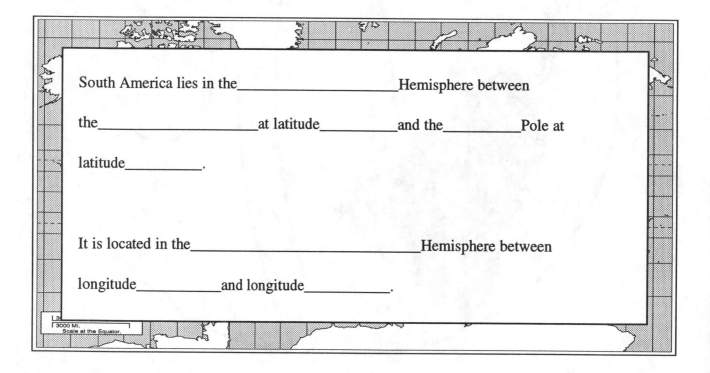

South America lies in the_____Hemisphere between

the_____at latitude_____and the_____Pole at

latitude_____.

It is located in the_____Hemisphere between

longitude_____and longitude_____.

L 3

3000 Mi.
Scale at the Equator.

Where on Earth Is South America? *(cont.)*

You can tell where things on the Earth are in two ways:

- You can give their exact or absolute location using latitude and longitude expressed in degrees (minutes and seconds).

- You can tell where they are in relation to other things.

Fill out the missing information to give the location of where you live in relation to other things:

I live
between_____and_____

near_____

and across
from_____.

Now, use the information from a map or globe to complete this description of the relative location of South America.

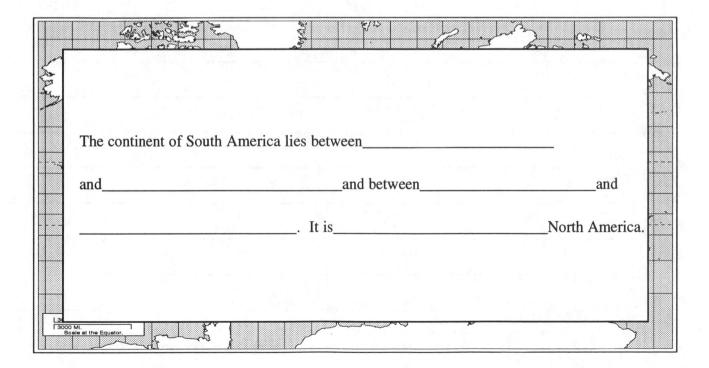

The continent of South America lies between_____

and_____and between_____and

_____. It is_____North America.

3000 Mi.
Scale at the Equator.

Where in South America Is ___?

Use information from a globe or map, an atlas, an encyclopedia, and your geography book to write both the exact and relative locations of five of the countries on the South American continent. See the next page for the names of countries to choose from.

1. _____

_____

_____

_____

2. _____

_____

_____

_____

3. _____

_____

_____

_____

_____

4. _____

_____

_____

_____

_____

5. _____

_____

_____

_____

_____

Countries of South America

The 14 countries of South America are listed below. Find them forwards, backwards, and diagonally in the word search below.

```
Y Q K L V N G H N J J F T L G F F R Z K J S F Y G B
P F C K V C R X S L B S C M R R Z H S Y Z Y V D V O
W C T X M H T Y Q Z Q H D Y B J W S W A V F X R P R
P N K C T W W Y H C X F X Z S D G Q Z R V X X B W X
C Y X H S Z D R H C O V R Z P H L X M G Q Z B W P H
S B J S N G H R X B M L K E U H J P F E W N O P F M
Z U W T Z U C N Z V B P U T N R B T Y N P H L C E X
L K R F K Y B T N E L J B M X C U Y R T R G I X S E
M M Z I Q A N R T N K H K K B T H G C I J C V G E F
P B Q Z N N N R A E M F F G V I L G U N S F I Y X I
W K E C U A D O R Z Z K P P A R A G U A Y N A R N I
C T C H N L M K K U I L K E F F Z R Z I Y Z J B A H
Z G F I G J Q E F E E L S R C M N H Z B A X G D K F
Y L G L M V D K R L Q W F U S H S H D K B N D K E N
J J J E F A L K L A N D I S L A N D S Q L Y A H R X
Y R Q Q Z W R S Q J P Q S Z R M Y V J P C H Z W P I
X T T F Q Q P P X J P B X Q H F G D V M Z W Z D M K
M T D L B D W E P O I K K N G F D U L U G F E I H O
H L T E C G B Z O I Y L Z R M K U T J L S W M U V U
L J G G K L J Y R E X L D T J U O L V C D E W Z C H
N U D R P M H F V C F Y K U D U K P M V T S U E I N
P D R W E S B J I Y L G C O U N T G D D T B P O I Y
I D C B N M T E I D B U K W D G V K L M H G R K U F
```

Cross off the countries as you find them: Columbia, Venezuela, Ecuador, Peru, Guyana, Suriname, French Guiana, Brazil, Bolivia, Paraguay, Chile, Argentina, Uruguay, Falkland Islands

Countries of South America *(cont.)*

Use information from an atlas, an encyclopedia, your geography book, or any other reference book to write two interesting facts about each South American country.

1. Argentina _____

   _____

2. Bolivia _____

   _____

3. Brazil _____

   _____

4. Chile _____

   _____

5. Columbia _____

   _____

6. Ecuador _____

   _____

7. Falkland Islands _____

   _____

Countries of South America *(cont.)*

8. French Guiana _____

   _____

9. Guyana _____

   _____

10. Paraguay _____

    _____

11. Peru _____

    _____

12 Suriname _____

    _____

13. Uruguay _____

    _____

14. Venezuela _____

    _____

Look at the Map

Use the numbered list of South American countries on pages 90 and 91 to label the map below. Write the number of each country on the map and use the list for a key.

South American Capital Cities

Use an atlas, an encyclopedia, your geography book, or any other reference book to find the capital city of each country listed below. Then write it in the space provided.

1. Argentina _____

2. Bolivia _____

3. Brazil _____

4. Chile_____

5. Columbia _____

6. Ecuador _____

7. Falkland Islands _____

8. French Guiana _____

9. Guyana_____

10. Paraguay_____

11. Peru _____

12. Suriname _____

13. Uruguay _____

14. Venezuela_____

Place

Physical Characteristics of South America

Major Bodies of Water

South America is surrounded by the *Atlantic Ocean* to the east and northeast, the *Pacific Ocean* to the west, and the *Caribbean Sea* to the northwest.

Use reference sources to label these major bodies of water on the map of South America.

```
500 Km
500 Mi.
```

Physical Characteristics of South America *(cont.)*

Mountains and Plains

Many things in South America seem bigger, higher, hotter, wetter, drier, and colder than on any other continent. TheI are the longest mountain range on Earth, running the entire length of the continent, and are higher than all of Earth's mountains except the Himalayas. In Peru and Bolivia where the Andes divide into two parallel ranges is the *altiplano*, a broad plateau. Because of the altitude, there is little oxygen and it is cold even in summer. On a narrow strip of coastal plain between the Andes and the Pacific Ocean lies the *Atacama Desert,* which is the driest place in the world. In the middle of the country lies the *Amazon Basin*, a hot and humid region of tropical forests which is nearly as large as the United States. Farther south are the grassy plains called *pampas* where cattle are raised and crops are grown. Even farther south are the rolling, treeless plateaus of *Patagonia.* At the very tip of the continent is *Cape Horn*, one of the world's stormiest places.

Use reference sources to label these landforms on the map of South America.

Physical Characteristics of South America *(cont.)*

Other Bodies of Water

South America has many rivers. A great many of them branch off from the *Amazon*, which is so huge that ocean-going ships can sail upstream 1,000 miles (1,600 km) from its mouth. There are two large lakes, *Lake Maracaibo* in Venezuela and *Lake Titicaca* on the Altiplano between Bolivia and Peru. The *Strait of Magellan* divides Tierra Del Fuego from the rest of the continent.

Use reference sources to draw in the rivers on the map on the next page. Then label the bodies of water with their numbers and use the list for a key.

1. Lake Maracaibo	8. Xingú River
2. Lake Titicaca	9. Mamoré River
3. Orinoco River	10. Ucayali River
4. Amazon River	11. San Francisco River
5. Rio Negro	12. Parana River
6. Purus River	13. Uruguay River
7. Madeira River	14. Strait of Magellan

Bonus Questions!

Into what body of water does the Amazon River empty?

_____

_____

Which South American country has two capital cities? What are the names of these two cities?

_____

_____

What is the name of the long, narrow South American country that borders on the Pacific Ocean?

_____

_____

Physical Characteristics of South America *(cont.)*

Other Bodies of Water

People in South America

Many different groups of people live in South America. Some of them are descended from the native Indians. Some are descended from the European explorers and the settlers who followed them. Some of them are more recent immigrants. There are also many people of mixed ancestry.

The people of South America live in many different environments. Some people live in large modern cities, some in towns, and still others in small villages. There are even groups of people who live within the tropical rainforest. Standards of living vary greatly throughout the continent. The wealthy make up a very small minority on the South American continent although these people hold most of the land. The majority of people living in South America live in primitive conditions and earn well below the Gross National Product (GNP) of their individual countries.

Much of the rain forests have been or are being cut down and burned to provide more farmland. This is having an adverse effect on the people and animals who live near and rely on these forests for survival. The loss of South American rain forests also has an adverse effect on the rest of the world because of the large amounts of oxygen produced from them. However, today many people, both in South America and around the world, are working together to save these rain forests.

Each South American country has an official language, but the people of these countries may also speak a native language or the language of their own original culture. Some dialect of Spanish is spoken throughout most of South America.

Do some research to find out where these languages are spoken:

Portuguese _____

English _____

Dutch _____

French _____

Find out how you can help to save the rain forests. Write your ideas below. Perhaps your class can have a "Save the Rain forest" project.

_____

_____

_____

_____

_____

_____

_____

People in South America *(cont.)*

Three groups of Indians built great civilizations in the Americas before the European explorers came. One of these civilizations was in South America. Do some research to find out as much as you can about the Inca civilization. Share your information with your class.

The Inca

_____

_____

_____

_____

_____

_____

_____

_____

_____

_____

_____

_____

_____

_____

_____

_____

_____

_____

Animals in South America

Read the clues and unscramble the names of South American animals.

1. _____ a slow-moving mammal that likes to hang upside down from the branches of trees (shlot)

2. _____ a fish with sharp teeth like razors (hairnap)

3. _____ an animal that catches its food with a long, sticky tongue (ratteena)

4. _____ a colorful bird of the rain forest (cwama)

5. _____ four-legged animal of the Andes (malla)

6. _____ a cat that roams the rain forest (garuja)

7. _____ a snake that crushes its prey before eating it (oba)

8. _____ a flightless bird that lives on the Falkland Islands (ginpune)

9. _____ a large lizard (gainua)

10. _____ a large, flightless bird that looks like an ostrich (hear)

11. _____ a fat, hoofed mammal found in the tropics (prait)

12. _____ a colorful tropical bird with a large beak (cutona)

13. _____ a shelled reptile hunted for food by native people in South America (lettru)

14. _____ a large water mammal of the Amazon (tenamea)

15. _____ a mammal that lives in the trees of the rain forests (dripes yeknom)

16. _____ the wild, camel-like ancestor of the llama and alpaca (acoguan)

17. _____ a relative of the llama (calapa)

18. _____ a pink, long-legged bird of the high Andes (minflaog)

People Depend on the Environment

Make a list of South America's natural resources.

_____

_____

_____

_____

_____

Then, create a symbol to go with each natural resource and make a key. Using your newly created symbols, show these resources on the map of South America on the next page.

Resource Key

People Depend on the Environment *(cont.)*

Resource Map

People Adapt to and Change the Environment

People adapt to and change the environment in many ways. Think of some possible solutions that may solve these environmental problems:

Very dry conditions for farming:

_____

_____

_____

_____

Hills too steep for crops:

_____

_____

_____

_____

Areas that flood:

_____

_____

_____

_____

Housing in hot climates:

_____

_____

_____

_____

People Adapt to and Change the Environment *(cont.)*

People adapt to and change the environment in many ways. Think of some possible solutions that may solve these environmental problems:

Housing in cold climates:

_____

_____

_____

Clothing in hot climates:

_____

_____

_____

Clothing in cold climates:

_____

_____

_____

Transportation in mountainous or hilly areas:

_____

_____

_____

Technology Impacts the Environment

Resources are things valued and used by people. Natural resources are the resources that occur in nature, such as minerals in the Earth, trees, water, and air.

The way people feel about and use natural resources changes as new technologies are developed. However, these developments depend on the wealth of the particular country.

Research how the lack of modern technology has affected the use of resources in South America.

	Resources Used	Effect of Lack of Technology
Cooking		
Heating		
Transportation		
Building Houses		

Technology Impacts the Environment *(cont.)*

	Resources Used	Effect of Lack of Technology
Building roads		
Land for farming		
Food for people		
Development of industry		
Waste disposal		
Electric power		

Movement Demonstrates Interdependence

Why do human activities require movement? _____

_____

_____

Do the people in your family go places?_____Choose two places and answer the following questions:

	Person #1	Person #2
Who?		
When?		
Where?		
How far?		
How often?		
Why?		
Mode of transportation?		

Movement Demonstrates Interdependence *(cont.)*

Use reference sources to figure the distances between these South American cities.

Caracas/Santiago _____

São Paulo/Lima _____

Rio de Janeiro/Bogotá _____

Sucre/La Paz _____

Buenos Aires/Bogota _____

Quito/Georgetown _____

Cordoba/Brasilia _____

Montevideo/Paramaribo _____

Cayenne/Recife _____

Santiago/Asunción _____

Fortaleza/São Paulo _____

Cordoba/Brasilia _____

Rio de Janeiro 2625 km.

Sao Paulo 1400 km.

Buenos Aires 2250 km.

Santiago 1890 km.

108

Movement Involves Linkages

List some of the ways people travel from place to place in the more rural areas of South America.

_____

_____

_____

_____

_____

_____

List some of the ways people travel from place to place in the urban areas of South America.

_____

_____

_____

_____

_____

_____

Bonus Question!

Why don't many people use cars to travel from one city to another?

_____

_____

_____

_____

_____

Movement Involves Linkages (cont.)

How will people travel around South America in the future?

_____

_____

_____

_____

Design your own future method of transportation. Explain it and then draw a picture of it below.

_____

_____

_____

_____

This Is How My Future Transportation Will Work:

_____

_____

_____

_____

This Is How My Future Transportation Will Look:

Movement Includes People, Ideas, and Products

People go places for business and for pleasure. Going somewhere for pleasure is called touring.

Where have you gone for pleasure?

_____

_____

_____

_____

Where would you like to go?

_____

_____

_____

_____

Ideas can travel too. List some of the different ways ideas travel from place to place.

_____

_____

_____

_____

Products also travel. What are some of the ways products travel?

_____

_____

_____

_____

Movement Includes People, Ideas, and Products *(cont.)*

Think about one of the places you would like to visit in South America. Design a cover for a travel brochure about that place. Sketch your design below. Write a description of the place that will make other people want to travel there too.

_____

_____

_____

_____

_____

The Mountains

People and Crops

A region is a portion of the Earth's surface that has characteristics unlike any other. The mountains and high plains (altiplanos) of the Andes form a region. The weather is cold even near the equator. Very few crops can be grown there.

Use reference books to find out about the crops that are grown on the altiplano. Write about them below.

_____

_____

_____

_____

_____

The air is thin at 13,000 feet (3,943 m). People who have lived there all their lives have developed physical adaptations that help them survive.

Use reference books to find out about the physical adaptations of the altiplano people. Write about them below.

_____

_____

_____

_____

_____

_____

_____

_____

_____

The Mountains *(cont.)*

Animals Across the Curriculum

Many animals live in the Andes Mountains. The *guanaco*, *alpaca*, and *llama* are all related. They supply wool, meat, and transportation for the Andean Indians. Other animals live there as well. The *flamingo* nests there, although its fledglings must survive temperatures that drop to near zero at night. The *puma* (mountain lion) hunts there. Rodents such as the *pika* and *gold-mantled squirrel* spend the summer evading *coyotes, hawks, eagles,* and *weasels*, while they fatten up for their winter hibernation that will last from five to seven months.

1. The Guanaco

Be ready to report on the guanaco. Find out what this animal eats, if it migrates, and if its territory has become smaller. Write down any other facts that you think are interesting.

_____

_____

_____

_____

_____

_____

_____

2. The Flamingo

Write a poem about the flamingo. This is a delicate-looking bird one would expect to find in a more temperate environment. Try to see a video, tape, or read an illustrated book about this bird before you write your poem.

_____

_____

_____

_____

_____

The Mountains *(cont.)*

Animals Across the Curriculum *(cont.)*

3. Put the names of the italicized animals on page 114 in ABC order and tell how many syllables are in each of the names.

_____   _____

_____   _____

_____   _____

_____   _____

_____   _____

4. **The Pika**

    Find out as much as you can about this little animal. Write your findings in the space provided below.

_____

_____

_____

_____

_____

_____

_____

_____

_____

_____

_____

_____

The Mountains *(cont.)*

Animals Across the Curriculum *(cont.)*

5. **The Puma**

The puma goes by many names in many countries. Read a few legends about different kinds of animals, for example "How the Bear Got His Stumpy Tail." After reading several stories, write your own legend about the puma. You may want to call your legend "How the Puma Got So Many Names."

_____

_____

_____

_____

_____

_____

_____

_____

_____

_____

_____

_____

_____

_____

_____

_____

_____

The Mountains *(cont.)*

Animals Across the Curriculum *(cont.)*

6. **The Eagle**

   What kind of eagles live in the Andes? Do they migrate to other areas during the year? What do they eat? Are they on the endangered species list? See what you can find out about the eagles of the Andes.

   _____

   _____

   _____

7. A Line Graph

   Animals are greatly affected by climate. Make a line graph that shows the average monthly high and low temperatures in the Andes. Keep track of your facts here as you do your research.

Hint: Use different colors to show highs and lows on your graph.

	High	Low
January		
February		
March		
April		
May		
June		
July		
August		
September		
October		
November		
December		

The Tropics

The Amazon Basin lies between the Guiana Highlands and the Brazilian Highlands. These highlands are really just rolling hills and plateaus, nowhere near as high as the highlands of the Andes Mountains. The Amazon Basin itself is almost as big as the United States. It is always hot and humid. The Amazon River and its tributaries flow through it, carrying water through the world's largest rain forest.

Find information about this area in reference books and answer these questions.

1. How long is the Amazon River?

   _____

2. How many tributaries does the Amazon River have?

   _____

3. How many miles (km) across is the mouth of the Amazon?

   _____

4. How many miles (km) upstream is the city of Manaus?

   _____

5. How many miles (km) upstream is Iquitos in Peru?

   _____

6. How many species of trees can be found in a single acre of rain forest?

   _____

The Tropics *(cont.)*

7. Name four different kinds of trees that grow in the rain forest.

    1._____   3. _____

    2._____   4. _____

8. What kind of tree does latex come from?

    _____

9. What happens to the rain forest near clearings or along riverbanks where light reaches the ground?

    _____

    _____

    _____

    _____

    _____

10. Why is the tropical rain forest in trouble?

    _____

    _____

    _____

    _____

    _____

The Tropics *(cont.)*

Meet with a partner or group to brainstorm ideas for helping to save the rain forest. List your ideas below.

_____

_____

_____

_____

Decide on the best of your ideas and formulate a plan for putting your idea into action. List the steps of your plan below.

1. _____

   _____

2. _____

   _____

3. _____

   _____

4. _____

   _____

5. _____

   _____

South American Fact Game

This game can be played in different ways:

Game 1—You can use a Jeopardy format. Students love this and they can set it up all by themselves or with just a little help. Run the answer cards on one color of paper and the question cards on another color for easy sorting.

Game 2—You can make a card game like rummy. All the cards should be run on one color for this. Shuffle the cards and deal five to each player. Put the leftovers facedown or in the middle of the table. Players draw from the stack and discard in another stack. The object of the game is to lay down pairs by matching questions and answers. You can make it more complicated by allowing students to challenge one another's matched pairs if they think the matches are incorrect. Have students keep track of the rules they make and write game directions.

Fact Game Cards

It is the longest river in South America.	What is the Amazon?
It is the second largest river on Earth.	What is the Amazon?
It is the highest navigable lake on Earth.	What is Lake Titicaca?

South American Fact Game (cont.)

Fact Game Cards (cont.)

It is the fourth largest continent.	What is South America?
They are the longest mountain range on Earth.	What are the Andes?
The largest tropical rain forest in the world is found there.	What is the Amazon River Basin?
This slow-moving animal hangs upside down from the branches of trees.	What is the sloth?
This fish has teeth like razors.	What is the piranha?
This spotted cat lives in the rain forest.	What is the jaguar?

South American Fact Game *(cont.)*

Fact Game Cards *(cont.*)

This animal hunts food with its sticky tongue.	What is the anteater?
This colorful bird lives in the rain forest.	What is the macaw?
This four-legged mammal lives in the Andes.	What is the llama?
This large snake crushes its prey.	What is the boa?
Portuguese is spoken in this South American country	What is Brazil?
This is the driest place on Earth.	What is the Atacama Desert?

South American Fact Game *(cont.)*

Fact Game Cards *(cont.)*

These are the grasslands of South America.	What are the pampas?
It is the capital city of Chile.	What is Santiago?
This South American country is the largest in land area.	What is Brazil?
It is the language spoken throughout most of South America.	What is Spanish?
He is a South American cowboy.	What is a gaucho?
It is Angel Falls in Venezuela.	What is the world's tallest waterfall?

South American Fact Game *(cont.)*

Fact Game Cards *(cont.)*

Let your students make their own question-and-answer fact cards. Students usually like to make extra hard ones in hopes of stumping each other, so have them write the book and page number where the information can be found for each card.

	Book:_____ Page: _____
	Book:_____ Page: _____
	Book:_____ Page: _____
	Book:_____ Page: _____
	Book:_____ Page: _____

The Geography Center

Putting the Center Together

You can set up your Geography Center in a corner of your classroom and make it as simple or as elaborate as you want. The center should have a map, a globe, and an atlas. (Several maps, a couple of globes, and multiple copies of the atlas would be even better.) A table and chairs will facilitate group activities and discussions. A supply of writing and drawing materials will also come in handy. A bookcase, shelf, or window sill can be utilized for storing reference books. The more reference books you can provide, the better the assigned projects will be. If you have access to a TV, VCR, and tapes, you can show movies about the places you are studying. There are many tapes of this variety available, and the visual learners in your class will really appreciate this. Cushions for sitting on the floor to read or view tapes add a cozy touch.

Making the Center Work

You can make the Geography Center part of your instructional day by scheduling groups to do center work. Change the materials daily or weekly or provide a set of task cards at the beginning of the unit and expect each student to work through them individually or as part of a group. (See pages 127–129.)

Use Portfolios

Have students make portfolios and store them in containers in an accessible area of your center. Try using the inexpensive but sturdy plastic crates that are available at local hardware stores. Make students responsible for their own progress by having them file their own work, both completed work and work in progress. Have students create attractive covers for their portfolios so the accumulated work can be attractively displayed at your school's open house.

Deck the Walls

Encourage artwork, creative writing, and exploratory math to go along with your geography unit and spread it throughout the curriculum. Display these products on a bulletin board in your Geography Center. Have students mount and post their own work. They can cut out letters and create colorful captions for the board.

Have another bulletin board reserved for posting newspaper and magazine articles dealing with the continent you are studying. Encourage your students to bring in these articles, share them, and discuss their meaning and importance.

The Geography Center *(cont.)*

Task Cards

Task Card #3

What is the highest mountain peak on the continent?

How tall is it?

In which country is it found?

Task Card #4

What is the largest country on the continent?

What countries or bodies of water border it?

What is its capital city?

Task Card #1

What is the longest river on the continent?

How long is it?

Through which country or countries does it flow?

Task Card #2

What is the most important mountain range on the continent?

How long is it?

In which country or countries are these mountains found?

The Geography Center *(cont.)*

Task Cards *(cont.)*

Task Card #7

What animals are associated with the continent?

In what country or countries do they live?

Are they in any danger in today's civilization?

Task Card #8

What variations in climate are found on the continent?

What variations in weather are found on the continent?

Can people live in all parts of the continent?

Task Card #5

What is the smallest country on the continent?

What countries or bodies of water border it?

What is its capital city?

Task Card #6

What is the largest lake on the continent?

In which country or countries is it found?

Which river is associated with it?

The Geography Center *(cont.)*

Task Card Response

Leave a stack of these task card response forms in the geography center for students to use.

Name _____ Date _____

Task Card #_____

Question #1

_____

_____

_____

_____

Question #2

_____

_____

_____

_____

Question #3

_____

_____

_____

_____

Bonus

I also learned_____

_____

_____

_____

The Culminating Activity: Making a Book

Method

You and your students can go about bookmaking in many different ways. Here are some suggestions:

- The book can be your students' showcase portfolios.

- Students can review and reflect upon the work they have accumulated in their portfolios, select the most representative samples or the pieces they like best, and put these things together in book form.

- The book can be a showcase portfolio based on the teacher's criteria.

- Have students select work from their portfolios, based on a list you develop.

- The book can be comprised of new material that sums up the unit.

- Have students complete various assignments meant specifically for inclusion in their books, showing their grasp of the material. (See pages 131–141.)

Contents

In most cases you will probably want your students to include maps, facts about both physical and political geography, research about animals, people, and resources. They can review or report on any books they have read about the continent, and they can write about what they have learned and how it has affected the way they view the world.

Cover

You can specify and provide the design for the cover so that all of the books will be uniform, or you can encourage your students to design a cover that is representative of the continent. A collage of pictures cut from magazines and travel brochures is an option that works well.

Be sure to laminate the finished covers so the books can be used as part of your classroom library or Geography Center reference shelf. Your students may also want to share their books with students in other classes.

Exciting ideas for binding and publishing follow on pages 142–144.

The Culminating Activity:
Making a Book (cont.)

Trace an outline map of the continent. Transfer information about its physical features from all of the maps you have made. You might want to use different colors to create a key.

Name _____ Date_____

Map of Physical Features

The Culminating Activity: Making a Book *(cont.)*

Use the information you have already gathered or do some new research to complete this page.

Name _____Date_____

Facts About Physical Features

Area: _____

_____

Highest Point: _____

_____

Lowest Point: _____

_____

Largest Island:_____

_____

Longest Rivers: _____

_____

Largest Lakes:_____

_____

Highest Waterfall:_____

_____

Largest Desert: _____

_____

Longest Reef: _____

_____

The Culminating Activity:
Making a Book *(cont.)*

Trace an outline map of the continent. Transfer information about its political features from all of the maps you have made. You might want to use a numbered list to create a key.

Name _____ Date_____

Map of Political Features

The Culminating Activity: Making a Book *(cont.)*

Use the information you have already gathered or do some new research to complete this page.

Name _____ Date _____

Facts About Political Features

Population: _____

Largest Country (by area): _____

Largest Country (by population): _____

Smallest Country (by area): _____

Smallest Country (by population): _____

Largest Metropolitan Areas (by population): _____

_____

_____

_____

_____

_____

Newest Countries: _____

_____

_____

_____

_____

_____

_____

_____

The Culminating Activity: Making a Book *(cont.)*

Use the information you have already gathered or do some new research to complete this page.

Name _____ Date _____

The People

The people of this continent belong to these ethnic groups:

_____

_____

_____

They speak these languages:

_____

_____

_____

They live in these different environments:

_____

_____

_____

Their ways of life have changed or are changing:

_____

_____

_____

_____

The Culminating Activity: Making a Book *(cont.)*

Pick the city on the continent that is most interesting to you. Use the information you have already gathered or do some new research to complete this page.

Name _____ Date_____

The city of_____.

This city is in _____

Area: _____

Population: _____

_____

Language(s): _____

_____

Ethnic Groups: _____

_____

Religious Groups: _____

_____

Famous Natural Features: _____

_____

_____

Famous Constructed Features: _____

_____

_____

_____

_____

The Culminating Activity: Making a Book *(cont.)*

Use the information you have already gathered or do some new research to complete this page.

Name _____ Date _____

The Animals

The best known animals of this continent are _____

_____

_____

The animals of this continent are important because _____

_____

_____

The animals that still live in their natural habitats are _____

_____

_____

The animals that are on the endangered species list are _____

_____

_____

_____

They are on the endangered species list because _____

_____

_____

_____

_____

The Culminating Activity: Making a Book *(cont.)*

Keep track of the books you read about the continent on this log.

Name _____ Date _____

Book Log

Title: _____ Fiction: _____

Author: _____ Nonfiction: _____

Illustrator: _____ Rating: _____

Title: _____ Fiction: _____

Author: _____ Nonfiction: _____

Illustrator: _____ Rating: _____

Title: _____ Fiction: _____

Author: _____ Nonfiction: _____

Illustrator: _____ Rating: _____

Title: _____ Fiction: _____

Author: _____ Nonfiction: _____

Illustrator: _____ Rating: _____

The Culminating Activity: Making a Book *(cont.)*

Use copies of this form to review your favorite nonfiction books about the continent you have been studying.

Name _____ Date_____

Book Review/Nonfiction

Title: _____

Author: _____

Illustrator: _____

Summary: _____

_____

_____

_____

_____

_____

Reasons I liked or did not like this book:_____

_____

_____

_____

_____

_____

_____

Bonus!

If you liked this book and think other people should read it, you can do one of two things. (1) Write a paragraph or two telling how a nonfiction book can help you understand a continent or a country and post it on the bulletin board in the Geography Center. (2) Make a poster advertising the book and post it on the bulletin board in the Geography Center.

The Culminating Activity: Making a Book *(cont.)*

Use copies of this form to review your favorite fiction books about the continent you have been studying.

Name _____ Date_____

Book Review/Fiction

Title: _____

Author: _____

Illustrator: _____

Summary: _____

_____

_____

_____

_____

_____

Reasons I liked or did not like this book:_____

_____

_____

_____

_____

_____

_____

_____

Bonus!

If you liked this book and think other people should read it, you can do one of two things. (1) Write a paragraph or two telling how a fiction book can help you understand a continent or a country and post it on the bulletin board in the Geography Center. (2) Make a poster advertising the book and post it on the bulletin board in the Geography Center.

The Culminating Activity:
Making a Book *(cont.)*

Write a reflective essay in which you discuss the ways that studying geography has given you a better understanding of the world and the people in it.

Name _____ Date_____

Title:_____

_____

_____

_____

_____

_____

_____

_____

_____

_____

_____

_____

_____

_____

_____

_____

_____

_____

_____

_____

_____

The Culminating Activity: Making a Book *(cont.)*

Book Binding Ideas

1. Stack all the pages of the book in a neat pile.

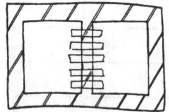

2. Place a blank sheet of paper on the top and bottom of the pages.

3. Leaving approximately 1/2" (1.25 cm) border, staple or sew all of the pages together on the left side.

4. Place two pieces of lightweight cardboard side by side. (Cereal boxes work well.) Each piece should be 1/2 to 1" (1.25 to 2.5 cm) larger than the size of the pages in the book.

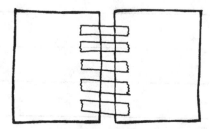

5. Leaving approximately 1" (2.5 cm) between them, tape the cardboard pieces together.

6. Put the cardboard on top of your covering material (e.g., fabric, wallpaper, contact paper, or wrapping paper). Glue the cardboard and covering material together, leaving a 1 to 1 1/2" (2.5 to 3.25 cm) material border.

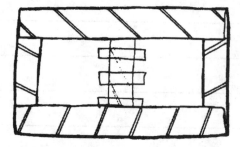

7. Fold up the edges of material over the cardboard and glue in place.

8. Glue the blank pages to the inside of the cardboard covers. Your book is ready to read and share.

The Culminating Activity: Making a Book *(cont.)*

Pop-Up Books

1. Fold a 8 1/2" x 11" (22 cm x 28 cm) piece of paper in half crosswise.

2. Measure and mark 2 3/4" (7 cm) from each side along the fold. Cut 2 3/4" (7 cm) slits at the marks.

3. Push cut area inside-out and crease to form the pop-up section.

4. Draw, color, and cut out the object to get "popped-up."

5. Glue it onto the pop-up section.

6. Glue two pages back to back, making sure the pop-up section is free.

7. Glue additional pages together, making as many pages (including pop-up pages) as you like. Be sure to include a free sheet on both the front and back so that those pages can be glued to a cover.

8. Glue a cover over the entire book.

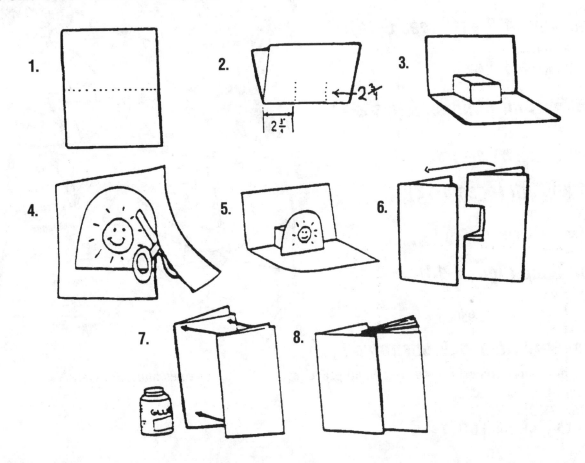

The Culminating Activity: Making a Book *(cont.)*

Real Markets for Student Writing

Student writing can be sent to the following addresses. Check your professional journals for more sources.

Children's Playmate (ages 5–8)

P.O. Box 567B
Indianapolis, Indiana 46206

Cricket (ages 6-12)

Cricket League
P.O. Box 300
Peru, Illinois 61354

Ebony Jr! (ages 6-12)

820 S. Michigan Avenue
Chicago, Illinois 60605

Flying Pencil Press (ages 8-14)

P.O. Box 7667
Elgin, Illinois 60121

Highlights for Children (ages 2-11)

803 Church Street
Honesdale, Pennsylvania 18431

Jack and Jill (ages 8-12)

P.O. Box 567B
Indianapolis, Indiana 46206

Stone Soup (ages 5-14)

P.O. Box 83
Santa Cruz, California 95063

National Written and Illustrated by...

(This is an awards contest for students in all grade levels. Write for rules and guidelines.)
Landmark Editions, Inc.
P.O. Box 4469
Kansas City, Missouri 64127

Software Review

Software: *Ecology Treks* (Sanctuary Woods)

Hardware: Macintosh 2MB (4MB for system 7) or 640K IBM PC with color graphics card, sound board, and hard drive

Grade Level: Intermediate

Summary: *Ecology Treks* is a program that will enable your students to study the connection between animals and their environments. The object of this piece of software is for students to overcome 11 different challenges as they travel through the Earth's various climate zones, one being the Brazilian rain forest. Included in this software is a visual almanac containing thousands of ecological facts. Lastly, it has several biosphere simulators, as well as an animated rain forest with sounds.

Bibliography

Argentina in Pictures. Lerner, 1989.

Ashford, Moyra. *Brazil.* Raintree, 1991.

Bender, Evelyn. *Brazil.* Chelsea House, 1990.

Bennett, Olivia. *A Family in Brazil.* Lerner, 1986.

Blair, David N. *Fear the Condor.* Dutton, 1992.

Carlson, Lori M., and Cynthia L. Ventura. *Where Angels Glide at Dawn: New Stories from Latin America.* Harper, 1990.

Carter, William E. *South America.* Watts, 1983.

Clark, Ann Nolan. *Secret of the Andes.* Viking, 1952.

Corwin, Judith Hoffman. *Latin American and Caribbean Crafts.* Watts, 1992.

Crossland, Bert. *Where on Earth Are We?* Book Links. September, 1994.

Delacre, Lulu. *Las Navidades: Popular Christmas Songs from Latin America.* Scholastic, 1990.

deTrevino, Elizabeth. *El Guero: A True Adventure Story.* Farrar, 1989.

Dickinson, Mary B. (Ed.). *National Geographic Picture Atlas of Our World.* National Geographic Society, 1993.

Dorros, Arthur. *Tonight Is Carnival.* Dutton, 1991.

DuBois, Jill. *Colombia.* Marshall, Cavendish, 1981.

Finger, Charles J. *Tales from Silver Lands.* Doubleday, 1965.

Galvin, Irene F. *Chile: Land of Poets and Patriots.* Macmillan, 1990.

Geographic Education National Implementation Projects. Guidelines, 1987.

Georges, D.V. *South America.* Childrens, 1986.

Gofen, Ethel C. *Argentina.* Marshall Cavendish, 1988.

Jacobsen, Karen. *Bolivia.* Childrens, 1991.

Karlowich, Robert. *Rise Up in Anger: Latin America Today.* Messner, 1985.

Kuss, Daniel. *Myths and Legends of Incas.* Marshall Cavendish, 1991.

Lepthien, Emilie. *Ecuador.* Childrens, 1986.

Lepthien, Emilie. *Peru.* Childrens, 1986.

Morrison, Marion. *Bolivia.* Childrens, 1988.

Morrison, Marion. *Uruguay.* Childrens, 1989.

Peterson, Marge. *Argentina: A Wild West Heritage.* Dillon, 1988.

Parnell, Helga. *Cooking the South American Way.* Lerner, 1992.

Siy, Alexandra. *The Waorani: People of the Ecuadoran Rain Forest.* Macmillan, 1993.

St. John, Jetty. *A Family in Peru.* Lerner, 1987.

Troughton, Joanna. *How the Birds Changed Their Feathers: A South American Indian Folktale.* Bedrick, 1986.

Van Laan, Nancy. *The Legend of El Dorado: A Latin American Tale.* Knopf, 1991.

Bibliography (cont.)

Technology

Broderbund. *MacGlobe & PC Globe and MacUSA & PC USA.* Available from Learning Services, (800) 877-9378. disk

Broderbund. *Where in the World Is Carmen Sandiego?* Available from Troll (800)526-5289. CD-ROM and disk

Bureau of Electronic Publishing Inc. *World Fact Book.* Available from Educational Resources, (800)624-2926. CD-ROM

DeLorme Publishing. *Global Explorer.* Available from DeLorme Publishing, 1995. CD-ROM

Discis. *Great Cities of the World, Volume 1 & 2.* Available from Learning Services, (800)877-9378. CD-ROM

Lawrence. *Nigel's World Adventures in World Geography.* Available from Educational Resources, (800)624-2926. CD-ROM and disk

Macmillan/McGraw-Hill. *World Atlas Action.* Available from Learning Services, (800)877-9378. disk

Magic Quest. *Time Treks and Earth Treks.* Available from Educational Resources, (800)624-2926. disk

MECC. *The Amazon Trail.* Available from MECC, (800)685-MECC; in Canada call (800)663-7731. CD-ROM and disk

Mindscape. *World Atlas.* Available from Educational Resources, (800)624-2926. disk

National Geographic. *Picture Atlas of the World.* Available from Educational Resources, (800)624-2926. CD-ROM

National Geographic. *Rain Forest.* Available from Educational Resources, (800)624-2926. laserdisc

National Geographic. STV: *World Geography.* Available from National Geographic Educational Technology, (800)368-2728. videodisc

Orange Cherry. *Time Traveler.* Available from Educational Resources, (800)624-2936. CD-ROM

Queue. *Atlas Explorer.* Available from Educational Resources, (800)624-2926. disk

Sanctuary Woods. *Ecology Treks.* Available from Learning Services, (800)877-3278. software and videodisc

Software Toolworks. *World Atlas.* Available from Learning Services, (800)877-9378. CD-ROM and disk

SVE. *Geography on Laserdisc.* Available from Learning Services, (800)877-9378. laserdisc

Answer Key

Page 89

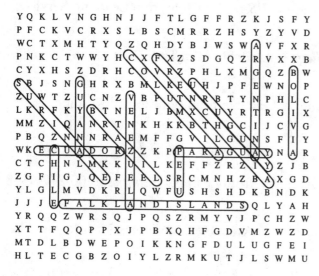

Page 93

1. Buenos Aires

2. La Paz/Sucre

3. Brasilia

4. Santiago

5. Bogota

6. Quito

7. Stanley

8. Cayenne

9. Georgetown

10. Asuncion

11. Lima

12. Paramaribo

13. Montevideo

14. Caracas

Page 100

1. sloth

2. piranha

3. anteater

4. macaw

5. llama

6. jaguar

7. boa

8. penguin

9. iguana

10. rhea

11. tapir

12. toucan

13. turtle

14. manatee

15. spider monkey

16. guanaco

17. alpaca

18. flamingo

Pages 118–119

1. 4,000 miles (6,400 km)

2. more than 1,000

3. 200 miles (320 km)

4. 1,000 miles (1,600 km)

5. 2,300 miles (3,680 km)

6. more than 100

7. answers will vary

8. the rubber tree

9. It becomes an impenetrable jungle.

10. Trees are being burned, bulldozed, and cut down to make roads and more farmland.

Africa

Table of Contents

Introduction *(cont.)*

Africa

This book was designed to present an overview of the geography of the continent of Africa. It is divided into five sections to match the themes of the Geographic Education National Implementation Project (GENIP), an educational project backed by the nation's most prestigious geographers.

Each section contains a selection of teaching pages, maps, activities, interesting facts, review questions, and puzzles or games. A plan for using the material to construct a geography center is also included, as well as ideas for putting together a book as a culminating activity.

You will also find a glossary of the specialized vocabulary used by geographers. This will make it easier for your students to talk about the world they live in.

A Word or Two About Maps

Projections

The landforms shown on maps and globes do not look exactly alike. This is because it is just as hard to "peel" a globe and flatten the Earth's "skin" out into a map as it is to peel an orange and flatten out its skin to make a smooth, even surface. Even if you can get the skin off the orange in one piece, the top and bottom edges must be broken and spread out.

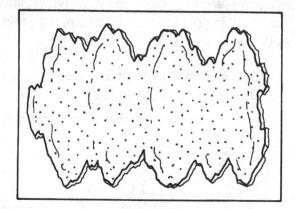

Different map makers (cartographers) have had different ideas about how to do this and have made different "projections." A projection is the way in which the map maker has chosen to flatten out the Earth's surface to make a flat map. Sometimes the map maker allows the breaks in the Earth's surface to show.

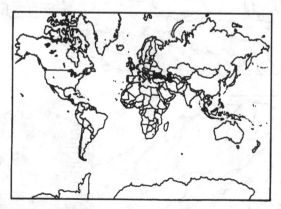

Sometimes the map maker stretches the Earth's "skin." This makes the countries near the poles look much bigger than they really are.

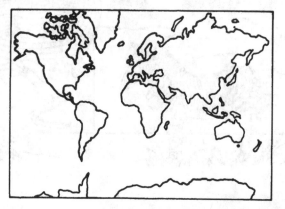

A Word or Two About Maps (cont.)

Projections (cont.)

Use your reference materials to find out the names of other common map projections and list them below. Research the advantages and disadvantages of each map projection you list and write them down below.

Map Projection	Advantages	Disadvantages

A Word or Two About Maps *(cont.)*

The Compass Rose

The compass rose is a small drawing that shows direction on a map. Most maps show north at the top and south at the bottom, west on the left and east on the right.

Look at maps to find some different styles of compass roses and then design your own. You can shrink your drawing and make multiple copies to use on the maps you make, color, or label.

154

Where on Earth Is Africa?

- Africa lies between the Atlantic Ocean and the Indian Ocean.

- Africa is the second largest continent, smaller only than Asia.

- The equator runs through the center of Africa.

- The Mediterranean Sea and the Red Sea form the northern boundaries of Africa.

Use these clues to find Africa on this map. Color it blue.

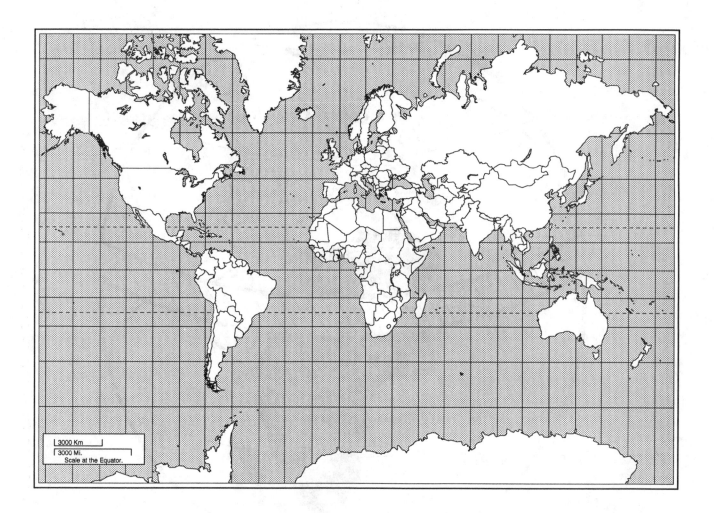

3000 Km
3000 Mi.
Scale at the Equator.

Where on Earth Is Africa? *(cont.)*

If you think of the Earth as a ball (a sphere or globe), you can draw a line around the middle (the equator) and separate the two halves into the top half (Northern Hemisphere) and the bottom half (Southern Hemisphere). Now you can talk about something as being in the Northern or Southern Hemisphere.

More lines are drawn around the Earth parallel to the equator and evenly spaced from the equator to the North and South Poles. They are called parallels or lines of latitude. They are numbered in degrees, starting with 0° at the equator and usually spaced at 15° intervals, ending with 90° N at the North Pole and 90° S at the South Pole.

(Geographers further divide their degrees into minutes and seconds so they can be very precise in locating the position of anything on the Earth's surface.)

If you divide the Earth into its Northern and Southern Hemispheres, Africa lies in the_____Hemisphere and in the_____Hemisphere.

Where on Earth Is Africa? *(cont.)*

You can also draw lines north and south around the Earth. These lines are called meridians or lines of longitude. They are usually shown 15° apart at the equator, but they all come together at the North and South Poles. (They also can be further divided into minutes and seconds, just like the parallels.)

The line that runs through Greenwich, England, is called the prime meridian (0°). Longitude is the distance east or west of the prime meridian. The line directly opposite the prime meridian is at 180° and is called the date line. If you are still thinking of the Earth as a ball (a sphere or globe), you can separate the two halves into the Western Hemisphere and the Eastern Hemisphere. (This is usually done along the meridians of 20° W and 160° E so all of Africa is in one hemisphere.)

If you divide the Earth into its Western and Eastern Hemisphere, Africa is in the_____Hemisphere.

Where on Earth Is Africa? *(cont.)*

You can tell where things on the Earth are in two ways:

- You can give their exact or absolute location using latitude and longitude expressed in degrees (minutes and seconds).

- You can tell where they are in relation to other things.

Fill out the missing information to give the exact location of where you live:

house number	street name	apartment number
city	state/country	zip code

Now, use information from a map or globe to complete this description of the exact location of Africa.

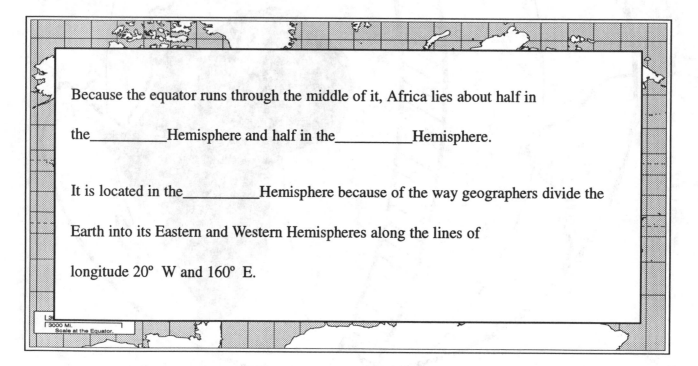

Because the equator runs through the middle of it, Africa lies about half in

the_____Hemisphere and half in the_____Hemisphere.

It is located in the_____Hemisphere because of the way geographers divide the

Earth into its Eastern and Western Hemispheres along the lines of

longitude 20° W and 160° E.

Where on Earth Is Africa? *(cont.)*

You can tell where things on the Earth are in two ways:

- You can give their exact or absolute location using latitude and longitude expressed in degrees (minutes and seconds).

- You can tell where they are in relation to other things.

Fill out the missing information of where you live in relation to other things:

I live

between_____and_____

near_____

and across

from_____.

Now, use the information from a map or globe to complete this description of the relative location of Africa.

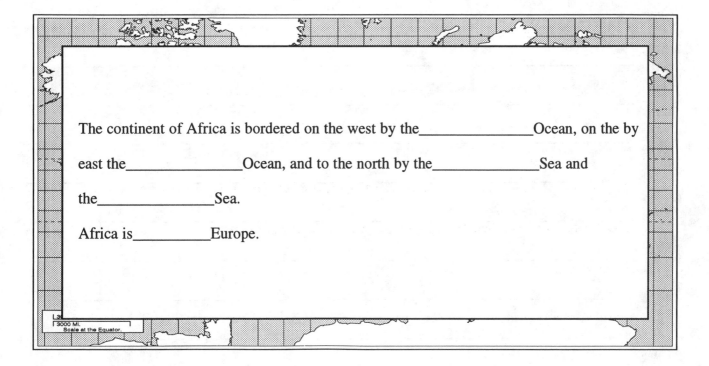

The continent of Africa is bordered on the west by the_____Ocean, on the by

east the_____Ocean, and to the north by the_____Sea and

the_____Sea.

Africa is_____Europe.

Where in Africa Is____?

Use information from a globe or map, an atlas, an encyclopedia, and your geography book to write both the exact and relative locations of five of the countries on the African continent. See the next page for the names of countries to choose from.

1. _____

_____

_____

2. _____

_____

_____

3. _____

_____

_____

4. _____

_____

_____

5. _____

_____

_____

Countries of Africa

There 57 countries of Africa listed below. Find them forwards, backwards, and diagonally in the word search below.

```
L M O R O C C O T H E G A M B I A G U I N E A S
I O A N G O L A L G E R I A A N E L E H T S S O
B Z Q W T E R T M G U I N E A B I S S A U O I U
Y A Y S A O T O M E A N D P R I N C I P E M E T
A M U I O E G Y P T R P L K E R I T R E A A R H
A B E N I N Z O X C V O S E N E G A L B Z L R A
Z I M B A B W E E T H I O P I A E N M M A I A F
Q Q W E R T Y U M I N O I N U E R A S D M A L R
F U G H E Q U A T O R I A L G U I N E A B J E I
C E N T R A L A F R I C A N R E P U B L I C O C
I M A U R I T A N I A M H S N B V U C X A O N A
V Q W N I G E R I A R R O A N T R Y U P I N E S
O E L I B E R I A S D R F O D K G H E J K G M W
R M N S U D A N V C O X B Z I A E V S D F O A A
Y D J I B O U T I M U A Q N W E E N R T Y H U Z
C A Z A I R E S O D G H A N A R F G Y D F T R I
O M N B V Z X C Z A A F S D D I W A L A M O I L
A Q W T A N Z A N I A E R E T Y U A K J H S T A
S M A Y O B T E A S N S D F B U R U N D I E I N
T N A M I B I A O G D B O T S W A N A D H L U D
S E Y C H E L L E S A E M A D A G A S C A R S D
```

Cross off the countries as you find them: Morocco, Algeria, Tunisia, Mauritania, Mali, Niger, Libya, Egypt, Chad, Sudan, Cape Verde, Senegal, Gambia, Guinea-Bissau, Guinea, Sierra Leone, Liberia, Ivory Coast, Burkina Faso, Ghana, Togo, Benin, Nigeria, Cameroon, Central African Republic, Sao Tome and Principe, Equatorial Guinea, Gabon, Congo, Zaire, Angola, Ethiopia, Djibouti, Somalia, Uganda, Kenya, Rwanda, Burundi, Tanzania, Seychelles, Comoros, Madagascar, Mauritius, Zambia, Malawi, Mozambique, Namibia, Botswana, Zimbabwe, South Africa, Swaziland, Lesotho

Countries of Africa *(cont.)*

Use information from an atlas, an encyclopedia, your geography book, or any other reference book to write two interesting facts about each African country listed below.

1. Algeria _____

_____

2. Angola _____

_____

3. Benin _____

_____

4. Botswana _____

_____

5. Burkina Faso _____

_____

6. Burundi _____

_____

7. Cameroon _____

_____

8. Cape Verde _____

_____

9. Central African Republic _____

_____

10. Chad _____

_____

11. Comoros _____

_____

Countries of Africa *(cont.)*

12. Congo _____

    _____

13. Ivory Coast _____

    _____

14. Djibouti _____

    _____

15. Egypt _____

    _____

16. Equatorial Guinea _____

    _____

17. Ethiopia _____

    _____

18. Gabon _____

    _____

19. Ghana _____

    _____

20. Guinea _____

    _____

21. Guinea-Bissau _____

    _____

22. Kenya _____

    _____

Countries of Africa *(cont.)*

23. Lesotho _____

_____

24. Liberia _____

_____

25. Libya _____

_____

26. Madagascar _____

_____

27. Malawi _____

_____

28. Mali _____

_____

29. Mauritania _____

_____

30. Mauritius _____

_____

31. Morocco _____

_____

32. Mozambique _____

_____

33. Namibia _____

_____

34. Niger _____

_____

Countries of Africa *(cont.)*

35. Nigeria _____

_____

36. Rwanda _____

_____

37. Sao Tome and Principe _____

_____

38. Senegal _____

_____

39. Seychelles _____

_____

40. Sierra Leone _____

_____

41. Somalia _____

_____

42. South Africa _____

_____

43. Sudan _____

_____

44. Swaziland _____

_____

45. Tanzania _____

_____

Countries of Africa *(cont.)*

46. Gambia _____

_____

47. Togo _____

_____

48. Tunisia _____

_____

49. Uganda _____

_____

50. Zaire _____

_____

51. Zambia _____

_____

52. Zimbabwe _____

_____

Bonus!

Many African nations changed their names when they became countries that colonized. How many can you find? What were their old names? What are they called now?

_____

_____

_____

_____

_____

_____

Look at the Map

Use the numbered list of African countries on pages 162–166 to label the map below. Write the number of each country on the map and use the list for a key.

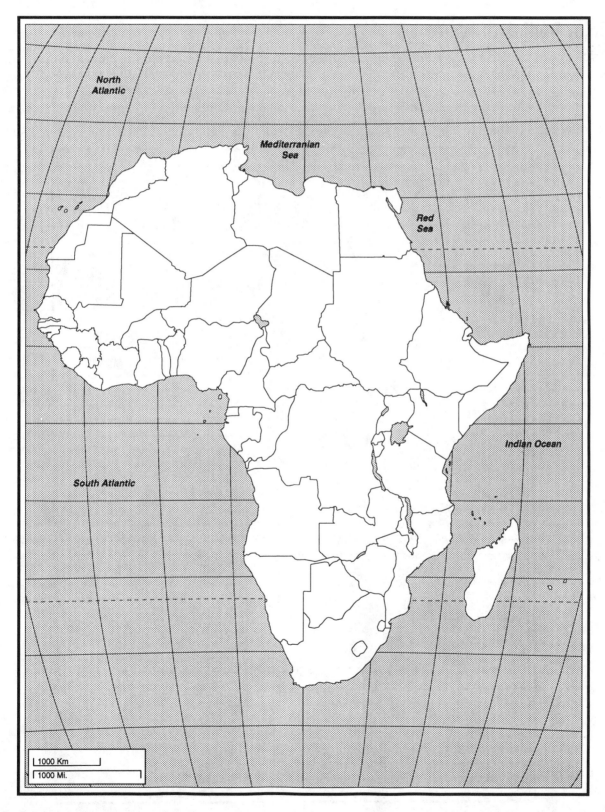

Physical Characteristics of Africa

Major Bodies of Water

Africa is surrounded by the *Atlantic Ocean* to the west, the *Indian Ocean* to the east, and the *Mediterranean Sea* to the north. It is separated from Asia on the northeast by the *Red Sea* and the *Gulf of Aden.*

Use reference sources to label these major bodies of water on the map of Africa.

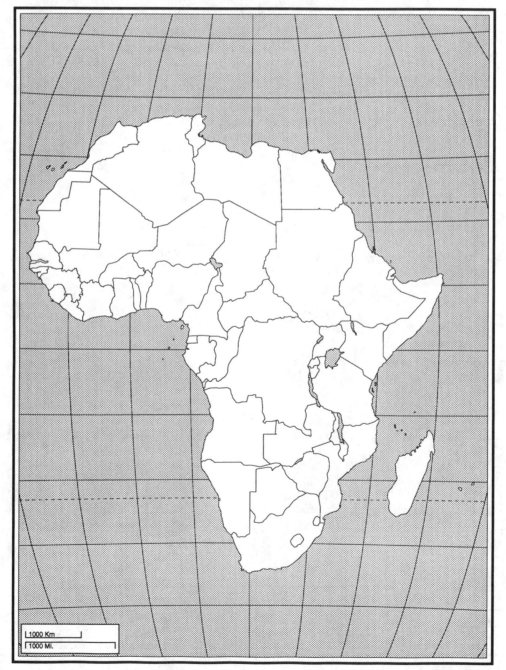

Physical Characteristics
of Africa *(cont.)*

Landforms

Africa is the second largest continent. Its coastlines are not as irregular as those of the other continents, and it has fewer mountains. *The Atlas Mountains* border on the Mediterranean Sea. *Mount Kilimanjaro,* the highest point in Africa, is a volcanic peak that rises near the east coast of the continent. Mount Kilimanjaro is near the *Great Rift Valley,* which runs north and south from the *Ethiopian Highlands* near the Red Sea almost to the Malawi River. This is an area where two of the Earth's plates are pulling apart, making a long wide depression on the Earth's surface.

Africa is largely desert. The *Sahara* sweeps across the north of Africa, filling more than a quarter of the continent. The *Sahel,* which is an arid grassland bordering the Sahara on the south, is turning into desert too. The *Kalahari Desert* and the *Namib Desert* cover much of southern Africa. In the middle of the continent, centered on the Equator, lies the *Congo Basin* covered with a rain forest that is one of the wettest places on Earth. Between the rain forest and the deserts are the savanna grasslands and great plains, which are home to most of Africa's large animals. The island of Madagascar is also part of Africa. It lies about 150 miles (240 km) off the southeast coast and is considered a continental fragment.

Use reference sources to label these landforms on the map of Africa.

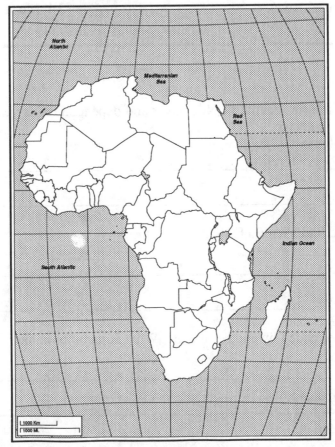

Physical Characteristics of Africa *(cont.)*

Other Bodies of Water

Africa has important lakes and rivers. The *Nile* is the longest river in the world, with a length of 4,145 miles (6,632 km). Other important rivers are the *Niger*, the *Congo*, the *Zambezi*, the *Senegal*, and the *Orange*. Lakes include *Victoria* and *Tanganyika*, two of the largest in the world. The *Mozambique Channel* divides Madagascar from the mainland.

Using reference sources and the map on page 171, draw the lakes and rivers listed below. Then label those lakes, rivers, and bodies of water with their numbers and use the list for a key.

1. Lake Tanganyika	8. Senegal River
2. Lake Victoria	9. Orange River
3. Lake Malawi	10. Niger River
4. Lake Chad	11. Nile River
5. Lake Volta	12. White Nile River
6. Congo River	13. Blue Nile River
7. Zambezi River	14. Mozambique Channel

Bonus Questions!

What ancient country grew up around the Nile River and depended on its yearly flooding for planting crops?

_____

_____

On which river will you find Victoria Falls?

_____

_____

Which river is sometimes called by another name? What is its other name?

_____

_____

Physical Characteristics
of Africa *(cont.)*

Other Bodies of Water

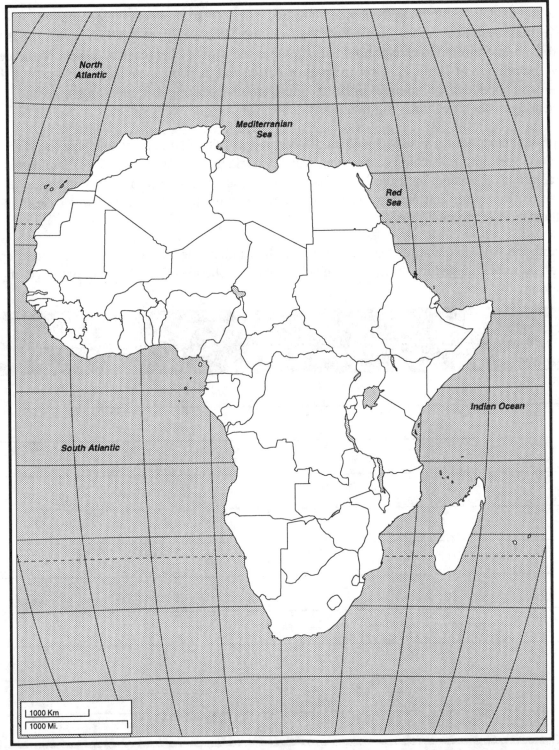

People in Africa

The oldest human fossils have been found in Africa, in Olduvai Gorge, which is located in the Great Rift Valley. Africa may turn out to be the place where the human race began. Certainly, many great civilizations developed there. Egypt is well known, of course. But, when Europeans first came to Africa, Timbuktu, in what is now Mali, was also a center of commerce and learning, as was Zimbabwe in the southeast.

Africa and its people can really be divided into two parts. First, there are the people who live around the Mediterranean Sea and across the Red Sea from the Middle Eastern Arab countries. In these countries, often referred to as North Africa, Arabic is the primary language and most of the people follow the religion of Islam. The second part of Africa and its people can be found south of the Sahara. This area is populated by hundreds of black ethnic groups speaking different languages and representing different cultures and religions.

European contact with Africa began about 500 years ago. The first contact involved the slave trade but soon developed into full-scale colonization, which was done without taking ethnic boundaries into consideration. It was not until the 1960s that most African countries won their independence and, when most of the Europeans left, had to face the problems of ethnic boundaries. In many cases, these problems have led to civil wars.

Research the African countries that have declared their independence from European countries. If the African country changed its name, write the old name and the new one. Use another page, if you need more room.

African Country		European Country
Old Name	New Name	

172

People in Africa *(cont.)*

Ethnic Groups

Pick an African ethnic group to learn about and answer these questions. Some suggested groups are listed below.

Arabs   **Pygmies**   **Masai**   **Ibo**

1. In which African environment does this group of people live?

   _____

2. Do they live the way their ancestors lived? If not, what changes have they made?

   _____

   _____

   _____

3. What are their homes like?

   _____

   _____

   _____

4. How do they earn a living? (What kind of work do they do?)

   _____

   _____

5. What religion do they practice?

   _____

6. Use the back of this page to tell about some of their customs.

   _____

   _____

   _____

   _____

   _____

Animals in Africa

Read the clues and unscramble the names of African animals. Circle the names of the animals that are on the endangered species list.

1. _____ large and ferocious-looking but really shy and friendly animals who live in both the lowlands and mountains (larislog)

2. _____ an animal easily recognized by its long neck (feragif)

3. _____ the pack animal of North Africa (macel)

4. _____ a large animal with a long trunk and two curving tusks (pantheel)

5. _____ a fierce carnivore of the grasslands (nilo)

6. _____ a spotted cat of the forests and plains (paroled)

7. _____ a type of anteater (radavkra)

8. _____ its name means river horse (pathopmipuso)

9. _____ an animal that is almost extinct because it is hunted for its horns (conshorier)

10. _____ a monkey that may have colorful markings on its body (bobnoa)

11. _____ is it black with white stripes or white with black stripes (razeb)

12. _____ there are many varieties of this grass-eating animal (lopteena)

13. _____ an animal that looks a lot like a raccoon (trielading muerl)

14. _____ an animal that is often confused with the alligator (dilorcoce)

15. _____ the ape that is ranked as the most intelligent of all animals (pamnizeech)

People Depend on the Environment

Make a list of Africa's natural resources.

_____

_____

_____

_____

_____

Then, create a symbol to go with each natural resource and make a key. Using your newly created symbols, show these resources on the map of Africa on the next page.

Resource Key

People Depend on the Environment *(cont.)*

Resource Map

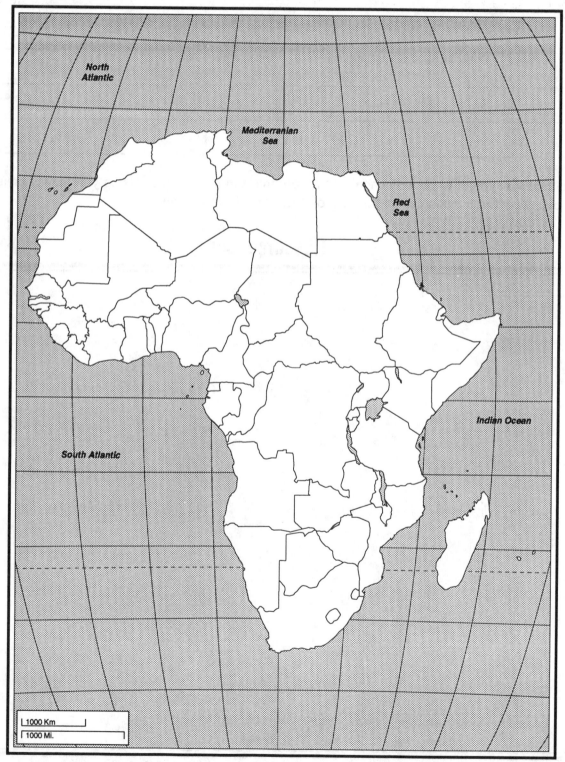

People Adapt to and Change the Environment

People adapt to and change the environment in many ways. Think of some possible solutions that may solve these environmental problems:

Very dry conditions for farming:

_____

_____

_____

_____

Hills too steep for crops:

_____

_____

_____

_____

Areas that flood:

_____

_____

_____

_____

Housing in hot climates:

_____

_____

_____

_____

People Adapt to and Change the Environment *(cont.)*

People adapt to and change the environment in many ways. Think of some possible solutions that may solve these environmental problems:

Housing in cold climates:

_____

_____

_____

_____

Clothing in hot climates:

_____

_____

_____

_____

Clothing in cold climates:

_____

_____

_____

_____

Transportation in mountainous or hilly areas:

_____

_____

_____

_____

Technology Impacts the Environment

Resources are things that are valued and used by people. Natural resources are resources that occur in nature, such as minerals in the Earth, trees, water, and air.

The way people feel about and use natural resources changes as new technologies are developed. However, the development and application of these technologies is affected by several factors: wealth, organization, and infrastructure. Infrastructure is what underlies new development. It consists of things like sewers, power sources and power lines, water purification plants, roads, tunnels, and bridges.

Work with a partner or in a group to figure out what kinds of infrastructure are needed for the uses of technology listed below.

Technology	Infrastructure Needed
Bathrooms with running water and flush toilets	
Radio reception	
Television reception	

Technology Impacts the Environment *(cont.)*

Work with a partner or in a group to figure out what kinds of infrastructure are needed for the uses of technology listed below.

Technology	Infrastructure Needed
Telephones	
Lights	
Train transportation	
Car and truck transportation	
Machines to assist with farming	

Movement Demonstrates Interdependence

Why does human activity require movement? _____

_____

_____

Do the people in your family go places?_____Choose two people and answer the following questions:

	Person #1	Person #2
Who?		
When?		
Where?		
How far?		
How often?		
Why?		
Mode of transportation?		

Movement Demonstrates
Interdependence *(cont.)*

Use reference sources to figure the distances between these African cities.

Algiers/Tunis _____

Cairo/Khartoum _____

Cape Town/Tripoli _____

Nairobi/Pretoria _____

Bangui/Mogadisho _____

Brazzaville/Rabat _____

Addis Ababa/Accra _____

Alexandria/Djibouti _____

Casablanca/Tripoli _____

Asmara/Abuja _____

Kampala/Kinshasa _____

Windhoek/Gaborone _____

Addis Ababa 2600km

Tunis 2750km

Nairobi 3060km

Capetown 5130km

Movement Involves Linkages

List some of the ways people travel from place to place in the less developed regions of Africa.

_____

_____

_____

_____

_____

List some of the ways people travel from place to place in the urban areas of Africa.

_____

_____

_____

_____

_____

_____

Bonus Question!

Why don't many people use cars to travel from one city to another?

_____

_____

_____

_____

_____

_____

_____

Movement Involves Linkages (cont.)

How will people travel around Africa in the future?

_____

_____

_____

_____

Design your own future method of transportation. Explain it and then draw a picture of it below.

_____

_____

_____

_____

This Is How My Future Transportation Will Work:

_____

_____

_____

_____

This Is How My Future Transportation Will Look:

_____

Movement Includes People, Ideas, and Products

People go places for business and for pleasure. Going somewhere for pleasure is called touring.

Where have you gone for pleasure?

_____

_____

_____

_____

Where would you like to go?

_____

_____

_____

_____

Ideas can travel too. List some of the different ways ideas travel from place to place.

_____

_____

_____

Products also travel. What are some of the ways products travel?

_____

_____

_____

_____

Includes People, Ideas, and Products *(cont.)*

Think about a place you would like to visit in Africa. Design a cover for a travel brochure about that place. Sketch your design below. Write a description of the place that will make other people want to travel there too.

_____

_____

_____

_____

_____

Savanna Grasslands

Animals Across the Curriculum

A region is a portion of the Earth's surface that has characteristics unlike any other. The savannas of Africa form a region. They are flat, sunny plains covered with long, thick grass and dotted with few trees. Most of the large animals of Africa live there.

Africa has more kinds of grassland animals than any other continent. The *elephant, rhinoceros,* and *hippopotamus* are three of the largest. The *giraffe* and *zebra* also live on the savannas, along with the *ostrich, aardvark, kudu, gnu,* and many other varieties of *antelope.* The *lion* is probably the best known and most ferocious of all African grassland animals.

1. The Elephant

Be ready to report on the elephant. Find out what this animal eats, if it migrates, and if its territory has become smaller. Write down any other facts that you think are interesting.

_____

_____

_____

_____

_____

_____

2. The Giraffe

Write a poem about the giraffe. This gentle, awkward-looking animal would seem like something out of a science-fiction story if we were not so used to what they look like. Try to see a video tape or read an illustrated book about this animal before you write your poem. Write your title and poem here and use another piece of paper to illustrate your poem when it is finished.

_____

_____

_____

_____

_____

_____

The Savanna Grasslands *(cont.)*

Animals Across the Curriculum

3. Put the names of the italicized animals on page 187 in ABC order and tell how many syllables are in each one.

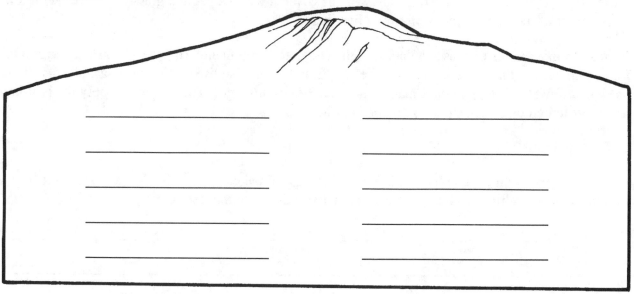

4. **The Hippopotamus and the Rhinoceros**

Compare and contrast these two huge animals. Where do they live? What do they eat? How much do they weigh? Do they have any enemies? What other interesting facts can you find out?

_____

_____

_____

_____

_____

_____

_____

_____

_____

The Savanna Grasslands *(cont.)*

Animals Across the Curriculum *(cont.)*

5. The Aardvark

The aardvark is a kind of anteater. Anteaters live in many places and go by many names. How is the aardvark different from the giant anteater or ant bear, the collared anteater, the echidna, and the pangolin? Find out as much information as you can about anteaters and list it below.

_____

_____

_____

_____

_____

_____

_____

_____

_____

_____

_____

_____

_____

_____

_____

_____

_____

_____

The Savanna Grasslands *(cont.)*

Animals Across the Curriculum *(cont.)*

6. Antelopes

How many kinds of antelopes live on the African savannas? What do they look like? How can you tell them apart?

_____

_____

_____

7. A Bar Graph

Many African countries are setting aside land for game reserves. Pick six countries and use a bar graph to compare their total land area with the land they have set aside for wild animals. Keep track of your facts here as you do your research.

Country	Total Land Area	Wild Animal Reserves

The Rain Forest

The Congo Basin lies on the equator in the middle of Africa, right where the continent narrows down on the Atlantic side near the Gulf of Guinea. Here is where the African rain forest grows. This is one of the wettest places on Earth; rain falls almost every day of the year. The rain forest covers a much smaller area than either the African deserts or the grasslands. The Congo River and its tributaries flow through it, and the basin is always hot and humid. The rain forest is still home to many exotic animals, but many of its native animals now live only in zoos around the world.

Find information about this area in reference books and answer these questions.

1. How long is the Congo River?

   _____

2. What is unique about this river?

   _____

3. How does it rank in comparison to other rivers?

   _____

4. What is the Congo River's other name?

   _____

5. What is Equatorial Guinea's chief export crop?

   _____

6. What is the capital city of Congo?

   _____

The Rain Forest *(cont.)*

Find information about this area in reference books and answer these questions.

7. Name four animals that live in the African rain forest.

1._____   3. _____

2._____   4. _____

8. From what European country did the people of Equatorial Guinea win their freedom?

_____

_____

_____

_____

9. What primitive ethnic group is associated with the African rain forest?

_____

_____

_____

_____

10. Why is the African rain forest in less trouble than the South American rain forests?

_____

_____

_____

_____

African Fact Game

This game can be played in different ways:

Game 1—You can use a Jeopardy format. Students love this, and they can set it up all by themselves or with just a little help. Run the answer cards on one color of paper and the question cards on another color for easy sorting.

Game 2—You can make a card game like rummy. All the cards should be run on one color for this. Shuffle the cards and deal five to each player. Put the leftovers facedown or in the middle of the table. Players draw from the stack and discard in another stack. The object of the game is to lay down pairs by matching questions and answers. You can make it more complicated by allowing students to challenge one another's matched pairs if they think the matches are incorrect. Have students keep track of the rules they make and write game directions.

Fact Game Cards

It is the highest point in Africa	What is Mt. Kilimanjaro?
It has the largest area of any country in Africa.	What is Sudan?
It has the most people of any country in Africa.	What is Nigeria?

African Fact Game *(cont.)*

Fact Game Cards *(cont.)*

It is the second largest continent.	What is Africa?
It is the longest river on Earth	What is the Nile?
It is one of the wettest places on Earth.	What is the Congo Basin?
It is the name of the cape at the southern tip of Africa?	What is the Cape of Good Hope?
These animals are hunted for their tusks and horns.	What are elephants and rhinoceroses?
It is a large island off the southeast coast of Africa.	What is Madagascar?

African Fact Game (cont.)

Fact Game Cards (cont.)

It is the largest desert in the world.	What is the Sahara?
It is a place in the desert where water and plants are found.	What is an oasis?
It is the bean from which chocolate is made.	What is cacao?
They are people who move from place to place to find water and grazing land.	What are nomads?
It is the capital city of Egypt.	What is Cairo?
They are a pride.	What is a group of lions called?

African Fact Game (cont.)

Fact Game Cards (cont.)

They are animals that are used for transportation in the desert.	What are camels?
It is an area of heavy rain forest.	What is the Congo Basin?
They are people who hunt endangered animals illegally	What are poachers?
Lake Assal, Djibouti, at 512 feet (155 m) below sea level.	What is the lowest point in Africa?
The place where archaeologists have found important fossils.	What is Olduvai Gorge?
It is the primary language of North Africa.	What is Arabic?

Fact Game Cards *(cont.)*

Let your students make their own question-and-answer fact cards. Students usually like to make extra hard ones in hopes of stumping each other, so have them write the book and page number where the information can be found for each card.

	Book:_____
	Page: _____
	Book:_____
	Page: _____
	Book:_____
	Page: _____
	Book:_____
	Page: _____
	Book:_____
	Page: _____

The Geography Center

Putting the Center Together

You can set up your Geography Center in a corner of your classroom and make it as simple or as elaborate as you want. The center should have a map, a globe, and an atlas. (Several maps, a couple of globes, and multiple copies of the atlas would be even better.) A table and chairs will facilitate group activities and discussions. A supply of writing and drawing materials will also come in handy. A bookcase, shelf, or window sill can be utilized for storing reference books. The more reference books you can provide, the better the assigned projects will be. If you have access to a TV, VCR, and tapes, you can show movies about the places you are studying. There are many tapes of this variety available, and the visual learners in your class will really appreciate this. Cushions for sitting on the floor to read or view tapes add a cozy touch.

Making the Center Work

You can make the Geography Center part of your instructional day by scheduling groups to do center work. Change the materials daily or weekly or provide a set of task cards at the beginning of the unit and expect each student to work through them individually or as part of a group. (See pages 199–201.)

Use Portfolios

Have students make portfolios and store them in containers in an accessible area of your center. Try using the inexpensive but sturdy plastic crates that are available at local hardware stores. Make students responsible for their own progress by having them file their own work, both completed work and work in progress. Have students create attractive covers for their portfolios so the accumulated work can be attractively displayed at your school's open house.

Deck the Walls

Encourage artwork, creative writing, and exploratory math to go along with your geography unit and spread it throughout the curriculum. Display these products on a bulletin board in your Geography Center. Have students mount and post their own work. They can cut out letters and create colorful captions for the board.

Have another bulletin board reserved for posting newspaper and magazine articles dealing with the continent you are studying. Encourage your students to bring in these articles, share them, and discuss their meaning and importance.

Task Cards

Task Card #3

What is the highest mountain peak on the continent?

How tall is it?

In which country is it found?

Task Card #4

What is the largest country on the continent?

What countries or bodies of water border it?

What is its capital city?

Task Card #1

What is the longest river on the continent?

How long is it?

Through which country or countries does it flow?

Task Card #2

What is the most important mountain range on the continent?

How long is it?

In which country or countries are these mountains found?

The Geography Center (cont.)

Task Cards (cont.)

Task Card #5

What is the smallest country on the continent?

What countries or bodies of water border it?

What's its capital city?

Task Card #6

What is the largest lake on the continent?

In which country or countries is it found?

Which river is associated with it?

Task Card #7

What animals are associated with the continent?

In what country or countries do they live?

Are they in any danger in today's civilization?

Task Card #8

What variations in climate are found on the continent?

What variations in weather are found on the continent?

Can people live in all parts of the continent?

The Geography Center *(cont.)*

Task Card Response

Leave a stack of these task card response forms in the geography center for students to use.

Name _____ Date_____

Task Card #_____

Question #1

_____

_____

_____

_____

Question #2

_____

_____

_____

_____

Question #3

_____

_____

_____

_____

Bonus

I also learned_____

_____

_____

_____

The Culminating Activity: Making a Book

Method

You and your students can go about bookmaking in many different ways. Here are some suggestions:

- The book can be your students' showcase portfolios.

- Students can review and reflect upon the work they have accumulated in their portfolios, select the most representative samples or the pieces they like best, and put these things together in book form.

- The book can be a showcase portfolio based on the teacher's criteria.

- Have students select work from their portfolios based on a list you develop.

- The book can be comprised of new material that sums up the unit.

- Have students complete various assignments meant specifically for inclusion in their books, showing their grasp of the material. (See pages 203–213.)

Contents

In most cases you will probably want your students to include maps, facts about both physical and political geography, research about animals, people, and resources. They can review or report on any books they have read about the continent, and they can write about what they have learned and how it has affected the way they view the world.

Cover

You can specify and provide the design for the cover so that all of the books will be uniform, or you can encourage your students to design a cover that is representative of the continent. A collage of pictures cut from magazines and travel brochures is an option that works well.

Be sure to laminate the finished covers so the books can be used as part of your classroom library or Geography Center reference shelf. Your students may also want to share their books with students in other classes.

Exciting ideas for binding and publishing follow on pages 214–216.

The Culminating Activity:
Making a Book (cont.)

Trace an outline map of the continent. Transfer information about its physical features from all of the maps you have made. You might want to use different colors to create a key.

Name _____ Date_____

Map of Physical Features

The Culminating Activity: Making a Book *(cont.)*

Use the information you have already gathered or do some new research to complete this page.

Name _____ Date_____

Facts About Physical Features

Area: _____

_____

Highest Point: _____

_____

Lowest Point: _____

_____

Largest Island:_____

_____

Longest River:_____

_____

Largest Lake: _____

_____

Tallest Waterfall:_____

_____

Largest Desert: _____

_____

Longest Reef: _____

_____

The Culminating Activity: Making a Book *(cont.)*

Trace an outline map of the continent. Transfer information about its political features from all of the maps you have made. You might want to use a numbered list to create a key.

Name _____Date_____

Map of Political Features

The Culminating Activity: Making a Book *(cont.)*

Use the information you have already gathered or do some new research to complete this page.

Name _____ Date_____

Facts About Political Features

Population: _____

Largest Country (by area): _____

Largest Country (by population): _____

Smallest Country (by area): _____

Smallest Country (by population): _____

Largest Metropolitan Area (by population):_____

_____

_____

_____

_____

_____

Newest Countries:_____

_____

_____

_____

_____

_____

_____

The Culminating Activity: Making a Book *(cont.)*

Use the information you have already gathered or do some new research to complete this page.

Name _____ Date_____

The People

The people of this continent belong to these ethnic groups:

_____

_____

_____

They speak these languages:

_____

_____

_____

They live in these different environments:

_____

_____

_____

_____

Their ways of life have changed or are changing:

_____

_____

_____

_____

_____

The Culminating Activity:
Making a Book *(cont.)*

Pick the city on the continent that is most interesting to you. Use the information you have already gathered or do some new research to complete this page.

Name _____Date_____

The city of_____.

This city is in _____

Area: _____

Population: _____

_____

Language(s): _____

_____

Ethnic Groups: _____

_____

Religious Groups: _____

_____

Famous Natural Features: _____

_____

_____

Famous Constructed Features: _____

_____

_____

_____

The Culminating Activity: Making a Book *(cont.)*

Use the information you have already gathered or do some new research to complete this page.

Name _____ Date_____

The Animals

The best known animals of this continent are _____

_____

_____

The animals of this continent are important because _____

_____

_____

The animals that still live in their natural habitats are _____

_____

_____

The animals that are on the endangered list are _____

_____

_____

_____

They are on the endangered list because _____

_____

_____

_____

_____

The Culminating Activity: Making a Book *(cont.)*

Keep track of the books you read about the continent on this log.

Name _____ Date _____

Book Log

Title: _____   Fiction: _____

Author: _____   Nonfiction: _____

Illustrator: _____   Rating: _____

Title: _____   Fiction: _____

Author: _____   Nonfiction: _____

Illustrator: _____   Rating: _____

Title: _____   Fiction: _____

Author: _____   Nonfiction: _____

Illustrator: _____   Rating: _____

Title: _____   Fiction: _____

Author: _____   Nonfiction: _____

Illustrator: _____   Rating: _____

The Culminating Activity: Making a Book _(cont.)_

Use copies of this form to review your favorite nonfiction books about the continent you have been studying.

Name _____ Date _____

Book Review/Nonfiction

Title: _____

Author: _____

Illustrator: _____

Summary: _____

_____

_____

_____

_____

Reasons I liked or did not like this book: _____

_____

_____

_____

_____

_____

_____

_____

Bonus!

If you liked this book and think other people should read it, you can do one of two things. (1) Write a paragraph or two telling how a nonfiction book can help you understand a continent or a country and post it on the bulletin board in the Geography Center. (2) Make a poster advertising the book and post it on the bulletin board in the Geography Center.

The Culminating Activity: Making a Book *(cont.)*

Use copies of this form to review your favorite fiction books about the continent you have been studying.

Name _____ Date_____

Book Review/Fiction

Title: _____

Author: _____

Illustrator: _____

Summary: _____

_____

_____

_____

_____

_____

Reasons I liked or did not like this book:_____

_____

_____

_____

_____

_____

Bonus!

If you liked this book and think other people should read it, you can do one of two things. (1) Write a paragraph or two telling how a fiction book can help you understand a continent or a country and post it on the bulletin board in the Geography Center. (2) Make a poster advertising the book and post it on the bulletin board in the Geography Center.

The Culminating Activity:
Making a Book *(cont.)*

Write a reflective essay in which you discuss the ways that studying geography has given you a better understanding of the world and the people in it.

Name _____ Date_____

Title:_____

_____

_____

_____

_____

_____

_____

_____

_____

_____

_____

_____

_____

_____

_____

_____

_____

_____

_____

_____

The Culminating Activity: Making a Book *(cont.)*

Book Binding Ideas

1. Stack all the pages of the book in a neat pile.

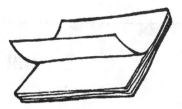

2. Place a blank sheet of paper on the top and bottom of the pages.

3. Leaving approximately 1/2" (1.25 cm) border, staple or sew all of the pages together on the left side.

4. Place two pieces of lightweight cardboard side by side. (Cereal boxes work well.) Each piece should be 1/2 to 1" (1.25 to 2.5 cm) larger than the size of the pages in the book.

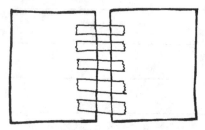

5. Leaving approximately 1" (2.5 cm) between them, tape the cardboard pieces together.

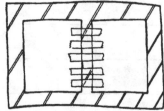

6. Put the cardboard on top of your covering material (e.g., fabric, wallpaper, contact paper, or wrapping paper). Glue the cardboard and covering material together, leaving a 1 to 1 1/2" (2.5 to 3.25 cm) material border.

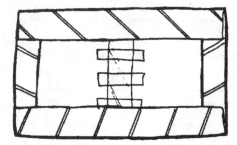

7. Fold up the edges of material over the cardboard and glue in place.

8. Glue the blank pages to the inside of the cardboard covers. Your book is ready to read and share.

The Culminating Activity: Making a Book (cont.)

Pop-Up Books

1. Fold a 8 1/2" x 11" (22 cm x 28 cm) piece of paper in half crosswise.

2. Measure and mark 2 3/4" (7 cm) from each side along the fold. Cut 2 3/4" (7 cm) slits at the marks.

3. Push cut area inside-out and crease to form the pop-up section.

4. Draw, color, and cut out the object to get "popped-up."

5. Glue it onto the pop-up section.

6. Glue two pages back to back, making sure the pop-up section is free.

7. Glue additional pages together, making as many pages (including pop-up pages) as you like. Be sure to include a free sheet on both the front and back so that those pages can be glued to a cover.

8. Glue a cover over the entire book.

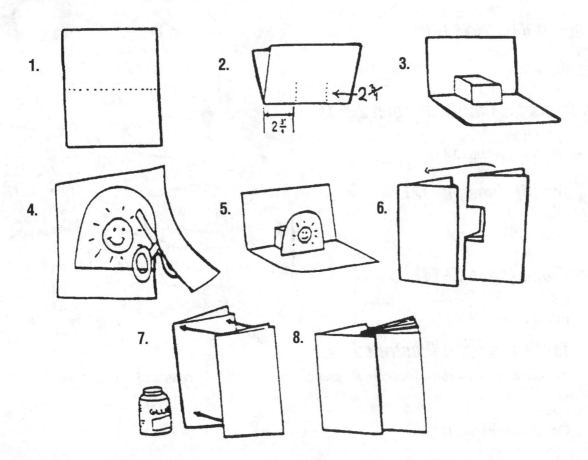

The Culminating Activity: Making a Book *(cont.)*

Real Markets for Student Writing

Student writing can be sent to the following addresses. Check your professional journals for more sources.

Children's Playmate (ages 5–8)

P.O. Box 567B
Indianapolis, Indiana 46206

Cricket (ages 6–12)

Cricket League
P.O. Box 300
Peru, Illinois 61354

Ebony Jr! (ages 6–12)

820 S. Michigan Avenue
Chicago, Illinois 60605

Flying Pencil Press (ages 8–14)

P.O. Box 7667
Elgin, Illinois 60121

Highlights for Children (ages 2–11)

803 Church Street
Honesdale, Pennsylvania 18431

Jack and Jill (ages 8–12)

P.O. Box 567B
Indianapolis, Indiana 46206

Stone Soup (ages 5–14)

P.O. Box 83
Santa Cruz, California 95063

National Written and Illustrated by...

(This is an awards contest for students in all grade levels. Write for rules and guidelines.)
Landmark Editions, Inc.
P.O. Box 4469
Kansas City, Missouri 64127

Software Review

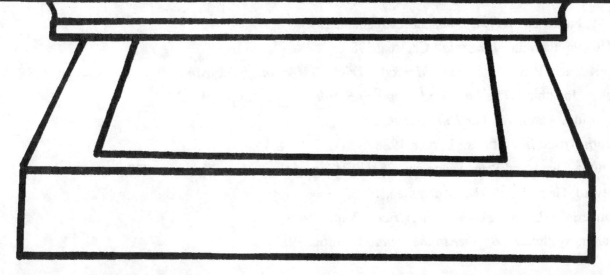

Software: *Where in the World Is Carmen Sandiego?* (Broderbund)

Hardware: 640K IBM PC with color graphics card, color monitor, sound card, and CD-ROM drive or 4MB Macintosh with CD-ROM drive

Grade Level: Intermediate

Summary: *Where in the World Is Carmen Sandiego?* is a simulation program where students will learn about world geography and world history. Carmen Sandiego and her group of villains are stealing priceless artifacts from around the world. It is the job of your students to recover the stolen artifacts, return them to their country of origin, and arrest the criminals responsible. By following clues and interviewing witnesses, your students will be able to track down the criminals.

Included in this software package is The World Almanac and Book of Facts to help students interpret clues and locate various places around the world. Students will be promoted as they solve cases, and when they have solved eighty cases, they will be retired from active duty.

Bibliography

Aardema, Verna. *Anansi Finds a Fool: An Ashanti Tale*. Dial, 1992.

Aardema, Verna. *Sebgugugu the Glutton: A Bantu Tale from Rwanda, Africa.* Eerdmans, 1993.

African Tales: Folklore of the Central African Republic. Telecraft, 1992.

Anderson, David. *The Origin of Life on Earth: An African Creation Myth.* Sights, 1991.

Arkhurst, Joyce Cooper. *The Adventures of Spider: West African Folktales*. Little, 1992.

Berger, Terry. *Black Fairy Tales.* Macmillan, 1974.

Brill, Marlene. *Libya.* Childrens, 1988.

Chaisson, John. *African Journey.* Macmillan, 1987.

Crossland, Bert. *"Where on Earth Are We?"* Book Links. September, 1994

Dickinson, Mary B. (Ed.). *National Geographic Picture Atlas of Our World*. National Geographic Society, 1993

Fox, Mary V. *Tunisia.* Childrens, 1990.

Geographic Education National Implementation Project. Guidelines, 1987.

Georges, D.V. *Africa.* Childrens, 1986.

Ghana in Pictures. Lerner, 1988.

Greeves, Nick. *When Hippo Was Hairy: And Other Tales from Africa.* Barron's, 1988.

Halliburton, Warren J. *Africa's Struggle to Survive.* Macmillan, 1993.

Halliburton, Warren J. *African Landscapes*. Macmillan, 1993.

Halliburton, Warren J. *City and Village Life.* Macmillan, 1993.

Hintz, Martin. *Morocco.* Childrens, 1985.

Jacobsoen, Karen. *Kenya.* Childrens, 1991.

Kurtz, Jane. *Ethiopia: The Roof of Africa.* Macmillan, 1991.

Laure, Jason. *Angola.* Childrens, 1993.

Laure, Jason. *Namibia.* Childrens, 1993.

Laure, Jason. *Zambia.* Childrens, 1989.

Levy, Patricia. *Nigeria.* Marshall Cavendish, 1993.

McCulla, Patricia. *Tanzania.* Chelsea, 1988.

McKissack, Patricia. *Monkey-Monkey's Trick: Based on an African Folk Tale.* Random, 1988.

Paton, Jonathan. *The Land and People of South Africa.* Harper, 1988.

Percefull, Aaron W. *The Nile.* Watts, 1984.

South Africa in Pictures. Lerner, 1988.

Stanley, Diane and Peter Vennema. *Shaka: King of the Zulus.* Morrow, 1988.

Stewart, Gail B. *Liberia.* Macmillan, 1992.

Timberlake, Lloyd. *Feminine in Africa.* Watts, 1986.

Walter, Mildred P. *Brother to the Wind.* Lothrop, 1985.

Bibliography *(cont.)*

Technology

Broderbund. *MacGlobe & PC Globe.* Available from Learning Services, (800)877-9378. disk

Broderbund. *Where in the World Is Carmen Sandiego?* Available from Troll (800)526-5289. CD-ROM and disk

Bureau of Electronic Publishing Inc. *World Fact Book.* Available from Educational Resources, (800)624-2926. CD-ROM

CLEARVUE. *The Earth, the Oceans, and Plants & Animals: Interactive, curriculum oriented CD-ROMs.* Available from Educational Resources, (800)624-2926. CD-ROM

DeLorme Publishing. *Global Explorer.* Available from DeLorme Publishing, 1995. CD-ROM

Impressions. *My First World Atlas.* Available from Educational Resources, (800)624-2926. disk

Lawrence. *Nigel's World Adventures in World Geography.* Available from Educational Resources, (800)624-2926. CD-ROM and disk

Magic Quest. *Time Treks and Earth Treks.* Available from Educational Resources, (800)624-2926. disk

MECC. *World GeoGraph.* Available from Educational Resources, (800)624-2926. disk

Mindscape. *World Atlas.* Available from Educational Resources, (800)624-2926. disk

National Geographic. *STV: World Geography.* Available from National Geographic Educational Technology, (800)328-2936. videodisc

National Geographic. *Zip Zap Map.* Available from Educational Resources, (800)624-2926. laserdisc and disk

Newton Technology. *GEOvista Tutor.* Available from William K. Bradford, (800)421-2009. disk

Orange Cherry. *Jungle Safari.* Available from Educational Resources, (800) 624-2926. disk

Orange Cherry. *Time Traveler.* Available from Educational Resources, (800)624-2926. CD-ROM

Pride in Learning. *Global Issues.* Available from Educational Resources, (800)624-2926. disk

Queue. *Atlas Explorer.* Available from Educational Resources, (800)624-2926. disk

Sanctuary Woods. *Ecology Treks.* Available from Learning Services, (800)624-2926. software and videodisc

Software Toolworks. *World Atlas.* Available from Learning Services, (800)877-9378. CD-ROM and disk

SVE. *Geography on Laserdisc.* Available from Learning Services, (800)877-9378. laserdisc.

Soleil. *Zurk's Learning Safari.* Available from Educational Resources, (800)624-2926. disk

Answer Key

Page 161

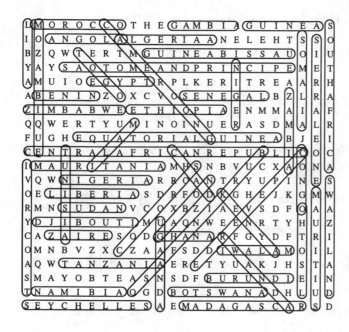

Pages 191–192

1. 2,900 miles (4,640 km)

2. no delta

3. 4th longest, 2nd in volume of water carried

4. the Zaire River

5. cacao

6. Brazzaville

7. (answers will vary)

8. Spain

9. the Pygmies

10. (answers will vary)

Page 174

1. gorillas

2. giraffe

3. camel

4. elephant

5. lion

6. leopard

7. aardvark

8. hippopotamus

9. rhinoceros

10. baboon

11. zebra

12. antelope

13. ringtailed lemur

14. crocodile

15. chimpanzee

Australia

Table of Contents

Introduction *(cont.)*

Australia

This book was designed to present an overview of the geography of the continent of Australia. It is divided into five sections to match the themes of the Geographic Education National Implementation Project (GENIP), an educational project backed by the nation's most prestigious geographers.

Each section contains a selection of teaching pages, maps, activities, interesting facts, review questions, and puzzles or games. A plan for using the material to construct a geography center is also included, as well as ideas for putting together a book as a culminating activity.

You will also find a glossary of the specialized vocabulary used by geographers. This will make it easier for your students to talk about the world they live in.

A Word or Two About Maps

Projections

The landforms shown on maps and globes do not look exactly alike. This is because it is just as hard to "peel" a globe and flatten the Earth's "skin" out into a map as it is to peel an orange and flatten out its skin to make a smooth, even surface. Even if you can get the skin off the orange in one piece, the top and bottom edges must be broken and spread out.

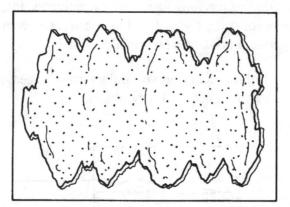

Different map makers (cartographers) have had different ideas about how to do this and have made different "projections." A projection is the way in which the map maker has chosen to flatten out the Earth's surface to make a flat map. Sometimes the map maker allows the breaks in the Earth's surface to show.

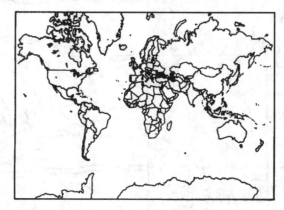

Sometimes the map maker stretches the Earth's "skin." This makes the countries near the poles look much bigger than they really are.

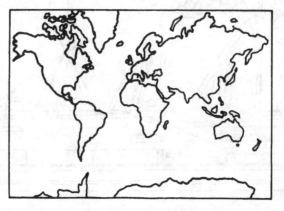

A Word or Two About Maps *(cont.)*

Projections *(cont.)*

Use your reference materials to find out the names of other common map projections and list them below. Research the advantages and disadvantages of each map projection you list and write them down below.

Map Projection	Advantages	Disadvantages

A Word or Two About Maps *(cont.)*

The Compass Rose

The compass rose is a small drawing that shows direction on a map. Most maps show north at the top and south at the bottom, west on the left and east on the right.

Look at maps to find some different styles of compass roses and then design your own. You can shrink your drawing and make multiple copies to use on the maps you make, color, or label.

Where on Earth Is Australia?

- Australia is the smallest of the seven continents.

- Australia lies in the Southern and Eastern Hemispheres between latitudes 10° S and 45° S and longitudes 110° E and 150° E.

- Australia is surrounded by the Pacific Ocean on the north, south, and east and by the Indian Ocean on the west.

- On Australia's northern side, the Great Barrier Reef extends almost to New Guinea.

Use these clues to find Australia on this map. Color it blue.

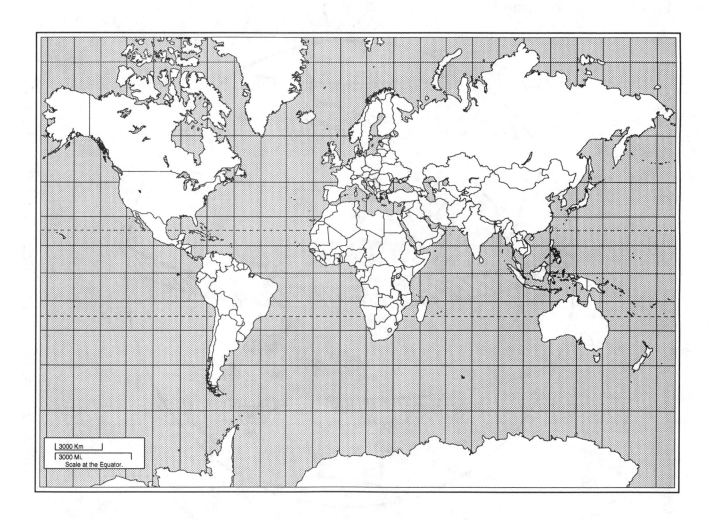

3000 Km
3000 Mi.
Scale at the Equator.

Where on Earth Is Australia? *(cont.)*

If you think of the Earth as a ball (a sphere or globe), you can draw a line around the middle (the equator) and separate the two halves into the top half (Northern Hemisphere) and the bottom half (Southern Hemisphere). Now you can talk about something as being in the Northern or Southern Hemisphere.

More lines are drawn around the Earth parallel to the equator and evenly spaced from the equator to the North and South Poles. They are called parallels or lines of latitude. They are numbered in degrees, starting with 0° at the equator and usually spaced at 15° intervals, ending with 90° N at the North Pole and 90° S at the South Pole.

(Geographers further divide their degrees into minutes and seconds so they can be very precise in locating the position of anything on the Earth's surface.)

If you divide the Earth into its Northern and Southern Hemispheres, Australia lies entirely in the_____Hemisphere.

Where on Earth
Is Australia? *(cont.)*

You can also draw lines north and south around the Earth. These lines are called meridians or lines of longitude. They are usually shown 15° apart at the equator, but they all come together at the North and South Poles. (They also can be further divided into minutes and seconds, just like the parallels.)

The line that runs through Greenwich, England, is called the prime meridian (0°). Longitude is the distance east or west of the prime meridian. The line directly opposite the prime meridian is at 180° and is called the date line. If you are still thinking of the Earth as a ball (a sphere or globe), you can separate the two halves into the Western Hemisphere and the Eastern Hemisphere. (This is usually done along the meridians of 20° W and 160° E so all of Africa is in one hemisphere.)

If you divide the Earth into its Western and Eastern Hemisphere, Australia lies entirely in the_____Hemisphere.

Where on Earth Is Australia? *(cont.)*

You can tell where things on the Earth are in two ways:

- You can give their exact or absolute location using latitude and longitude expressed in degrees (minutes and seconds).

- You can tell where they are in relation to other things.

Fill out the missing information to give the exact location of where you live:

house number	street name	apartment number
city	state/country	zip code

Now, use information from a map or globe to complete this description of the exact location of Australia.

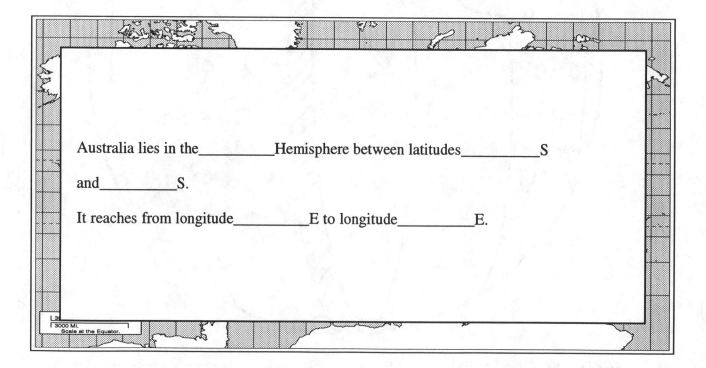

Australia lies in the_____Hemisphere between latitudes_____S

and_____S.

It reaches from longitude_____E to longitude_____E.

Where on Earth Is Australia? *(cont.)*

You can tell where things on the Earth are in two ways:

- You can give their exact or absolute location using latitude and longitude expressed in degrees (minutes and seconds).

- You can tell where they are in relation to other things.

Fill out the missing information to give the location of where you live in relation to other things:

I live
between_____and_____

near_____

and across
from_____.

Now, use information from a map or globe to complete this description of the relative location of Australia.

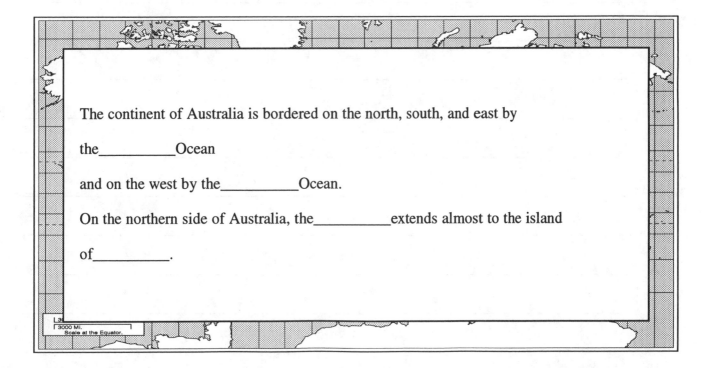

The continent of Australia is bordered on the north, south, and east by

the_____Ocean

and on the west by the_____Ocean.

On the northern side of Australia, the_____extends almost to the island

of_____.

3000 MI.
Scale at the Equator.

Where in Oceania Is_____?

As well as being a continent and a country, Australia is part of Oceania, the more than 25,000 islands spread across the Pacific Ocean. Use information from a globe or map, an atlas, an encyclopedia, and your geography book to write both the exact and relative locations of five of the islands in Oceania. See the next page for the names of some of these islands to choose from.

1. _____

_____

_____

_____

2. _____

_____

_____

_____

3. _____

_____

_____

_____

4. _____

_____

_____

_____

5. _____

_____

_____

_____

Islands of Oceania

There are 18 islands of Oceania listed below. Find them forwards, backwards, and diagonally in the word search.

```
P P H N E W C A L E D O N I A Z X L S S M V G W
T A B A G H C G V W S R N Y X V Q Z O O A A I M
D B P M W E F Q Y C K L K N D N D X L C R N L P
H T H U A A A C O O K I S L A N D S O I S U B S
Z B O N A R I S K V X P V C X N F C M E H A E Q
S B E T H N I I T V Y B S T K E G N O T A T R B
Q F N D P W E A A E K F V Z J W S Q N Y L U T P
M I I L Q G C W N N R P T M G Z T S I I L V I W
B J X V L V J K G A I I C R R E Y S S I H S X
W I I V Z P N J V U I S S G L A F Q L L S G L B
F I S M M M P J V P I S L L N L C N A A L S A B
S S L X B F B R W P Y N L A A A X S N N A X N G
R L A C B Z S L K V T D E A N N T F D D N M D W
Q A N B M I D W A Y I S L A N D D L S S D J S N
R N D W T C H W W J Q R L G C D S S R N S T B X
J D S B V C X C A R O L I N E I S L A N D S Y T
X S T A U M O T U I S L A N D S T O N G A H G Y
Q W E R T Y U I O P A S Z X C V N B M L K J H F
A S D F G H J K L Z X V P O I U Y T R E W Q M E
J K P L C R R Y U J H G T Y J K H G F C V B O P
A B C D E F G H I J K Z G G B V C E A A S Z P U
```

Cross off the islands as you find them: Marshall Islands, Mariana Islands, Caroline Islands, Solomon Islands, Fiji Islands, Gilbert Islands, Midway Island, New Zealand, New Caledonia, Phoenix Islands, Vanuatu, Society Islands, Cook Islands, Hawaiian Islands, Tonga, Tuamotu Islands, Easter Island, Papua New Guinea

Islands of Oceania *(cont.)*

Use information from an atlas, an encyclopedia, your geography book, or any other reference book to write two interesting facts about each island or group of islands.

1. Marshall Islands _____

   _____

2. Mariana Islands _____

   _____

3. Caroline Islands _____

   _____

4. Solomon Islands _____

   _____

5. Fiji Islands _____

   _____

6. Gilbert Islands _____

   _____

7. Midway Island _____

   _____

8. New Zealand _____

   _____

9. New Caledonia _____

   _____

Islands of Oceania *(cont.)*

10. Phoenix Islands _____

_____

11. Vanuatu _____

_____

12. Society Islands _____

_____

13. Cook Islands _____

_____

14. Hawaiian Islands _____

_____

15. Tonga _____

_____

16. Tuamotu Islands _____

_____

17. Easter Island _____

_____

18. Papua New Guinea _____

Look at the Map

Use the numbered list of the islands of Oceania on pages 234–235 to label the map below. Write the number of each island or group of islands on the map and use the list for a key.

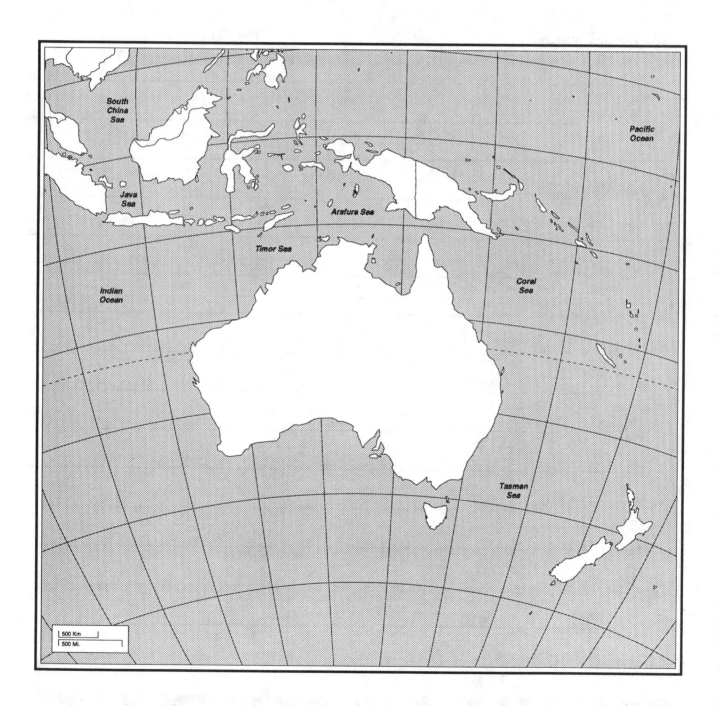

New Zealand—Australia's Neighbor to the East

Use information from an atlas, an encyclopedia, your geography book, or any other reference book to identify the places and people in or around New Zealand.

1. North Island _____

   _____

2. South Island _____

   _____

3. Tasman Sea _____

   _____

4. Lake Taupo _____

   _____

5. Cook Strait _____

   _____

6. Auckland _____

   _____

7. Wellington _____

   _____

8. Southern Alps _____

   _____

9. Mount Cook _____

   _____

10. Maori _____

   _____

Physical Characteristics of Australia

Major Bodies of Water

Australia lies below the equator with the *Indian Ocean* to the west and the *Pacific Ocean* to the north and east. The *Coral Sea* lies between the Great Barrier Reef on the northeast edge of Australia and the Pacific Ocean itself, bounded by an arc of islands that consists of Papua New Guinea, the Solomons, Vanuatu, and New Caledonia. The *Tasman Sea* lies between Australia and New Zealand on the southeast side of the continent. On the south side of Australia is one of those places where two oceans come together with no particular boundary. Somewhere between Australia and Antarctica, the Pacific and Indian Oceans meet and blend.

Use reference sources to label these major bodies of water on the map of Australia.

Physical Characteristics of Australia *(cont.)*

Mountains, Plains, and Reefs

Australia is an ancient continent. Its highlands have been worn down through the ages. Its highest mountain range, the *Great Dividing Range,* runs the length of the east coast. The highest peak of that range, *Mount Kosciusko,* reaches an altitude of only 7,310 feet (2,217 m). To the west of these mountains, there is an area where wheat is grown. As the air from the Pacific rises over the mountains and deposits its moisture in the form of rain, the water sinks into the ground, forming The *Great Artesian Basin.* About a third of Australia depends on artesian wells for its water supply. The great plains and deserts of central and western Australia lie beyond. This is a land of dust, blazing heat, and little vegetation. Australians call it the *outback.* It is divided on the map into areas such as the *Great Sandy Desert*, the *Great Victoria Desert*, and the *Tatami Desert.* In the outback, and almost exactly in the middle of Australia, is *Ayers Rock*, which is 1,000 feet (303 m) high. In contrast to this hot dry area, one of Australia's most impressive features is the *Great Barrier Reef.* It lies along the Queensland coast in the Coral Sea. It is 1,250 miles (2,000 km) long, the longest reef in the world.

Use reference sources to label these physical characteristics on the map of Australia.

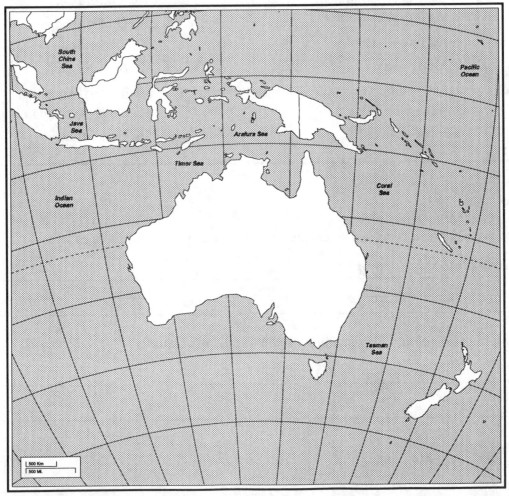

Physical Characteristics of Australia *(cont.)*

Other Bodies of Water

Australia's rivers have a hard time in the hot, dry outback. On many maps, they are drawn with dotted lines. Some of the lakes are drawn that way too. The *Murray River* and its branches form Australia's largest river system. The *Darling River,* Australia's longest, feeds into the Murray River.

Many of Australia's bodies of water occur around the edges of the continent. The large inward dip in Australia's south coast is called the *Great Australian Bight,* and the narrow body of water separating the island of Tasmania from the mainland is called *Bass Strait.*

Use reference sources to draw in the rivers and lakes on the map on the next page. Then label the bodies of water with their numbers and use the list for a key.

1. Lake Mackay	9. Victoria River
2. Lake Disappointment	10. Arafura Sea
3. Lake Carnegie	11. Gulf of Carpentaria
4. Darling River	12. Timor Sea
5. Murray River	13. Spencer Gulf
6. Lachlan River	14. Shark Bay
7. Ashburton River	15. Great Australian Bight
8. Fitzroy River	16. Bass Strait

Bonus Questions!

What does it mean when lakes and rivers are drawn on a map with dotted lines?

_____

_____

Which important line of latitude runs through the middle of Australia?

_____

_____

Place

Physical Characteristics of
Australia *(cont.)*

Other Bodies of Water

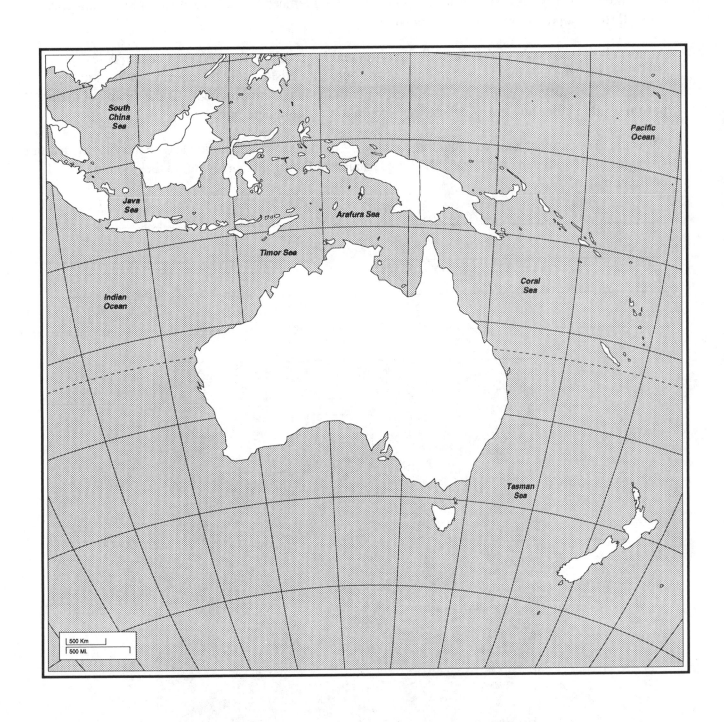

People in Australia

Australia was first discovered and settled by the people who are now called the aborigines. They probably came from Asia by way of what is now Indonesia about 40,000 years ago.

Australia was claimed for England by Captain Cook who discovered it in 1770. For a long time it was used as a penal colony, a place to send convicts. Then it became a destination for adventurous people who went to seek their fortunes. It remained a colony of Great Britain until 1901, when it became an independent country. Australia is now a self-governing member of the British Commonwealth and is going through a period of growing nationalism.

Almost all of the people of Australia live in cities and towns along the southeast coast. A few people who farm the land live on the eastern edge of the outback. Historically the aborigines lived in the outback, where they developed a way of dealing with the harsh environment. Today, many of them have moved to cities and towns, where they live in almost complete poverty.

Australia the continent and Australia the country fill up the same land area. The country is divided into six states and two federal territories. List these states and territories below and label them on the political map of Australia.

_____   _____

_____   _____

_____   _____

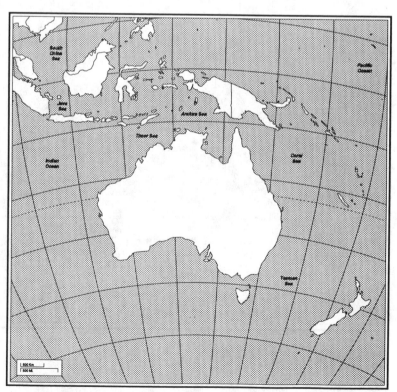

People in Australia *(cont.)*

The Aborigines

The Australian aborigines developed a way of life that allowed them to survive in the outback. Although they live in a very primitive manner, they have complex and interesting social and religious customs. Some of the problems that Australia is facing today have to do with tourists visiting sacred places of the aborigines. See what you can find out about these people.

Survival Skills

_____

_____

_____

_____

Sacred Places

_____

_____

_____

_____

Similarity to Native Americans

_____

_____

_____

_____

Animals in Australia

Read the clues and unscramble these words related to the Australian animals.

1. _____ an animal that carries its young in a pouch (rampuslia)
2. _____ a marsupial that looks like a teddy bear (loaka)
3. _____ the tree that provides for food and shelter for the koala (calypteus)
4. _____ an animal that hops on two strong back legs (nogakroa)
5. _____ a small kangaroo-like marsupial (ballway)
6. _____ a thick, burrowing marsupial that lives on the island of Tasmania (mobtaw)
7. _____ an unusual mammal living in the waters around Australia (godung)
8. _____ an egg-laying mammal with webbed feet and a bill like a duck (spytalup)
9. _____ a large flightless bird that looks like an ostrich; related to the cassowary (mue)
10. _____ an egg-laying mammal that is also called the spiny anteater (andchie)
11. _____ a kind of lizard (kniks)
12. _____ the Australian wild dog (doing)
13. _____ a large flightless bird that looks like an ostrich; related to the emu (sowcarsay)
14. _____ a bird with a cry like a laughing donkey (burakokoar)
15. _____ small marsupials with long narrow noses and tails like rats (candiboots)
16. _____ a bird with a beautiful lyre-shaped tail (dribelry)
17. _____ ferocious and ugly little animal that is native to Tasmania (sTanmania viled)
18. _____ a bird that uses vines to "stitch" its nest together (dribvarwee)

People Depend on the Environment

Make a list of Australia's natural resources.

_____

_____

_____

_____

Then create a symbol to go with each natural resource and make a key. Using your newly created symbols, show these resources on the map of Australia on the next page.

Resource Key

People Depend on the Environment *(cont.)*

Resource Map

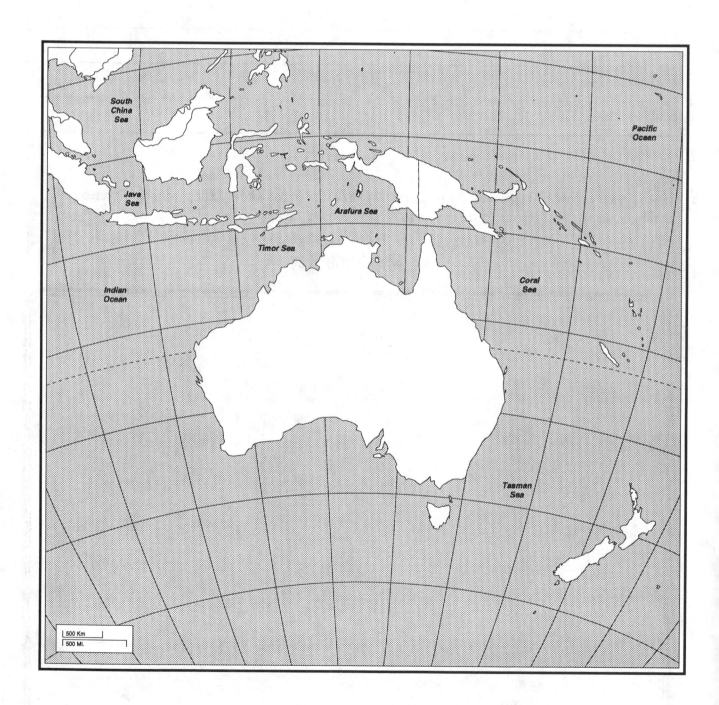

People Adapt to and Change the Environment

People adapt to and change the environment in many ways. Think of some possible solutions that may solve these environmental problems:

Very dry conditions for farming:

_____

_____

_____

_____

Hills too steep for crops:

_____

_____

_____

_____

Areas that flood:

_____

_____

_____

_____

Housing in hot climates:

_____

_____

_____

_____

People Adapt to and Change the Environment *(cont.)*

People adapt to and change the environment in many ways. Think of some possible solutions that may solve these environmental problems:

Housing in cold climates:

_____

_____

_____

_____

Clothing in hot climates:

_____

_____

_____

_____

Clothing in cold climates:

_____

_____

_____

_____

Transportation in mountainous or hilly areas:

_____

_____

_____

_____

Technology Impacts the Environment

Resources are things that are valued and used by people. Natural resources are the resources that occur in nature, such as minerals in the Earth, trees, water, and air.

The way people feel about and use natural resource changes as new technologies are developed.

Research how the use of natural resources has already changed in Australia and how it may change in the future.

Type of Resource	Past	Present	Future
Fuel for heating			
Fuel for ships			
Fuel for trains			
Fuel for cars			

Technology Impacts the Environment *(cont.)*

Type of Resource	Past	Present	Future
Materials for building			
Materials for containers			
Propellant for spray cans			
Material for paper			
Treatment of the air			
Use of water			

Movement Demonstrates Interdependence

Why do human activities require movement? _____

_____

_____

Do the people in your family go places?_____Choose two people and answer the following questions:

	Person #1	Person #2
Who?		
When?		
Where?		
How far?		
How often?		
Why?		
Mode of transportation?		

Movement Demonstrates Interdependence *(cont.)*

Use reference sources to figure the distances between these Australian cities, as well as between Australian cities and cities in other countries around the world.

Melbourne/Sydney _____

Sydney/Brisbane _____

Canberra/Perth _____

Melbourne/Wellington, New Zealand _____

Sydney/Tokyo _____

Sydney/Manilla _____

Melbourne/Honolulu _____

Melbourne/Mexico City _____

Perth/Rome _____

Melbourne/Miami _____

Sydney/London _____

Brisbane/Hong Kong _____

Melbourne 3125 km

Perth 2600 km

Sydney 3110 km

Brisbane 2930 km

Movement Involves Linkages

List some of the ways people traveled from place to place in Australia in the past.

_____

_____

_____

_____

_____

_____

List some of the ways people travel from place to place in Australia in the present.

_____

_____

_____

_____

_____

_____

_____

Bonus Question!

Why did methods of transportation change?

_____

_____

_____

_____

_____

_____

Movement Involves Linkages (cont.)

How will people travel around Australia in the future?

_____

_____

_____

_____

Design your own future method of transportation. Explain it and then draw a picture of it below.

_____

_____

_____

_____

This Is How My Future Transportation Will Work:

_____

_____

_____

_____

This Is How My Future Transportation Will Look:

Movement Includes People, Ideas, and Products

People go places for business and for pleasure. Going somewhere for pleasure is called touring.

Where have you gone for pleasure?

_____

_____

_____

_____

Where would you like to go?

_____

_____

_____

_____

Ideas can travel too. List some of the different ways ideas travel from place to place.

_____

_____

_____

_____

Products also travel. What are some of the ways products travel?

_____

_____

_____

_____

_____

Movement Includes People, Ideas, and Products *(cont.)*

Think about one of the places you would like to visit in Australia. Design a cover for a travel brochure about that place. Sketch your design below. Write a description of the place that will make other people want to travel there too.

_____

_____

_____

_____

The Land Time Forgot

Australia as a Region

A region is a portion of the Earth's surface that has characteristics unlike any other. The whole continent of Australia is itself a region. Its age has allowed the mountains to weather. Its isolation has given it unusual animals. Its physical features and climate have made life very different for both its native people and its current population.

The weather is hot, dry, and dusty. Water is scarce, but is attainable from artesian wells. These wells are used for watering sheep and cattle, which makes possible enormous sheep and cattle ranches.

Use reference books to find out about artesian wells. What are they? How do they work? Write about them below.

_____

_____

_____

_____

_____

_____

Children go to school, no matter where they live. How do they go to school in the outback?
Use reference books to find out about education in different parts of Australia. Write about it below.

_____

_____

_____

_____

_____

_____

_____

_____

_____

The Land Time Forgot *(cont.)*

The Aborigines Across the Curriculum

The word "aborigines" was formerly used to refer to the original people of any geographical area. Now, however, *aborigines* are understood to be the native people of Australia, and the word is restricted by scientists to that usage. The aborigines live in the Australian *outback*, where they maintain a delicate balance with their environment. They trap rare rainfall by building little dams, and they carry water in the shells of huge eggs laid by the *emu* and the *cassowary*, birds of the outback that look like ostriches. They invented the weapon known as the *boomerang* and use it for hunting today but used it also for warfare in the past. *Ayers Rock* in the *Northern Territory* is one of their most sacred places.

1. **The Aborigines**
   Be ready to report on the aborigines. Find out what these people hunt, if they migrated, what their family groups are like, and how they live today. Write down any other facts that you think are interesting.

   _____

   _____

   _____

   _____

   _____

2. **The Outback**
   Write a poem about the outback. This is a wild and harsh environment, but it is also full of color and excitement. Try to see a video tape or read an illustrated book about this interesting place before you write your poem.

   _____

   _____

   _____

   _____

   _____

The Land Time Forgot *(cont.)*

The Aborigines Across the Curriculum *(cont.)*

3. Put the italicized terms on page 258 in ABC order and tell how many syllables are in each of them.

4. The Boomerang

Find out as much as you can about this weapon. Write your findings on the lines below. (Hint: There are two kinds.)

The Land Time Forgot *(cont.)*

The Aborigines Across the Curriculum *(cont.)*

5. Ayers Rock

Ayers Rock is a sacred place to the aborigines. Read about some places that people have thought were sacred. Make up a story explaining how Ayers Rock became a sacred place. Call your story "The Biggest Rock on Earth."

_____

_____

_____

_____

_____

_____

_____

_____

_____

_____

_____

_____

_____

_____

_____

_____

_____

_____

_____

The Land Time Forgot *(cont.)*

The Aborigines Across the Curriculum *(cont.)*

6. Scientists

What kind of scientists study people like the aborigines? What else do they study? How do they learn to be this kind of scientist? See what you can find out about these scientists.

_____

_____

_____

_____

7. Emu/Cassowary/Ostrich

These three birds are very much alike. Make a chart to compare their characteristics. Keep track of your facts here as you do your research.

	Emu	Cassowary	Ostrich
Country			
Height			
Weight			
Size of egg			
Unusual habits			

The Great Barrier Reef

The Great Barrier Reef is the longest reef in the world. People go from all over the world to snorkel and scuba dive there. It is home to many varieties of sea life, both plants and animals.

Find information about the Great Barrier Reef in reference books and answer these questions.

1. What is a reef?

   _____

2. How long is the Great Barrier Reef?

   _____

3. Where is it located?

   _____

4. How was it built?

   _____

5. How long did it take?

   _____

6. How many species of fish live on the Great Barrier Reef?

   _____

The Great Barrier Reef *(cont.)*

7. How many kinds of coral live there?

   _____

8. Name four kinds of coral that live on the Great Barrier Reef.

   _____

   _____

   _____

   _____

9. How far is the Great Barrier Reef from the shore?

   _____

10. What are some reasons the Great Barrier Reef is in trouble?

   _____

   _____

   _____

   _____

   _____

   _____

   _____

The Great Barrier Reef *(cont.)*

Meet with a partner or group to brainstorm ideas for helping to save the Great Barrier Reef. List your ideas below.

_____

_____

_____

_____

_____

Decide on the best of your ideas and formulate a plan for putting your idea into action. List the steps of your plan below.

1. _____

_____

_____

2. _____

_____

_____

3. _____

_____

_____

4. _____

_____

_____

5. _____

_____

_____

Australian Fact Game

This game can be played in different ways:

Game 1—You can use a Jeopardy format. Students love this, and they can set it up all by themselves or with just a little help. Run the answer cards on one color of paper and the question cards on another color for easy sorting.

Game 2—You can make a card game like rummy. All the cards should be run on one color for this. Shuffle the cards and deal five to each player. Put the leftovers facedown or in the middle of the table. Players draw from the stack and discard in another stack. The object of the game is to lay down pairs by matching questions and answers. You can make it more complicated by allowing students to challenge one another's matched pairs if they think the matches are incorrect. Have students keep track of the rules they make and write game directions.

Fact Game Cards

It is the smallest continent in the world.	What is Australia?
It is a weapon used in hunting.	What is a boomerang?
It is the only continent that is only one country.	What is Australia?

Australian Fact Game (cont.)

Fact Game Cards (cont.)

This area is called the "outback."	What are the huge deserts and plains?
This is known as the land "down under."	What is Australia?
This is the largest and most well-known rock in the outback.	What is Ayers Rock?
It is the largest coral reef in the world.	What is the Great Barrier Reef?
It is a large island off the southeast end of Australia.	What is Tasmania?
They are the native people of Australia.	Who are the aborigines?

Australian Fact Game (cont.)

Fact Game Cards (cont.)

These animals have pouches in which they carry their babies.	What are marsupials?
It lives in eucalyptus trees and looks like a teddy bear.	What is a koala?
It jumps along with the help of strong back legs and a heavy tail.	What is a kangaroo?
It is a bird that looks a lot like an ostrich.	What is an emu?
It is the capital city of Australia.	What is Canberra?
It is the capital city of New Zealand.	What is Wellington?

Australian Fact Game (cont.)

Fact Game Cards (cont.)

This is the official language of Australia.	What is English?
This is the wild dog of the outback.	What is the dingo?
This is the name given to the huge sheep and cattle ranches of the outback.	What are stations?
This is the longest and highest chain of mountains in Australia.	What is the Great Dividing Range?
This body of water separates Tasmania from the main continent.	What is Bass Strait?
Australis is the Latin word for southern.	From what word does Australia get its name?

Australian Fact Game *(cont.)*

Fact Game Cards *(cont.)*

Let your students make their own question-and-answer fact cards. Students usually like to make extra hard ones in hopes of stumping each other, so have them write the book and page number where the information can be found on the question card.

	Book:_____ Page: _____
	Book:_____ Page: _____
	Book:_____ Page: _____
	Book:_____ Page: _____
	Book:_____ Page: _____

The Geography Center

Putting the Center Together

You can set up your Geography Center in a corner of your classroom and make it as simple or as elaborate as you want. The center should have a map, a globe, and an atlas. (Several maps, a couple of globes, and multiple copies of the atlas would be even better.) A table and chairs will facilitate group activities and discussions. A supply of writing and drawing materials will also come in handy. A bookcase, shelf, or window sill can be utilized for storing reference books. The more reference books you can provide, the better the assigned projects will be. If you have access to a TV, VCR, and tapes, you can show movies about the places you are studying. There are many tapes of this variety available, and the visual learners in your class will really appreciate this. Cushions for sitting on the floor to read or view tapes add a cozy touch.

Making the Center Work

You can make the Geography Center part of your instructional day by scheduling groups to do center work. Change the materials daily or weekly or provide a set of task cards at the beginning of the unit and expect each student to work through them individually or as part of a group. (See pages 271–273.)

Use Portfolios

Have students make portfolios and store them in containers in an accessible area of your center. Try using the inexpensive but sturdy plastic crates that are available at local hardware stores. Make students responsible for their own progress by having them file their own work, both completed work and work in progress. Have students create attractive covers for their portfolios so the accumulated work can be attractively displayed at your school's open house.

Deck the Walls

Encourage artwork, creative writing, and exploratory math to go along with your geography unit and spread it throughout the curriculum. Display these products on a bulletin board in your Geography. Center. Have students mount and post their own work. They can cut out letters and create colorful captions for the board.

Have another bulletin board reserved for posting newspaper and magazine articles dealing with the continent you are studying. Encourage your students to bring in these articles, share them, and discuss their meaning and importance.

The Geography Center *(cont.)*

Task Cards

Task Card #1

What is the longest river on the continent?

How long is it?

Through which state/territory or states/territories does it flow?

Task Card #3

What is the highest mountain peak on the continent?

How tall is it?

In which state/territory is it found?

Task Card #2

What is the most important mountain range on the continent?

How long is it?

In which state/territory or states/territories are these mountains found?

Task Card #4

What is the largest state/territory on the continent?

What states/territories or bodies of water border it?

What is its capital city?

Task Cards (cont.)

Task Card #7

What animals are associated with the continent?

In what state/territory or states/territories do they live?

Are they in any danger in today's civilization?

Task Card #8

What variations in climate are found on the continent?

What variations in weather are found on the continent?

Can people live in all parts of the continent?

Task Card #5

What is the smallest state/territory on the continent?

What states/territories or bodies of water border it?

What is its capital city?

Task Card #6

What is the largest lake on the continent?

In which state/territory or states/territories is it found?

Which river is associated with it?

The Geography Center *(cont.)*

Task Card Response

Leave a stack of these task card response forms in the geography center for students to use.

Name _____ Date _____

Task Card # _____

Question #1

_____

_____

_____

_____

Question #2

_____

_____

_____

_____

Question #3

_____

_____

_____

_____

Bonus

I also learned _____

_____

_____

_____

The Culminating Activity: Making a Book

Method

You and your students can go about bookmaking in many different ways. Here are some suggestions:

- The book can be your students' showcase portfolios.

- Students can review and reflect upon the work they have accumulated in their portfolios, select the most representative samples or the pieces they like best, and put these things together in book form.

- The book can be a showcase portfolio based on the teacher's criteria.

- Have students select work from their portfolios based on a list you develop.

- The book can be comprised of new material that sums up the unit.

- Have students complete various assignments meant specifically for inclusion in their books, showing their grasp of the material. (See pages 275–285.)

Contents

In most cases you will probably want your students to include maps, facts about both physical and political geography, research about animals, people, and resources. They can review or report on any books they have read about the continent, and they can write about what they have learned and how it has affected the way they view the world.

Cover

You can specify and provide the design for the cover so that all of the books will be uniform, or you can encourage your students to design a cover that is representative of the continent. A collage of pictures cut from magazines and travel brochures is an option that works well.

Be sure to laminate the finished covers so the books can be used as part of your classroom library or Geography Center reference shelf. Your students may also want to share their books with students in other classes.

Exciting ideas for binding and publishing follow on pages 286–288.

The Culminating Activity:
Making a Book *(cont.)*

Trace an outline map of the continent. Transfer information about its physical features from all of the maps you have made. You might want to use different colors to create a key.

Name _____Date_____

Map of Physical Features

The Culminating Activity: Making a Book *(cont.)*

Use the information you have already gathered or do some new research to complete this page.

Name _____ Date_____

Facts About Physical Features

Area: _____

_____

Highest Point: _____

_____

Lowest Point: _____

_____

Largest Island:_____

_____

Longest River:_____

_____

Largest Lake: _____

_____

Tallest Waterfall: _____

_____

Largest Desert: _____

_____

Longest Reef: _____

_____

The Culminating Activity: Making a Book *(cont.)*

Trace an outline map of the continent. Transfer information about its political features from all of the maps you have made. You might want to use a numbered list to create a key.

Name _____Date_____

Map of Political Features

The Culminating Activity: Making a Book *(cont.)*

Use the information you have already gathered or do some new research to complete this page.

Name _____ Date_____

Facts About Political Features

Population: _____

Largest State/Territory (by area): _____

Largest State/Territory (by population): _____

Smallest State/Territory (by area): _____

Smallest State/Territory (by population): _____

Largest Metropolitan Area (by population):_____

_____

_____

_____

_____

_____

Newest States/Territories: _____

_____

_____

_____

_____

_____

_____

The Culminating Activity: Making a Book *(cont.)*

Use the information you have already gathered or do some new research to complete this page.

Name _____Date_____

The People

The people of this continent belong to these ethnic groups:

_____

_____

_____

They speak these languages:

_____

_____

_____

They live in these different environments:

_____

_____

_____

_____

Their ways of life have changed or are changing:

_____

_____

_____

_____

_____

The Culminating Activity: Making a Book *(cont.)*

Pick the city on the continent that is most interesting to you. Use the information you have already gathered or do some new research to complete this page.

Name _____Date_____

The city of_____.

This city is in _____

Area: _____

Population: _____

_____

Language(s): _____

_____

Ethnic Groups: _____

_____

Religious Groups:_____

_____

Famous Natural Features:_____

_____

_____

Famous Constructed Features: _____

_____

_____

_____

The Culminating Activity: Making a Book *(cont.)*

Use the information you have already gathered or do some new research to complete this page.

Name _____ Date_____

The Animals

The best known animals of this continent are _____

_____

_____

The animals of this continent are important because _____

_____

_____

The animals that still live in their natural habitats are _____

_____

_____

The animals that are on the endangered list are _____

_____

_____

_____

They are on the endangered list because _____

_____

_____

_____

_____

_____

The Culminating Activity: Making a Book *(cont.)*

Keep track of the books you read about the continent on this log.

Name _____ Date_____

Book Log

Title: _____   Fiction: _____

Author: _____   Nonfiction: _____

Illustrator: _____   Rating: _____

Title: _____   Fiction: _____

Author: _____   Nonfiction: _____

Illustrator: _____   Rating: _____

Title: _____   Fiction: _____

Author: _____   Nonfiction: _____

Illustrator: _____   Rating: _____

Title: _____   Fiction: _____

Author: _____   Nonfiction: _____

Illustrator: _____   Rating: _____

The Culminating Activity: Making a Book *(cont.)*

Use copies of this form to review your favorite nonfiction books about the continent you have been studying.

Name _____Date_____

Book Review/Nonfiction

Title: _____

Author: _____

Illustrator: _____

Summary: _____

_____

_____

_____

_____

_____

Reasons I liked or did not like this book:_____

_____

_____

_____

_____

_____

Bonus!

If you liked this book and think other people should read it, you can do one of two things. (1) Write a paragraph or two telling how a nonfiction book can help you understand a continent or a country and post it on the bulletin board in the Geography Center. (2) Make a poster advertising the book and post it on the bulletin board in the Geography Center.

The Culminating Activity: Making a Book *(cont.)*

Use copies of this form to review your favorite fiction books about the continent you have been studying.

Name _____ Date_____

Book Review/Fiction

Title: _____

Author: _____

Illustrator: _____

Summary: _____

_____

_____

_____

_____

_____

Reasons I liked or did not like this book:_____

_____

_____

_____

_____

_____

_____

Bonus!

If you liked this book and think other people should read it, you can do one of two things. (1) Write a paragraph or two telling how a fiction book can help you understand a continent or a country and post it on the bulletin board in the Geography Center. (2) Make a poster advertising the book and post it on the bulletin board in the Geography Center.

The Culminating Activity:
Making a Book *(cont.)*

Write a reflective essay in which you discuss the ways that studying geography has given you a better understanding of the world and the people in it.

Name _____ Date _____

Title: _____

_____

_____

_____

_____

_____

_____

_____

_____

_____

_____

_____

_____

_____

_____

_____

_____

_____

_____

The Culminating Activity: Making a Book *(cont.)*

Book Binding Ideas

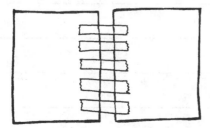

1. Stack all the pages of the book in a neat pile.

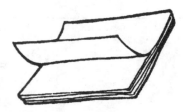

2. Place a blank sheet of paper on the top and bottom of the pages.

3. Leaving approximately 1/2" (1.25 cm) border, staple or sew all of the pages together on the left side.

4. Place two pieces of lightweight cardboard side by side. (Cereal boxes work well.) Each piece should be 1/2 to 1" (1.25 to 2.5 cm) larger than the size of the pages in the book.

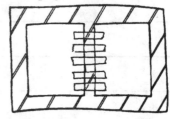

5. Leaving approximately 1" (2.5 cm) between them, tape the cardboard pieces together.

6. Put the cardboard on top of your covering material (e.g., fabric, wallpaper, contact paper, or wrapping paper). Glue the cardboard and covering material together, leaving a 1 to 1 1/2" (2.5 to 3.25 cm) material border.

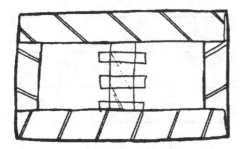

7. Fold up the edges of material over the cardboard and glue in place.

8. Glue the blank pages to the inside of the cardboard covers. Your book is ready to read and share.

The Culminating Activity:
Making a Book *(cont.)*

Pop-Up Books

1. Fold a 8 1/2" x 11" (22 cm x 28 cm) piece of paper in half crosswise.

2. Measure and mark 2 3/4" (7 cm) from each side along the fold. Cut 2 3/4" (7 cm) slits at the marks.

3. Push cut area inside-out and crease to form the pop-up section.

4. Draw, color, and cut out the object to get "popped-up."

5. Glue it onto the pop-up section.

6. Glue two pages back to back, making sure the pop-up section is free.

7. Glue additional pages together, making as many pages (including pop-up pages) as you like. Be sure to include a free sheet on both the front and back so that those pages can be glued to a cover.

8. Glue a cover over the entire book.

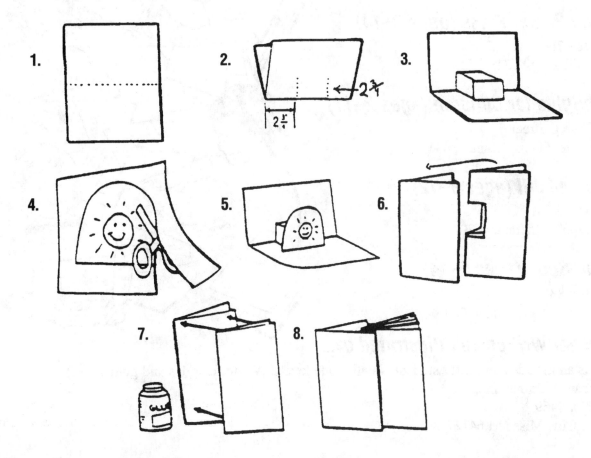

The Culminating Activity: Making a Book *(cont.)*

Real Markets for Student Writing

Student writing can be sent to the following addresses. Check your professional journals for more sources.

Children's Playmate (ages 5–8)

P.O. Box 567B
Indianapolis, Indiana 46206

Cricket (ages 6–12)

Cricket League
P.O. Box 300
Peru, Illinois 61354

Ebony Jr! (ages 6–12)

820 S. Michigan Avenue
Chicago, Illinois 60605

Flying Pencil Press (ages 8–14)

P.O. Box 7667
Elgin, Illinois 60121

Highlights for Children (ages 2–11)

803 Church Street
Honesdale, Pennsylvania 18431

Jack and Jill (ages 8–12)

P.O. Box 567B
Indianapolis, Indiana 46206

Stone Soup (ages 5–14)

P.O. Box 83
Santa Cruz, California 95063

National Written and Illustrated by...

(This is an awards contest for students in all grade levels. Write for rules and guidelines.)
Landmark Editions, Inc.
P.O. Box 4469
Kansas City, Missouri 64127

Software Review

Software: *From Alice to Ocean: Alone Across the Outback* (Claris)

Hardware: Macintosh computer (4MB) and CD-ROM player

Grade Level: Intermediate Level

Summary: *From Alice to Ocean: Alone Across the Outback*, allows your students to follow Robyn Davidson's 1,700 mile (2,720 km) trek across the Australian outback. She makes her journey with her dog and four camels. The adventure is narrated by Robyn and documented by a National Geographic photographer. Included in the program software is an on-screen map to allow students to track Robyn's progress across the outback. The software also includes text on plant and animal life, aboriginal culture, the environment, etc. Using this program your students will have the opportunity to experience the Australian outback without having to really be there.

Bibliography

Arnold, Caroline. *A Walk on the Great Barrier Reef.* Carolrhoda, 1988.

Baillie, Allan. *Adrift.* Viking, 1992.

Baker, Jeannie. *Where the Forest Meets the Sea.* Greenwillow, 1988.

Browne, Rolle. *A Family in Australia.* Lerner, 1987.

Browne, Rolle. *An Aboriginal Family.* Lerner, 1985.

Crossland, Bert. *Where on Earth Are We?* Book Links. September, 1994.

Czernecki, Stefan, and Timothy Rhodes. *The Singing Snake.* Hyperion, 1993.

Dickinson, Mary B (Ed.) *National Geographic Picture Atlas of Our World.* National Geographic Society, 1993.

Dolce, Laura. *Australia.* Chelsea, 1990.

Fatchen, Max. *The Country Mail Is Coming: Poems from Down Under.* Little, 1990.

Fox, Mary B. *New Zealand.* Childrens, 1991.

Garret, Dan. *Australia.* Raintree, 1990.

Geographic Education National Implementation Project. Guidelines, 1987.

Germaine, Elizabeth, and Ann L. Burckhardt. *Cooking the Australian Way.* Lerner, 1990.

Gittins, Anne. *Tales from the South Pacific Islands.* Stemmer, 1977.

Gleeson, Libby. *Eleanor, Elizabeth.* Holiday, 1990.

Gleitzman, Morris. *Misery Guts.* Harcourt, 1993.

Kelleher, Victor. *Bailey's Bones.* Dial, 1989.

Kelly, Andrew. *Australia.* Watts, 1989.

Keyworth, Valerie. *New Zealand: Land of the Long White Cloud.* Macmillan, 1990.

Klwin, Robin. *All in the Blue Clouded Weather.* Viking, 1992.

Lepthien, Emilie U. *Australia.* Childrens, 1982.

Lepthien, Emilie U. *The Philippines.* Childrens, 1986.

Margolies, Barbara A. *Warriors, Wigmen, and the Crocodile People: Journeys in Papua New Guinea.* Macmillan, 1993.

Nance, John. *Lobo of the Tasaday: A Stone Age Boy Meets the Modern World.* Pantheon, 1982.

Reynolds, Jan. *Down Under: Vanishing Cultures.* Harcourt, 1992.

Scholes, Katherine. *The Landing: A Night of Birds.* Doubleday, 1990.

Te Kanawa, Kiri. *Land of the Long White Cloud: Maori Myths, Tales, and Legends.* Arcade, 1990.

Thiele, Colin. *Shadow Shark.* Harper, 1988.

Thiele, Colin. *Storm Boy.* Harper, 1978.

Topek, Lily R. *Philippines.* Marshall Cavendish, 1991.

Trezise, Percy, and Dick Roughsey. *Turramulh the Giant Quinkin.* Stevens, 1988.

Wheatley, Nadia. *My Place.* Kane-Miller, 1992.

Wiremu, Graham. *The Maoris of New Zealand.* Rourke, 1987.

Wrightson, Patricia. *Moon-Dark.* Macmillan, 1988.

Bibliography *(cont.)*

Technology

Broderbund. *MacGlobe & PC Globe.* Available from Learning Services, (800)877-9378. disk

Broderbund. *Where in the World Is Carmen Sandiego?* Available from Troll, (800)526-5289. CD-ROM and disk

Bureau of Electronic Publishing Inc. *World Fact Book.* Available from Educational Resources, (800)624-2926. CD-ROM

Claris Corporation. *From Alice to Ocean: Alone Across the Outback.* Available from Educational Resources, (800)624-2926. CD-ROM

CLEARVUE. *The Earth, the Oceans, and Plants & Animals:* Interactive, curriculum oriented CD-ROMs. Available from Educational Resources, (800)624-2926. CD-ROM

DeLorme Publishing. *Global Explorer.* Available from DeLorme Publishing, 1995. CD-ROM

Impressions, My First World Atlas. Available from Educational Resources, (800)624-2926.

Lawrence. *Nigel's World Adventures in World Geography.* Available from Educational Resources, (800)624-2926. CD-ROM and disk

Learningways, Inc. *Explore-Australia.* Available from William K. Bradford Publishing Co., (800)421-2009. disk

Magic Quest. *Time Treks and Earth Treks.* Available from Educational Resources, (800)624-2926. disk, CD-ROM, and laserdisc

MECC. *Odell Down Under.* Available from MECC, (800)685-MECC. disk.

MECC. *World GeoGraph.* Available from Educational Resources, (800)624-2926. disk

Mindscape. *World Atlas.* Available from Educational Resources, (800)624-2926. disk

National Geographic. *STV: World Geography.* Available from National Geographic Educational Technology, (800)328-2936. videodisc

National Geographic. *Zip Zap Map.* Available from Educational Resources, (800)624-2926. laserdisc and disk

Newton Technology. *GEOvista Tutor.* Available from William K. Bradford, (800)421-2009. disk

Orange Cherry. *Time Traveler.* Available from Educational Resources, (800)624-2926. CD-ROM

Pride in Learning. *Global Issues.* Available from Educational Resources, (800)624-2926. disk

Queue. *Atlas Explorer.* Available from Educational Resources, (800)624-2926. disk

Sanctuary Woods. *Ecology Treks.* Available from Learning Services, (800)624-2926. software and videodisc

Software Toolworks. *World Atlas.* Available from Learning Services, (800)877-9378. CD-ROM and disk

SVE. *Geography on Laserdisc.* Available from Learning Services, (800)877-9378. laserdisc.

Answer Key

Page 233

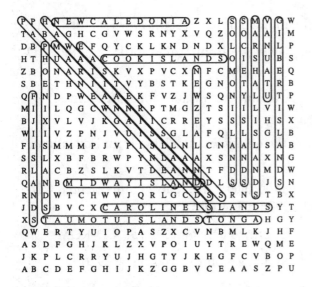

Page 244

1. marsupial
2. koala
3. eucalyptus
4. kangaroo
5. wallaby
6. wombat
7. dugong
8. platypus
9. emu
10. echidna
11. skink
12. dingo
13. cassowary
14. kookaburra
15. bandicoots
16. lyrebird
17 Tasmanian devil
18. weaverbird

Pages 262–263

1. an island built from the skeletons of coral polyps
2. 1,250 miles (2,000 km)
3. in the Coral Sea off the northeast coast of Australia
4. tiny coral polyps
5. millions of years
6. about 1,500 species
7. about 400 kinds
8. rose coral

   brain coral

   mushroom coral

   fan coral
9. between 10 miles (16 km) and 150 miles (190 km) from the shore
10. answers will vary

Antarctica

Table of Contents

Introduction *(cont.)*

Antarctica

This book was designed to present an overview of the geography of the continent of Antarctica. It is divided into five sections to match the themes of the Geographic Education National Implementation Project (GENIP), an educational project backed by the nation's most prestigious geographers.

Each section contains a selection of teaching pages, maps, activities, interesting facts, review questions, and puzzles or games. A plan for using the material to construct a geography center is also included, as well as ideas for putting together a book as a culminating activity.

You will also find a glossary of the specialized vocabulary used by geographers. This will make it easier for your students to talk about the world they live in.

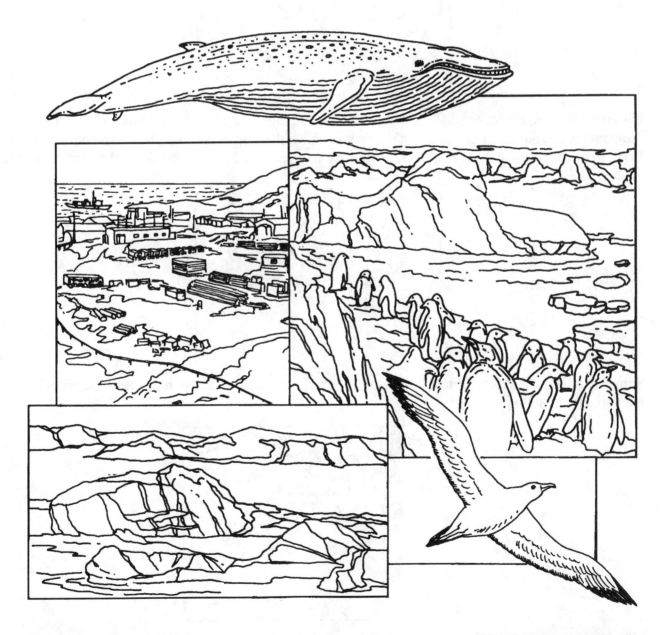

A Word or Two About Maps

Projections

The landforms shown on maps and globes do not look exactly alike. This is because it is just as hard to "peel" a globe and flatten the Earth's "skin" out into a map as it is to peel an orange and flatten out its skin to make a smooth, even surface. Even if you can get the skin off the orange in one piece, the top and bottom edges must be broken and spread out.

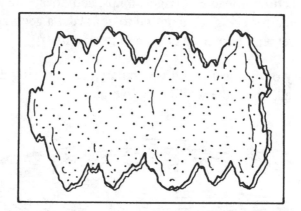

Different map makers (cartographers) have had different ideas about how to do this and have made different "projections." A projection is the way in which the map maker has chosen to flatten out the Earth's surface to make a flat map. Sometimes the map maker allows the breaks in the Earth's surface to show.

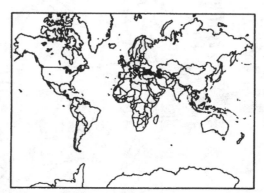

Sometimes the map maker stretches the Earth's "skin." This makes the countries near the poles look much bigger than they really are.

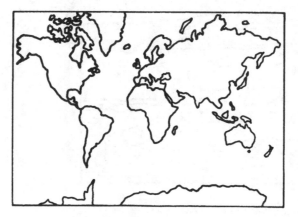

A Word or Two About Maps *(cont.)*

Projections *(cont.)*

Use your reference materials to find out the names of other common map projections and list them below. Research the advantages and disadvantages of each map projection you list and write them down below.

Map Projection	Advantages	Disadvantages

A Word or Two About Maps *(cont.)*

The Compass Rose

The compass rose is a small drawing that shows direction on a map. Most maps show north at the top and south at the bottom, west on the left and east on the right.

Look at maps to find some different styles of compass roses and then design your own. You can shrink your drawing and make multiple copies to use on the maps you make, color, or label.

Where on Earth Is Antarctica?

- Antarctica is surrounded by three of Earth's Oceans: the Pacific Ocean, the Atlantic Ocean, and the Indian Ocean.
- Although Antarctica lies entirely in the Southern Hemisphere, it is found in both the Western and Eastern Hemispheres.
- Except for Antarctica's one peninsula that reaches toward South America, Antarctica lies almost entirely within the Antarctic Circle.
- Only Europe and Australia are smaller than Antarctica.

Use these clues to find Antarctica on this map. Color it blue.

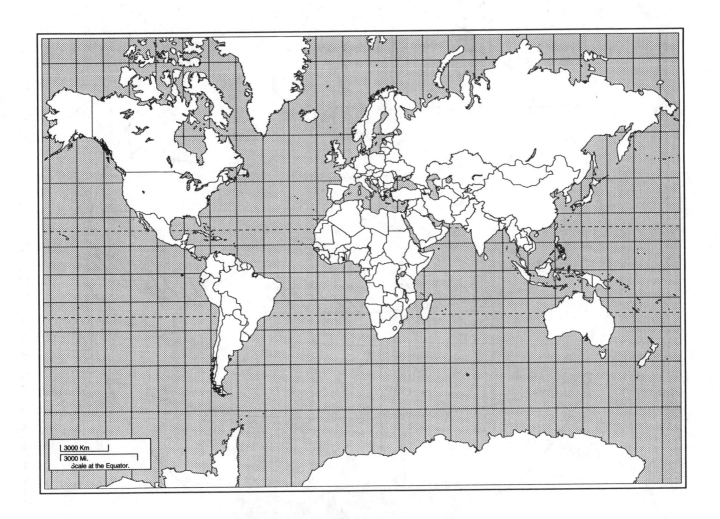

3000 Km
3000 Mi.
Scale at the Equator.

Where on Earth Is Antarctica? *(cont.)*

If you think of the Earth as a ball (a sphere or globe), you can draw a line around the middle (the equator) and separate the two halves into the top half (Northern Hemisphere) and the bottom half (Southern Hemisphere). Now you can talk about something as being in the Northern or Southern Hemisphere.

More lines are drawn around the Earth parallel to the equator and evenly spaced from the equator to the North and South Poles. They are called parallels or lines of latitude. They are numbered in degrees, starting with 0° at the equator and usually spaced at 15° intervals, ending with 90° N at the North Pole and 90° S at the South Pole.

(Geographers further divide their degrees into minutes and seconds so they can be very precise in locating the position of anything on the Earth's surface.)

If you divide the Earth into its Northern and Southern Hemispheres, Antarctica lies in
the_____Hemisphere.

Where on Earth Is Antarctica? *(cont.)*

You can also draw lines north and south around the Earth. These lines are called meridians or lines of longitude. They are usually shown 15° apart at the equator, but they all come together at the North and South Poles. (They also can be further divided into minutes and seconds, just like the parallels.)

The line that runs through Greenwich, England, is called the prime meridian (0°). Longitude is the distance east or west of the prime meridian. The line directly opposite the prime meridian is at 180° and is called the date line. If you are still thinking of the Earth as a ball (a sphere or globe), you can separate the two halves into the Western Hemisphere and the Eastern Hemisphere. (This is usually done along the meridians of 20° W and 160° E so all of Africa is in one hemisphere.)

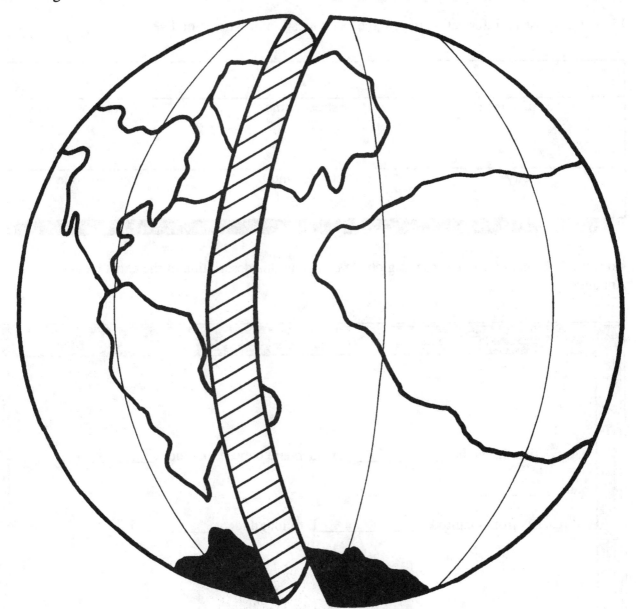

If you divide the Earth into its Western and Eastern Hemispheres, Antarctica lies in the

_____Hemisphere.

Where on Earth Is Antarctica? *(cont.)*

You can tell where things on the Earth are in two ways:

- You can give their exact or absolute location using latitude and longitude expressed in degrees (minutes and seconds).

- You can tell where they are in location to other things.

Fill out the missing information to give the exact location of where you live:

house number	street name	apartment number
city	state/country	zip code

Now, use information from a map or globe to complete this description of the exact location of Antarctica.

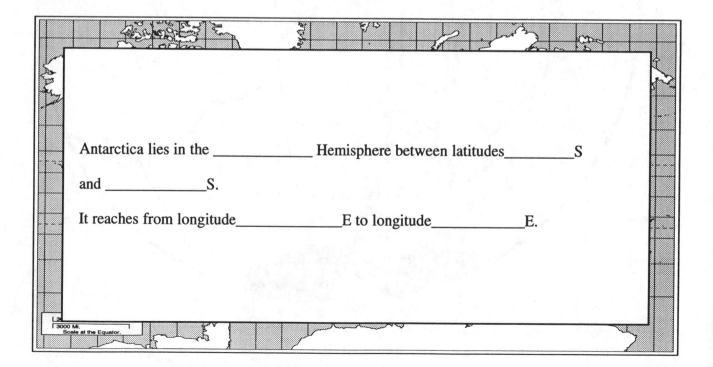

Antarctica lies in the _____ Hemisphere between latitudes_____S

and _____S.

It reaches from longitude_____E to longitude_____E.

Where on Earth Is Antarctica? *(cont.)*

You can tell where things on the Earth are in two ways:

- You can give their exact or absolute location using latitude and longitude expressed in degrees (minutes and seconds).
- You can tell where they are in relation to other things.

Fill out the missing information to give the relative location of where you live:

I live
between_____and_____

near_____

and across
from_____.

Now, use information from a map or globe to complete this description of the realitive location of Antarctica

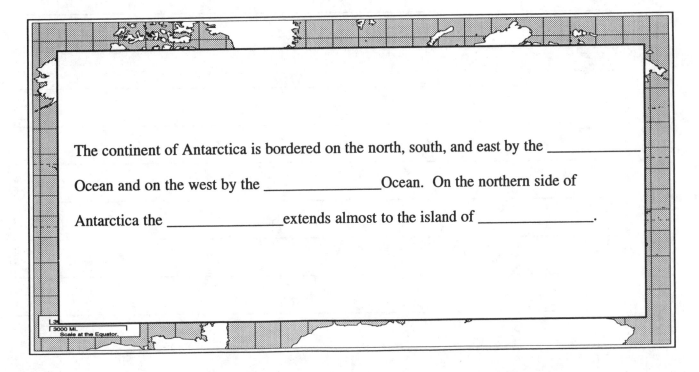

The continent of Antarctica is bordered on the north, south, and east by the _____

Ocean and on the west by the _____Ocean. On the northern side of

Antarctica the _____extends almost to the island of _____.

Where In Antarctica Is ___?

The nations of the world (38 of them, at least) have agreed to use Antarctica for only peaceful, scientific purposes and not to press their claims to this continent. Nevertheless, names have been given to many of Antarctica's outstanding features. Use information from a map or globe, an atlas, an encyclopedia, and your geography book to write both the exact and relative location of five features of the continent of Antarctica. See the next page for the names of some features to choose from.

1. _____

_____

_____

_____

2. _____

_____

_____

_____

3. _____

_____

_____

_____

4. _____

_____

_____

_____

5 _____

_____

_____

_____

Features of Antarctica

There are 29 names that have been given to a variety of places (features) on the continent of Antarctica listed below. Find them forwards, backwards, and diagonally in the word search below.

```
A Q U E E N M A U D L A N D C O A T S L A N D S Q W
N W E R T Y U M R O N N E I C E S H E L F I O H D P
T R A N S A N T A R C T I C M O U N T A I N S A N S
A P S V D F G B E R K N E R I S L A N D H E V C A N
R O F I L C H N E R I C E S H E L F L M N N I K L I
C L V N X P Z R O O S E V E L T I S L A N D C L S A
T A W S E O R T O Y U I B O P L K J H G F E T E I T
I R S O A I Z X C S V B N Y M N B V C X Z R O T R N
C P N N V B C X Z A S S D F R G H J K L P B R O E U
P L L M E R X A N D Q S W E R D T Y U I O Y I N D O
E A S A D P R T Y U I W E D D E L L S E A L A I N N
N T O S I L W I L K E S L A N D U A Y T R A L C A H
I E D S F A M E R Y I C E S H E L F N W E N A E X T
N A X I N E W S C H W A B E N L A N D D C D N S E R
S U H F J A M E R I C A N H I G H L A N D Y D H L O
U Q W M O U N T E R E B U S A D M U N S E N S E A W
L Q U E E N M A U D M O U N T A I N S Q W E R L T S
A R O S S I C E S H E L F P A L M E R L A N D F U L
R I S S E R L A R S E N I C E S H E L F B V C X Z L
B E L L I N G S H A U S E N S E A A S D F G H J K E
```

Cross off the places as you find them: Antarctic Peninsula, Palmer Land, Polar Plateau, Queen Maud Land, Transantarctic Mountains, Marie Byrd Land, Mount Erebus, Berkner Island, Coats Land, New Schwabenland, American Highland, Roosevelt Island, Ross Sea, Ross Ice Shelf, Victoria Land, Queen Maud Mountains, Shackleton Ice Shelf, Amery Ice Shelf, Enderby Land, Riiser-Larsen Ice Shelf, Weddell Sea, Ronne Ice Shelf, Filchner Ice Shelf, Vinson Massif, Alexander Island, Admunsen Sea, Bellingshausen Sea, Ellsworth Mountains, Wilkes Land

Features of Antarctica *(cont.)*

Use information from an atlas, an encyclopedia, your geography book, or any other reference book to write one interesting fact about each feature.

1. Admunsen Sea _____

   _____

2. Alexander Island _____

   _____

3. American Highland _____

   _____

4. Amery Ice Shelf _____

   _____

5. Antarctic Peninsula _____

   _____

6. Bellingshausen Sea _____

   _____

7. Berkner Island _____

   _____

Features of Antarctica *(cont.)*

8. Coats Land _____

   _____

9. Ellsworth Mountains _____

   _____

10. Enderby Land_____

    _____

11. Filchner Ice Shelf_____

    _____

12. Marie Byrd Land _____

    _____

13. Mount Erebus_____

    _____

14. New Schwabenland _____

    _____

15. Palmer Land_____

    _____

Features of Antarctica *(cont.)*

16. Polar Plateau _____

    _____

17. Queen Maud Land _____

    _____

18. Queen Maud Mountains _____

    _____

19. Riiser-Larsen Ice Shelf _____

    _____

20. Ronne Ice Shelf _____

    _____

21. Roosevelt Island _____

    _____

22. Ross Ice Shelf _____

    _____

23. Ross Sea _____

    _____

Features of Antarctica *(cont.)*

24. Shackleton Ice Shelf _____

    _____

25. Transantarctic Mountains_____

    _____

26. Victoria Land _____

    _____

27. Vinson Massif _____

    _____

28. Weddell Sea _____

    _____

29. Wilkes Land_____

    _____

Bonus Question!

Why aren't there any countries or cities on the continent of Antarctica? _____

_____

Look at the Map

Use the numbered list of Antarctic features on pages 306–309 to label the map below. Write the number of each feature on the map and use the list for a key.

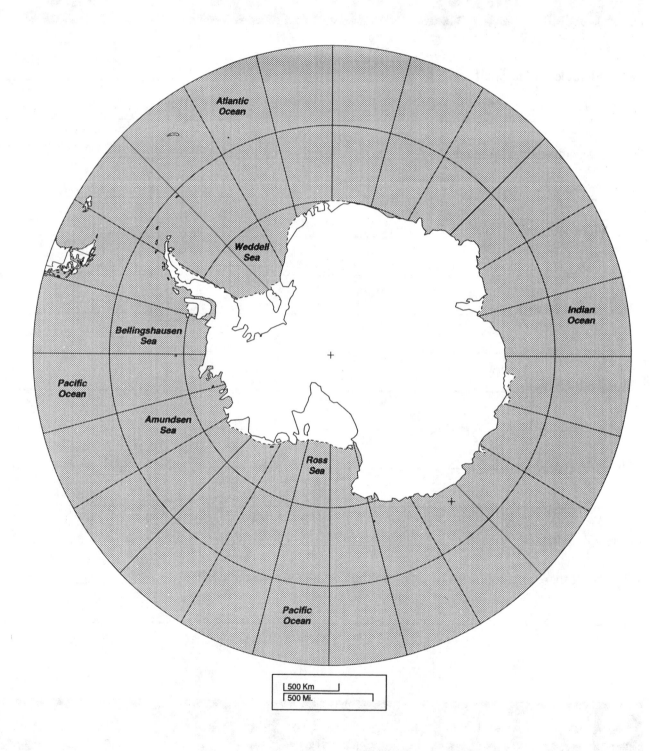

Physical Characteristics of Antarctica

Major Bodies of Water

Antarctica is bordered by the southernmost waters of the *Atlantic Ocean*, the *Pacific Ocean*, and the *Indian Ocean*.

(Some scientists like to think of the water closely surrounding the continent as a separate ocean they call the *Antarctic Ocean*. The water in this area is much colder and less salty than the rest of the world's oceans, and it freezes over in the winter forming a solid ice pack that floats on the surface. The place where this cold water meets the warmer waters of the other oceans is called the Antarctica Convergence. Nevertheless, most maps do not show a separate Antarctic Ocean.)

Use reference sources to label the major bodies of water on the map of Antarctica.

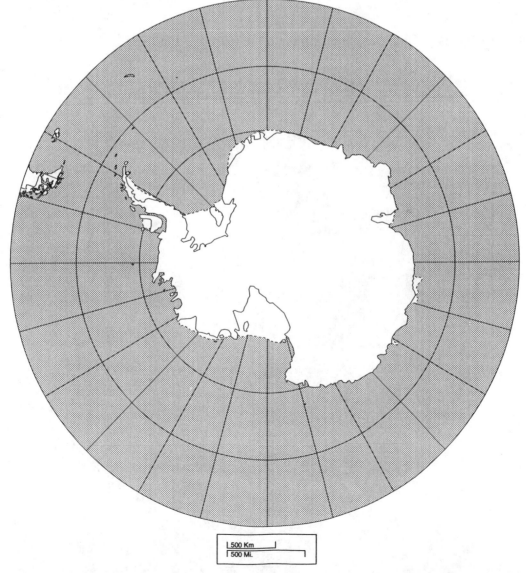

500 Km
500 Mi.

Physical Characteristics of Antarctica *(cont.)*

Landforms

Antarctica is the fifth largest continent. Only Australia and Europe are smaller. Antarctica is about twice the size of Australia, the smallest continent. The whole continent of Antarctica is covered by a thick icecap. This icecap is an average of two miles (3.2 km) thick and contains more fresh water than all the rest of the world. The ice moves slowly toward the sea in great frozen rivers called glaciers.

The *Transantarctica Mountains* cross the whole continent. They are probably an extension of the Andes Mountains that run the length of South America. This mountain chain contains a number of mountain ranges such as the *Ellsworth Mountains* and *Queen Maud Mountains*. The Transantarctic Mountains divide the continent into two regions: West Antarctica and East Antarctica. The *Antarctica Peninsula* extends north from West Antarctica to within 600 miles (960 km) of the tip of South America.

Use reference sources to label these landforms on the map of Antarctica.

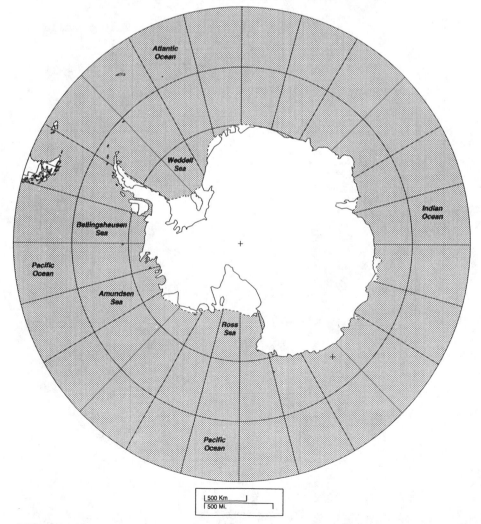

Physical Characteristics of Antarctica *(cont.)*

Other Bodies of Water

Unlike the other continents, Antarctica has no lakes or rivers that we can see. Everything is just frozen ice. There are two huge bays, the *Ross Sea* and the *Weddell Sea*, that cut into West Antarctica from both sides. Two smaller seas, *Bellingshausen Sea* and *Admunsen Sea* can be found near the base of the Antarctica Peninsula. Smaller bays indent the coast of East Antarctica. See how many you can find on a map of Antarctica.

Use reference sources to make your own list of smaller bays around the edge of East Antarctica. Then write their names below. Using the map on the next page, label the bodies of water with their numbers and use the list for a key.

1. Ross Sea	9.	
2. Weddell Sea	10.	
3. Bellingshausen Sea	11.	
4. Admunsen Sea	12.	
5.	13.	
6.	14.	
7.	15.	
8.	16.	

Bonus Question!

The lowest point in the world is on the continent of Antarctica. Does it have a special name? Where is it located? How many feet (meters) below sea level is it?

_____

_____

_____

_____

_____

_____

_____

_____

Physical Characteristics of
Antarctica *(cont.)*

Other Bodies of Water

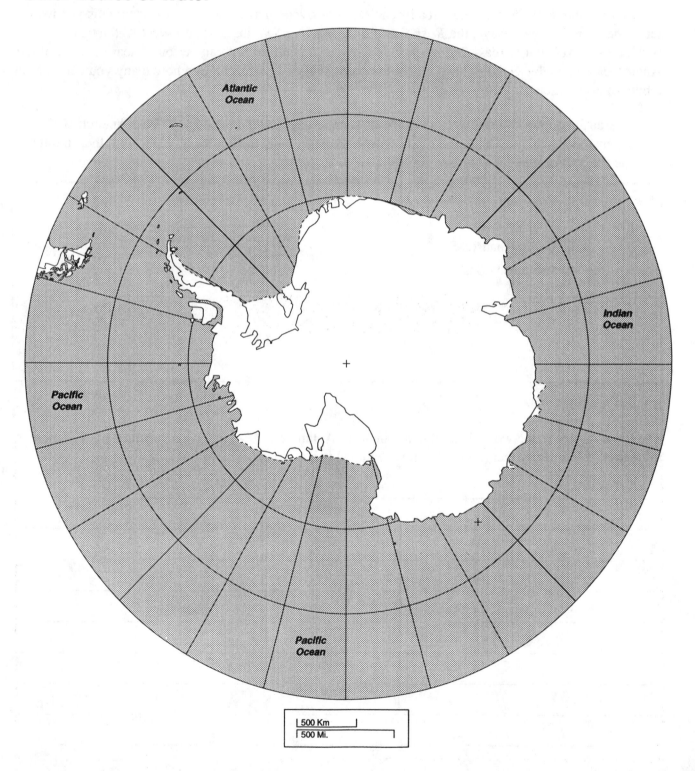

People in Antarctica

There are no native people on the continent of Antarctica. The only people who have spent much time there are hunters, explorers, and scientists. Seal hunters first sighted parts of the Antarctic Peninsula in the early 1800s. The explorers arrived later in the 1800s and first reached the South Pole in the early 1900s. The scientists came later, and today there are more than 40 scientific settlements in Antarctica.

In 1911, groups of explorers led by Roald Amundsen of Norway and Robert F. Scott of Great Britain took part in a great race to be the first humans to reach the South Pole. Amundsen reached it first on December 14, 1911, and returned safely. Scott's team was nearly overcome by misfortunes on the way to the pole. They reached the South Pole on January 18, 1912, to find the Norwegian flag and a note to Scott from Amundsen. Scott and all of his men died before they could finish their return journey.

The next important Antarctica exploration was headed by American Admiral Richard E. Byrd in 1928. He established a base called Little America on the Ross Ice Shelf. Exploration had become much easier and safer because of the invention of the radio and the airplane. Byrd and three companions were the first to fly over the South Pole. They also used dog sleds to explore thousands of square miles of Antarctica, always linked by radio to their home base. Byrd's group combined science with exploration as they studied the ice cap, weather, the Earth's magnetism, and geology.

How many countries have scientific bases in Antarctica? Do some research about them. Write the names of five of the countries that have bases there. Where are they located?

Location of Base	Country

People in Antarctica *(cont.)*

Use information from an atlas, an encyclopedia, your geography book, and any other reference book to answer the questions that follow.

1. What mineral resources are believed to lie beneath the Earth in Antarctica? What have people decided to do about them? Why?_____

   _____

   _____

   _____

   _____

   _____

2. Why are scientists worried about the effect of global warming on Antarctica? What is the "green-house effect"?_____

   _____

   _____

   _____

   _____

3. What is the ozone layer? How is it connected with Antarctica? _____

   _____

   _____

   _____

   _____

People in Antarctica *(cont.)*

4. What natural resources are thought to lie underneath the ice cap of Antarctica?

_____

_____

_____

_____

5. What two things have kept people from trying to exploit the mineral resources of Antarctica?

_____

_____

_____

_____

6. What is the Antarctica Treaty? _____

_____

_____

_____

_____

7. What was the 1987 Montreal Protocol? _____

_____

_____

_____

_____

South Pole vs North Pole

How are the North and South Polar regions different from one another? Use reference books to help you answer these questions.

1. What is different about what the North and South Polar regions are made of?

   _____

   _____

   _____

2. Compare their temperatures. Is one pole colder than the other?

   _____

   _____

   _____

3. Compare the animal life of both poles. How are they similar or different?

   _____

   _____

   _____

4. Are the same explorers associated with both poles?

   _____

   _____

   _____

5. Are natural resources being handled the same way on both poles? Why or why not?

   _____

   _____

   _____

Animals in Antarctica

Read the clues and unscramble the names of some Antarctic animals. Circle the names of the animals that are on the endangered species list.

1. _____ an animal that strains shellfish from the water with its teeth (breatrace lase)

2. _____ a vicious carnivore; chief enemy of the penguin (prodale sale)

3. _____ the southernmost mammal; it stays close to the continent while other southern mammals range far to sea (ledleWd asel)

4. _____ the largest of the seals; they may weigh more than four tons (lephante asel)

5. _____ the rarest of the five kinds of Antarctica seals (soRs eals)

6. _____ a whale that hunts in packs of up to 40; attacks penguins, seals, fish, and even whales larger than itself (lerlik welah)

7. _____ a type of whale that strains plankton from sea water with a bony sieve hanging from roof of its mouth (leneba hawel)

8. _____ the biggest creature that has ever lived; it weighs 150 tons and eats three tons of krill, small shrimp-like sea animals, each day (lube lehaw)

9. _____ a hawklike bird that feeds on penguin chicks and eggs (thouS laroP kaus)

10. _____ the largest Antarctica penguin which can weigh as much as 100 pounds when fully grown (preemor gipnune)

11. _____ a small penguin that fashions its nest from pebbles (léAdie nepuing)

12. _____ a bird that migrates to Antarctica every summer from its breeding grounds in the Arctic (rent)

13. _____ six kinds of these birds live in the Antarctic (letper)

People Depend on the Environment

Make a list of Antarctica's natural resources.

_____

_____

_____

_____

_____

Why have people decided not to use Antarctica's resources?

_____

_____

_____

_____

_____

_____

How has that decision been enforced?

_____

_____

_____

_____

_____

_____

_____

_____

_____

People Adapt to and Change the Environment

People adapt to and change the environment in many ways. Think of some possible solutions that may solve these environmental problems:

Availability of food, water, and other supplies:

_____

_____

_____

Housing in cold climates:

_____

_____

_____

_____

Clothing in cold climates:

_____

_____

_____

_____

Caring for illness and injury in remote areas:

_____

_____

_____

_____

People Adapt to and Change the Environment *(cont.)*

Severe weather conditions:

_____

_____

_____

_____

Surviving natural disasters:

_____

_____

_____

_____

Transportation in mountainous or hilly areas:

_____

_____

_____

_____

Transportation on snow or ice:

_____

_____

_____

_____

Technology Impacts the Environment

Resources are things that are valued and used by people. Natural resources are the resources that occur in nature, such as minerals in the Earth, trees, water, and air.

Since the natural resources of Antarctica are not being used, people have realized that other things are even more important.

Research to find the things that people think are even more important than the chance to use Antarctica's resources and tell why they think so.

_____

_____

_____

_____

_____

_____

_____

More Important Than Using Resources

_____

_____

_____

_____

Why?_____

_____

_____

_____

_____

Movement Demonstrates Interdependence

Why do human activities require movement? _____

_____

_____

Do the people in your family go places? _____ Choose two people and answer the following questions:

	Person #1	Person #2
Who?		
When?		
Where?		
How far?		
How often?		
Why?		
Mode of transportation?		

Movement Demonstrates Interdependence *(cont.)*

Use reference sources to figure the distances between the South Pole and major cities in countries around the world.

South Pole/New York _____

South Pole/London _____

South Pole/Paris _____

South Pole/Rome _____

South Pole/Tokyo _____

South Pole/Sydney _____

South Pole/Los Angeles _____

South Pole/Mexico City _____

South Pole/Hong Kong _____

South Pole/Cairo _____

South Pole/Moscow _____

South Pole/New Delhi _____

Movement Involves Linkages

List some of the ways people traveled from place to place in Antarctica in the past.

_____

_____

_____

_____

_____

List some of the ways people travel from place to place in Antarctica in the present.

_____

_____

_____

_____

_____

Bonus Question!

Why did methods of transportation change?

_____

_____

_____

_____

_____

_____

_____

Movement Involves Linkages *(cont.)*

How will people travel around Antarctica in the future?

_____

_____

_____

_____

_____

Design your own future method of transportation. Explain it and then draw a picture of it below.

_____

_____

_____

_____

_____

This Is How My Future Transportation Will Work:

_____

_____

_____

_____

This Is How My Future Transportation Will Look:

Movement Includes People, Ideas, and Products

People go places for business and for pleasure. Going somewhere for pleasure is called touring.

Where have you gone for pleasure?

_____

_____

_____

_____

_____

Where would you like to go?

_____

_____

_____

_____

_____

Ideas can travel too. List some of the different ways ideas travel from place to place.

_____

_____

_____

_____

_____

Products also travel. What are some of the ways products travel?

_____

_____

_____

Movement Includes People, Ideas, and Products *(cont.)*

What kind of person would want to visit Antarctica? Design a cover for a travel brochure that would appeal to that person. Sketch your design below. Write a description of Antarctica that would make someone decide to travel there.

_____

_____

_____

_____

_____

East Antarctica

Animals Across the Curriculum

A region is a portion of the Earth's surface that has characteristics unlike any other. However, it is hard to tell East Antarctica from West Antarctica except on a map. The Transantarctica Mountains divide the continent into two natural regions. East Antarctica is the largest region of the continent. It faces Africa, the Indian Ocean, and Australia. The South Pole is in East Antarctica, about 300 miles (480 km) from the Transantarctic Mountains. Most of East Antarctica is a high plateau surrounded by mountains and glaciers.

Only a few insects and microscopic organisms actually live on the Antarctic continent. The larger animals live in the waters around the continent, some of them coming ashore only briefly to breed and to care for their young. These animals include the *crabeater seal, leopard seal, Weddell seal, Ross seal,* and *elephant seal* or *sea elephant*. There are several varieties of whale such as the *killer whale, baleen whale*, and *blue whale*, which is a type of *baleen whale*. The *emperor penguins, Adelie penguin*, and *tern* are some of the birds who visit the continent.

1. **The Elephant Seal**

Be ready to report on the elephant seal. Find out what this animal eats, if it migrates, and if its territory has become smaller. Describe its appearance. Write down any other facts that you think are interesting.

_____

_____

_____

_____

_____

_____

_____

_____

_____

_____

_____

_____

_____

_____

East Antarctica *(cont.)*

Animals Across the Curriculum *(cont.)*

2. The Emperor Penguin

Write a short, humorous poem about the emperor penguin. This large, "well-dressed" bird looks as if it were going to a formal dance. Try to see a video tape or read an illustrated book about this animal before you write your poem. Use another piece of paper for an illustration.

_____

_____

_____

_____

_____

_____

_____

3. Put the names of the italicized animals on page 330 in ABC order and tell how many syllables are in each of the names.

_____   _____

_____   _____

_____   _____

_____   _____

East Antarctica *(cont.)*

Animals Across the Curriculum *(cont.)*

4. The Leopard Seal and the Killer Whale

Compare and contrast these two carnivores. What do they eat? How much do they weigh? Do they have any enemies? What else can you find out?

_____

_____

_____

_____

_____

_____

_____

_____

_____

_____

_____

_____

_____

_____

_____

_____

_____

_____

_____

_____

_____

East Antarctica *(cont.)*

Animals Across the Curriculum *(cont.)*

5. The Adélie Penguin

The Adélie penguin is a small bird with some interesting habits. One of these is its use of pebbles in its courtship ritual. Another is its curiosity about people. Still another is its refusal to abandon its eggs through fair and foul weather. Make up and write a legend explaining the origin of one of the Adélie penguin's habits. Call your legend "Why the Adélie Penguin?"

_____

_____

_____

_____

_____

_____

_____

_____

_____

_____

_____

_____

_____

_____

_____

_____

_____

_____

_____

_____

_____

East Antarctica *(cont.)*

Animals Across the Curriculum *(cont.)*

6. The Tern

This bird migrates thousands of miles (km) each year. Where does it come from? Where does it go? How far does it fly?

_____

_____

_____

_____

_____

_____

_____

_____

_____

7. A Bar Graph

Use a bar graph to compare the sizes (length and weight) of five Antarctic seals. Keep track of your facts here as you do your research.

Seal	Length	Weight

West Antarctica

West Antarctica lies mostly within the Western Hemisphere and faces the Pacific Ocean and South America. The long finger-like mountainous ridge of the Antarctic Peninsula extends northward from West Antarctica toward the tip of South America.

Find information about this area in reference books and answer these questions.

1. How far is it from the end of the Antarctic Peninsula to the tip of South America?

_____

2. Is most of West Antarctica's land mass above or below sea level?

_____

3. What is the name of Antarctica's only active volcano?

_____

4. How high is it?

_____

5. Where is it located?

_____

6. What is the name of Antarctica's highest peak?

_____

West Antarctica (cont.)

7. How high is it?

   _____

8. Where is it located?

   _____

9. What is the area's average yearly temperature?

   _____

10. What is the lowest temperature that has been recorded there?

   _____

11. What plants are found on the Antarctic continent? Where?

   _____

12. What is Antarctica's largest land animal?

   _____

Antarctica Fact Game

This game can be played in different ways:

Game 1—You can use a Jeopardy format. Students love this, and they can set it up all by themselves or with just a little help. Run the answer cards on one color of paper and the question cards on another color for easy sorting.

Game 2—You can make a card game like rummy. All the cards should be run on one color for this. Shuffle the cards and deal five to each player. Put the leftovers facedown or in the middle of the table. Players draw from the stack and discard in another stack. The object of the game is to lay down pairs by matching questions and answers. You can make it more complicated by allowing students to challenge one another's matched pairs if they think the matches are incorrect. Have students keep track of the rules they make and write game directions.

Fact Game Cards

It is the third smallest continent.	What is Antarctica?
It is the only continent that contains no countries at all.	What is Antarctica?
It is the continent on which the South Pole is located.	What is Antarctica?

Antarctica Fact Game (cont.)

Fact Game Cards (cont.)

It is Antarctica's only active volcano.	What is Mount Erebus?
It is the highest point on the Antarctic continent.	What is Vinson Massif?
It is the finger of land that reaches toward South America.	What is the Antarctic Peninsula?
They are the two seas that cut into West Antarctica.	What are the Weddell Sea and the Ross Sea?
This is the mountain range that crosses the continent of Antarctica.	What is the Transantarctic mountain range?
It is where the cold water around Antarctica meets the warmer oceans to the north.	What is the Antarctic Convergence?

Fact Game Cards (cont.)

It is a slow-moving river of ice.	What is a glacier?
It is the most common of the Antarctic seals.	What is the crabeater seal?
It is the world's largest seal.	What is the elephant seal?
It is the most vicious of the seals.	What is a leopard seal?
It is the largest creature that has ever lived.	What is the blue whale?
It is also called an orca.	What is a killer whale?

Antarctica Fact Game (cont.)

Fact Game Cards (cont.)

It is the bird that courts his mate with a pebble.	What is the Adélie penguin?
It is a large penguin that can weigh as much as 100 pounds (45 kg).	What is the emperor penguin?
He was the first explorer to sail around Antarctica.	Who was Captain James Cook?
He was the first explorer to reach the South Pole.	Who was Roald Amundsen?
He was the second explorer to reach the South Pole.	Who was Robert Scott?
He called his base Little America.	Who was Admiral Richard E. Byrd?

Antarctica Fact Game (cont.)

Fact Game Cards (cont.)

Let your students make their own question-and-answer fact cards. Students usually like to make extra hard ones in hopes of stumping each other, so have them write the book and page number where the information can be found on the question card.

	Book:_____ Page: _____
	Book:_____ Page: _____
	Book:_____ Page: _____
	Book:_____ Page: _____
	Book:_____ Page: _____

The Geography Center

Putting the Center Together

You can set up your Geography Center in a corner of your classroom and make it as simple or as elaborate as you want. The center should have a map, a globe, and an atlas. (Several maps, a couple of globes, and multiple copies of the atlas would be even better.) A table and chairs will facilitate group activities and discussions. A supply of writing and drawing materials will also come in handy. A bookcase, shelf, or window sill can be utilized for storing reference books. The more reference books you can provide, the better the assigned projects will be. If you have access to a TV, VCR, and tapes, you can show movies about the places you are studying. There are many tapes of this variety available, and the visual learners in your class will really appreciate this. Cushions for sitting on the floor to read or view tapes add a cozy touch.

Making the Center Work

You can make the Geography Center part of your instructional day by scheduling groups to do center work. Change the materials daily or weekly or provide a set of task cards at the beginning of the unit and expect each student to work through them individually or as part of a group. (See pages 343–345.)

Use Portfolios

Have students make portfolios and store them in containers in an accessible area of your center. Try using the inexpensive but sturdy plastic crates that are available at local hardware stores. Make students responsible for their own progress by having them file their own work, both completed work and work in progress. Have students create attractive covers for their portfolios so the accumulated work can be attractively displayed at your school's open house.

Deck the Walls

Encourage artwork, creative writing, and exploratory math to go along with your geography unit and spread it throughout the curriculum. Display these products on a bulletin board in your Geography Center. Have students mount and post their own work. They can cut out letters and create colorful captions for the board.

Have another bulletin board reserved for posting newspaper and magazine articles dealing with the continent you are studying. Encourage your students to bring in these articles, share them, and discuss their meaning and importance.

Task Cards

Task Card #3

Describe a glacier.

Name several of the continent's glaciers.

Through which part of the continent do they move?

Task Card #4

What is the most important mountain range on the continent?

How long is it?

In which part of the continent is it found?

Task Card #1

What is the highest mountain peak on the continent?

How tall is it?

In which mountain range is it found?

Task Card #2

What is the largest ice shelf on the continent?

How large is it?

Does it remain part of the continent all year long?

The Geography Center (cont.)

Task Cards (cont.)

Task Card #7

What oceans border the continent?

What smaller bodies of water are important to it?

Does it have any rivers?

Task Card #8

What animals are associated with the continent?

In what part of the continent do they live?

Are they in any danger in today's civilization?

Task Card #5

What variations in climate are found on the continent?

What variations in weather are found on the continent?

Can people live in all parts of the continent?

Task Card #6

What plants are found on the continent?

Where are they found?

Why do these plants grow where they do?

The Geography Center (cont.)

Task Card Response

Leave a stack of these task card response forms in the Geography Center for students to use.

Name _____ Date _____

Task Card #_____

Question #1

_____

_____

_____

_____

Question #2

_____

_____

_____

_____

Question #3

_____

_____

_____

_____

Bonus

I also learned_____

_____

_____

_____

The Culminating Activity: Making a Book

Method

You and your students can go about bookmaking in many different ways. Here are some suggestions:

- The book can be your students' showcase portfolios.

- Students can review and reflect upon the work they have accumulated in their portfolios, select the most representative samples or the pieces they like best, and put these things together in book form.

- The book can be a showcase portfolio based on the teacher's criteria.

- Have students select work from their portfolios, based on a list you develop.

- The book can be comprised of new material that sums up the unit.

- Have students complete various assignments meant specifically for inclusion in their books, showing their grasp of the material. (See pages 347–357.)

Contents

In most cases you will probably want your students to include maps, facts about both physical and political geography, research about animals, people, and resources. They can review or report on any books they have read about the continent, and they can write about what they have learned and how it has affected the way they view the world.

Cover

You can specify and provide the design for the cover so that all of the books will be uniform, or you can encourage your students to design a cover that is representative of the continent. A collage of pictures cut from magazines and travel brochures is an option that works well.

Be sure to laminate the finished covers so the books can be used as part of your classroom library or Geography Center reference shelf. Your students may also want to share their books with students in other classes.

Exciting ideas for binding and publishing follow on pages 358–360.

The Culminating Activity:
Making a Book *(cont.)*

Trace an outline map of the continent. Transfer information about its physical features from all of the maps you have made. You might want to use different colors to create a key.

Name _____ Date _____

Map of Physical Features

The Culminating Activity:
Making a Book *(cont.)*

Use the information you have already gathered or do some new research to complete this page.

Name _____Date_____

Facts About Physical Features

Area: _____

_____

Highest Point: _____

_____

Lowest Point: _____

_____

Largest Ice Shelf: _____

_____

Longest Peninsula: _____

_____

Largest Sea:_____

_____

Tallest Glacier: _____

_____

Thickest Ice: _____

_____

Longest Mountain Range:_____

_____

The Culminating Activity: Making a Book *(cont.)*

Trace an outline map of the continent. Transfer information about its territorial calims and research stations from all of the maps you have made. You might want to use a numbered list to create a key.

Name _____ Date_____

Map of Territorial Claims and Research Stations

The Culminating Activity: Making a Book *(cont.)*

Use the information you have already gathered or do some new research to complete this page.

Name _____ Date _____

Facts About Territorial Claims and Research Stations

Population: _____

Largest Territorial Claim (by area): _____

Smallest Territorial Claim (by area): _____

Largest Research Station (by area): _____

Largest Research Station (by population): _____

Smallest Research Station (by area): _____

Smallest Research Station (by population): _____

_____

_____

_____

_____

_____

Newest Research Station: _____

_____

_____

_____

_____

_____

The Culminating Activity:
Making a Book *(cont.)*

Use the information you have already gathered or do some new research to complete this page.

Name _____ Date_____

The People

The people of this continent belong to these regions:

_____

_____

_____

They speak these languages:

_____

_____

_____

They live in these different environments:

_____

_____

_____

Their ways of life have changed or are changing:

_____

_____

_____

_____

The Culminating Activity: Making a Book *(cont.)*

Pick the research station on the continent that is most interesting to you. Use the information you have already gathered or do some new research to complete this page.

Name _____ Date_____

The Research Station

Area: _____

Population: _____

Country: _____

Language(s): _____

Constructed Features: _____

_____

Kinds of Research: _____

_____

_____

_____

_____

When most research takes place: _____

_____

_____

_____

_____

_____

The Culminating Activity: Making a Book *(cont.)*

Use the information you have already gathered or do some new research to complete this page.

Name _____ Date _____

The Animals

The best known animals of this continent are _____

_____

_____

The animals of this continent are important because _____

_____

_____

The animals that still live in their natural habitats are _____

_____

_____

The animals that are on the endangered species list are _____

_____

_____

_____

They are on the endangered species list because _____

_____

_____

_____

_____

The Culminating Activity: Making a Book *(cont.)*

Keep track of the books you read about the continent on this log.

Name _____ Date _____

Book Log

Title: _____   Fiction: _____

Author: _____   Nonfiction: _____

Illustrator: _____   Rating: _____

Title: _____   Fiction: _____

Author: _____   Nonfiction: _____

Illustrator: _____   Rating: _____

Title: _____   Fiction: _____

Author: _____   Nonfiction: _____

Illustrator: _____   Rating: _____

Title: _____   Fiction: _____

Author: _____   Nonfiction: _____

Illustrator: _____   Rating: _____

The Culminating Activity: Making a Book *(cont.)*

Use copies of this form to review your favorite nonfiction books about the continent you have been studying.

Name _____Date_____

Book Review/Nonfiction

Title: _____

Author: _____

Illustrator: _____

Summary: _____

_____

_____

_____

_____

_____

Reasons I liked or did not like this book:_____

_____

_____

_____

_____

_____

Bonus!

If you liked this book and think other people should read it, you can do one of two things. (1) Write a paragraph or two telling how a nonfiction book can help you understand a continent or a country and post it on the bulletin board in the Geography Center. (2) Make a poster advertising the book and post it on the bulletin board in the Geography Center.

The Culminating Activity: Making a Book *(cont.)*

Use copies of this form to review your favorite fiction books about the continent you have been studying.

Name _____ Date _____

Book Review/Fiction

Title: _____

Author: _____

Illustrator: _____

Summary: _____

_____

_____

_____

_____

Reasons I liked or did not like this book: _____

_____

_____

_____

_____

_____

Bonus!

If you liked this book and think other people should read it, you can do one of two things. (1) Write a paragraph or two telling how a fiction book can help you understand a continent or a country and post it on the bulletin board in the Geography Center. (2) Make a poster advertising the book and post it on the bulletin board in the Geography Center.

The Culminating Activity:
Making a Book (cont.)

Write a reflective essay in which you discuss the ways that studying geography has given you a better understanding of the world and the people in it.

Name _____Date_____

Title:_____

_____

_____

_____

_____

_____

_____

_____

_____

_____

_____

_____

_____

_____

_____

_____

_____

_____

_____

_____

The Culminating Activity:
Making a Book *(cont.)*

Book Binding Ideas

1. Stack all the pages of the book in a neat pile.

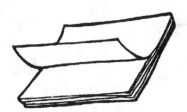

2. Place a blank sheet of paper on the top and bottom of the pages.

3. Leaving approximately 1/2" (1.25 cm) border, staple or sew all of the pages together on the left side.

4. Place two pieces of lightweight cardboard side by side. (Cereal boxes work well.) Each piece should be 1/2 to 1" (1.25 to 2.5 cm) larger than the size of the pages in the book.

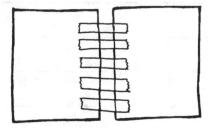

5. Leaving approximately 1" (2.5 cm) between them, tape the cardboard pieces together.

6. Put the cardboard on top of your covering material (e.g., fabric, wallpaper, contact paper, or wrapping paper). Glue the cardboard and covering material together, leaving a 1 to 1 1/2" (2.5 to 3.25 cm) material border.

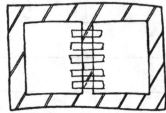

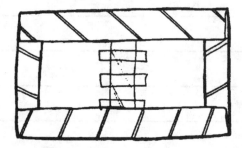

7. Fold up the edges of material over the cardboard and glue in place.

8. Glue the blank pages to the inside of the cardboard covers. Your book is ready to read and share.

The Culminating Activity: Making a Book (cont.)

Pop-Up Books

1. Fold a 8 1/2" x 11" (22 cm x 28 cm) piece of paper in half crosswise.

2. Measure and mark 2 3/4" (7 cm) from each side along the fold. Cut 2 3/4" (7 cm) slits at the marks.

3. Push cut area inside-out and crease to form the pop-up section.

4. Draw, color, and cut out the object to get "popped-up."

5. Glue it onto the pop-up section.

6. Glue two pages back to back, making sure the pop-up section is free.

7. Glue additional pages together, making as many pages (including pop-up pages) as you like. Be sure to include a free sheet on both the front and back so that those pages can be glued to a cover.

8. Glue a cover over the entire book.

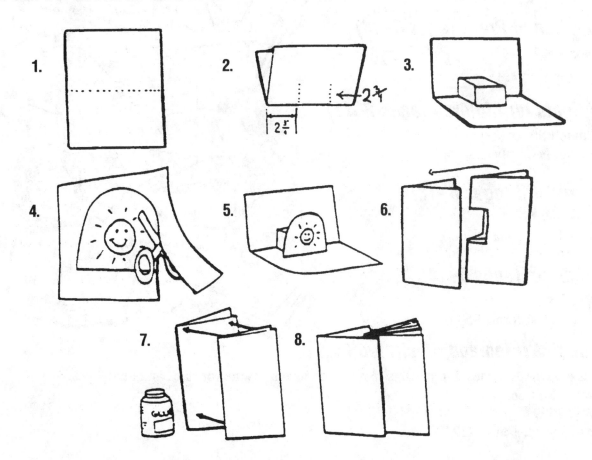

The Culminating Activity: Making a Book *(cont.)*

Real Markets for Student Writing

Student writing can be sent to the following addresses. Check your professional journals for more sources.

Children's Playmate (ages 5–8)

P.O. Box 567B
Indianapolis, Indiana 46206

Cricket (ages 6–12)

Cricket League
P.O. Box 300
Peru, Illinois 61354

Ebony Jr! (ages 6–12)

820 S. Michigan Avenue
Chicago, Illinois 60605

Flying Pencil Press (ages 8–14)

P.O. Box 7667
Elgin, Illinois 60121

Highlights for Children (ages 2–11)

803 Church Street
Honesdale, Pennsylvania 18431

Jack and Jill (ages 8–12)

P.O. Box 567B
Indianapolis, Indiana 46206

Stone Soup (ages 5–14)

P.O. Box 83
Santa Cruz, California 95063

National Written and Illustrated by...

(This is an awards contest for students in all grade levels. Write for rules and guidelines.)
Landmark Editions, Inc.
P.O. Box 4469
Kansas City, Missouri 64127

Software Review

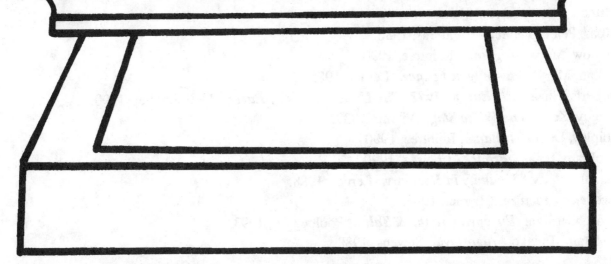

Software: *Picture Atlas of the World* (National Geographic Society)

Hardware: CD-ROM player, Macintosh or IBM/Windows compatible computer (4MB)

Grade Level: Intermediate

Summary: *Picture Atlas of the World* is a program that will allow your students instant information about any continent, country, city, etc., in the world. The main menu offers several options for students to locate information—Mapping Our World, World Map, and Countries A-Z. In Mapping Our World, your students have the option of listening to three animated explanations of latitude and longitude, cartography, and time zones.

When your students want to go somewhere specific in the world, all they have to do is just click on the world map to that continent, and it will appear with several options to choose from. Because of the written text, sound, and video, this piece of software becomes an excellent tool in doing research or just exploring the world.

Bibliography

Allen, Peter. *The Origins of World War II.* Watts, 1992.

Atkinson, Ian. *The Viking Ships.* Cambridge Univ. Pr, 1979.

Bains, Rae. *Europe.* Troll, 1985.

Barker, Peter. *Eastern Europe.* Silver Burdett, 1979.

Biel, Timothy. *The Black Death.* Lucent Books, 1990.

Cairns, Trevor. *Europe Rules the World.* Cambridge U Pr., 1981.

Caran, Betty. *Romania.* Childrens, 1988.

Crossland, Bert. *Where on Earth Are We?* Book Links, 1994.

Cross, Esther and Wilbur Cross. *Portugal.* Childrens, 1986.

Dickinson, Mary B. (Ed.). *National Geographic Picture Atlas of Our World.* National Geographic Society, 1993.

DuBois, Jill. *Greece.* Marshall Cavendish, 1992.

Dunnan, Nancy. *One Europe.* Millbrook, 1992.

Ecke, Worlfgang. *The Face at the Window.* Prentice Hall, 1979.

Europe at the Time of Greece & Rome. Raintree Steck-V, 1988.

Finland in Pictures. Lerner, 1991.

Flint, David. *The Baltic States: Estonia, Latvia, Lithuania.* Millbook, 1992.

Fradin, Dennis B. *The Netherlands.* Childrens, 1983.

Garett, Dan. *Germany.* Raintree, 1992.

Greene, Carol. *Austria.* Childrens, 1986.

Hargrove, Jim. *Germany.* Childrens, 1992.

Harris, Jonathan. *The Land and People of France.* Harper, 1989.

Horejs, Vit. *Twelve Iron Sandals: And Other Czechoslovak Tales.* Prentice Hall, 1985.

Hubley, Penny, and John Hubley. *A Family in Italy.* Lerner, 1987.

James, Ian. *Inside Italy.* Watts, 1988.

Kuniczak, W.S. *The Glass Mountain: Twenty-Six Ancient Polish Folktales and Fables.* Hippocrene, 1992.

Mayer, Marianna. *The Prince and the Princess: A Bohemian Fairy Tale.* Bantam, 1989.

Miller, Arthur. *Spain.* Chelsea, 1989.

Milner, Cate. *France.* Raintree, 1990.

Moss, Peter. *France.* Childrens, 1986.

Peplow, Mary. *England.* Raintree, 1990.

Regan, Mary. *A Family in France.* Lerner, 1985.

Roberts, Elizabeth. *Europe 1992: The United States of Europe?* Gloucester, 1990.

Seredy, Kate. *The White Stag.* Viking, 1937.

Shipley, Debra. *Ireland.* Raintree, 1990.

Sookram, Brian. *France.* Chelsea, 1990.

St. John, Jetty. *A Family in Hungary.* Lerner, 1988.

Sweden in Pictures. Lerner, 1990.

Swift, Carolyn. *European Myths & Tales.* Poolbeg Pr., 1993.

Yokatani, Takako. *Yugoslavia.* Stevens, 1988.

Bibliography *(cont.)*

Technology

Broderbund. *MacGlobe & PC Globe.* Available from Learning Services, (800)877-9378. disk

Broderbund. *Where in the World Is Carmen Sandiego?* Available from Troll (800)526-5289. CD-ROM and disk

Bureau of Electronic Publishing Inc. *World Fact Book.* Available from Educational Resources, (800)624-2926. CD-ROM

CLEARVUE. *The Earth, the Oceans, and Plants & Animals:* Interactive, curriculum oriented CD-ROMs. Available from Educational Resources, (800)624-2926. CD-ROM

DeLorme Publishing. *Global Explorer.* Available from DeLorme Publishing, 1995. CD-ROM

Impressions. *My First World Atlas.* Available from Educational Resources, (800)624-2926.

Lawrence. *Nigel's World Adventures in World Geography.* Available from Educational Resources, (800)624-2926. CD-ROM and disk

Magic Quest. *Time Treks and Earth Treks.* Available from Educational Resources, (800)624-2926.

MECC. *World GeoGraph.* Available from Educational Resources, (800)624-2926. disk

Mindscape. *World Atlas.* Available from Educational Resources, (800)624-2926. disk

National Geographic. *STV: World Geography.* Available from National Geographic Educational Technology, (800)328-2936. videodisc

Newton Technology. *GEOvista Tutor.* Available from William K. Bradford, (800)421-2009. disk

Orange Cherry. *Time Traveler.* Available from Educational Resources, (800)624-2926. CD-ROM

Partnership Plus. Vol. 3: *World Hot Spots.* Educational Resources, (800)624-2926. disk

Pride in Learning. *Global Issues.* Available from Educational Resources, (800)624-2926. disk

Queue. *Atlas Explorer.* Available from Educational Resources, (800)624-2926. disk

Sanctuary Woods. *Ecology Treks.* Available from Learning Services, (800)624-2926. software and videodisc

Software Toolworks. *World Atlas.* Available from Learning Services, (800)877-9378. CD-ROM and disk

SVE. *Geography on Laserdisc.* Available from Learning Services, (800)877-9378. laserdisc.

Answer Key

Page 305

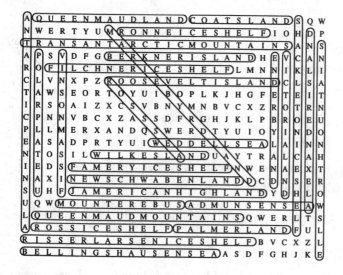

```
A Q U E E N M A U D L A N D C O A T S L A N D S Q W
N W E R T Y U M R O N N E I C E S H E L F I O D P
T R A N S A N T A R C T I C M O U N T A I N S A N S
A P S V D F G B E R K N E R I S L A N D H E N A S N
R O F I L C H N E R I C E S H E L F L M N N I K I
C L V N X P Z R O O S E V E L T I S L A N D C L S A
T A W S E O R T O Y U I B O P L K J H G F E T E T N
I R S O A I Z X C S V B N Y M N B V C X Z O E R O T
C P N N V B C X Z A S S D F R G H J K L P B R O N U
P L L M E R X A N D Q S W E R D T Y U I O Y I N I N
E A A D P R T Y U I W E D D E L L S E A L I O C I A
N T O S I L W I L K E S L A N D U A Y T R A L C A R
I E D S F A M E R Y I C E S H E L F N W E N A E N C
N A X I N E W S C H W A B E N L A N D O C D N S E T
S U H F J A M E R I C A N H I G H L A N D Y D H L I
U Q W M O U N T E R E B U S A D M U N S E N S E A C
L Q U E E N M A U D M O U N T A I N S Q W E R L T S
A R O S S I C E S H E L F P A L M E R L A N D F U L
R I S S E R L A R S E N I C E S H E L F B V C X Z L
B E L L I N G S H A U S E N S E A A S D F G H J K E
```

8. near the point where the mountains of the peninsula extend into the Antarctic mainland

9. below 0 F (below -18 C)

10. -127 F (-87 C) in August, 1960

11. mosses, lichens, three types of flowering plants on the edges of the continent and on the Antarctic Peninsula

12. a wingless insect, less than a tenth of an inch long

Page 319

1. crabeater seal
2. leopard seal
3. Weddell seal
4. elephant seal
5. Ross seal
6. killer whale
7. baleen whale
8. blue whale
9. South Polar skua
10. emperor penguin
11. Adelie penguin
12. tern
13. petrel

Pages 335–336

1. about 600 miles (960 km)
2. below sea level
3. Mount Erebus
4. 12,280 feet (3,725 m)
5. on Ross Island in the Ross Sea
6. Vinson Massif
7. 16,864 feet (5,059 m)

Asia

Table of Contents

Introduction *(cont.)*

Asia

This book was designed to present an overview of the geography of the continent of Asia. It is divided into five sections to match the themes of the Geographic Education National Implementation Project (GENIP), an educational project backed by the nation's most prestigious geographers.

Each section contains a selection of teaching pages, maps, activities, interesting facts, review questions, and puzzles or games. A plan for using the material to construct a geography center is also included, as well as ideas for putting together a book as a culminating activity.

You will also find a glossary of the specialized vocabulary used by geographers. This will make it easier for your students to talk about the world they live in.

A Word or Two About Maps

Projections

The landforms shown on maps and globes do not look exactly alike. This is because it is just as hard to "peel" a globe and flatten the Earth's "skin" out into a map as it is to peel an orange and flatten out its skin to make a smooth, even surface. Even if you can get the skin off the orange in one piece, the top and bottom edges must be broken and spread out.

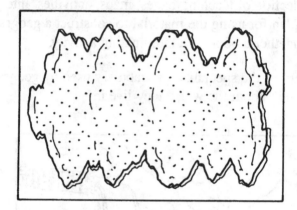

Different map makers (cartographers) have had different ideas about how to do this and have made different "projections." A projection is the way in which the map maker has chosen to flatten out the Earth's surface to make a flat map. Sometimes the map maker allows the breaks in the Earth's surface to show.

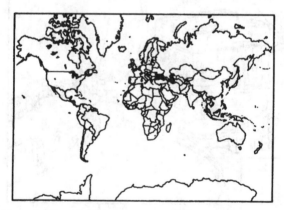

Sometimes the map maker stretches the Earth's "skin." This makes the countries near the poles look much bigger than they really are.

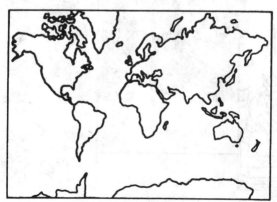

A Word or Two About Maps *(cont.)*

Projections *(cont.)*

Use your reference materials to find out the names of other common map projections and list them below. Research the advantages and disadvantages of each map projection you list and write them down below.

Map Projection	Advantages	Disadvantages

A Word or Two About Maps *(cont.)*

The Compass Rose

The compass rose is a small drawing that shows direction on a map. Most maps show north at the top and south at the bottom, west on the left and east on the right.

Look at maps to find some different styles of compass roses and then design your own. You can shrink your drawing and make multiple copies to use on the maps you make, color, or label.

Where on Earth Is Asia?

- Asia is the largest of the continents.

- Together with Europe, Asia forms the landmass sometimes called Eurasia.

- Except for the islands of Indonesia which extend south of the equator, Asia lies in the Northern Hemisphere, reaching well above the Arctic Circle.

- Most of Asia lies in the Eastern Hemisphere except for the part that stretches around into the Western Hemisphere near Alaska in North America.

Use these clues to find Asia on this map. Color it blue.

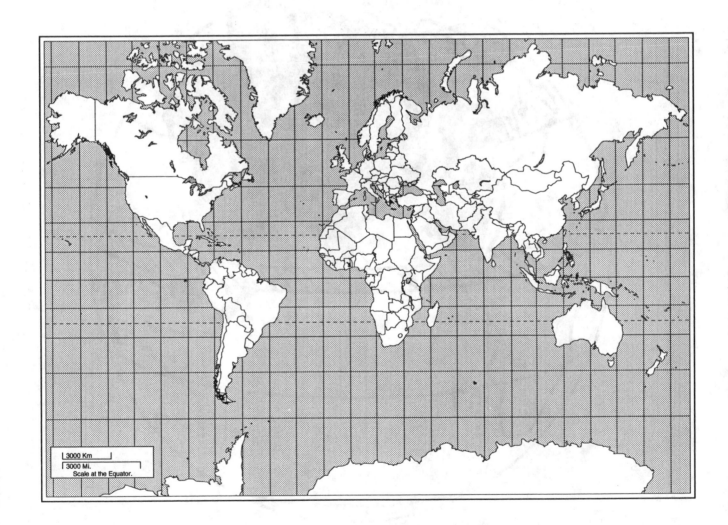

3000 Km
3000 Mi.
Scale at the Equator.

Where on Earth Is Asia? *(cont.)*

If you think of the Earth as a ball (a sphere or globe), you can draw a line around the middle (the equator) and separate the two halves into the top half (Northern Hemisphere) and the bottom half (Southern Hemisphere). Now you can talk about something as being in the Northern or Southern Hemisphere.

More lines are drawn around the Earth parallel to the equator and evenly spaced from the equator to the North and South Poles. They are called parallels or lines of latitude. They are numbered in degrees, starting with 0° at the equator and usually spaced at 15° intervals, ending with 90° N at the North Pole and 90° S at the South Pole.

(Geographers further divide their degrees into minutes and seconds so they can be very precise in locating the position of anything on the Earth's surface.)

If you divide the Earth into its Northern and Southern Hemispheres, Asia lies almost entirely in the_____Hemisphere.

Where on Earth Is Asia? *(cont.)*

You can also draw lines north and south around the Earth. These lines are called meridians or lines of longitude. They are usually shown 15° apart at the equator, but they all come together at the North and South Poles. (They also can be further divided into minutes and seconds, just like the parallels.)

The line that runs through Greenwich, England, is called the prime meridian (0°). Longitude is the distance east or west of the prime meridian. The line directly opposite the prime meridian is at 180° and is called the date line. If you are still thinking of the Earth as a ball (a sphere or globe), you can separate the two halves into the Western Hemisphere and the Eastern Hemisphere. (This is usually done along the meridians of 20° W and 160° E so all of Africa is in one hemisphere.)

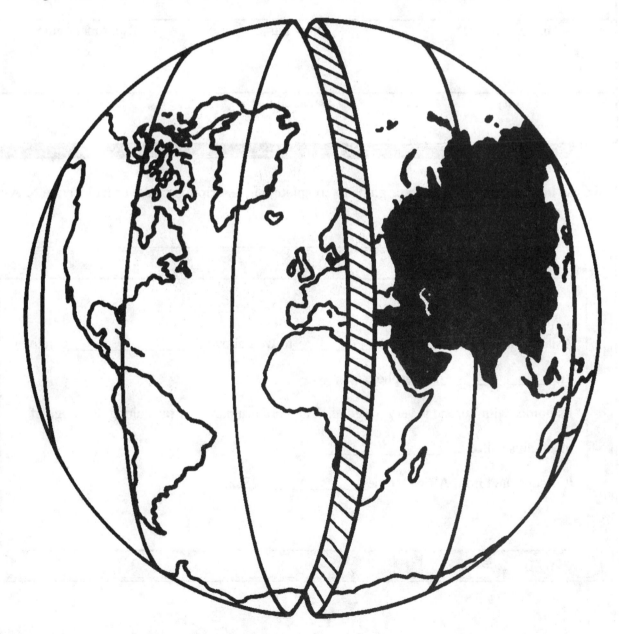

If you divide the Earth into its Western and Eastern Hemispheres, Asia lies almost entirely in the_____Hemisphere.

Where on Earth Is Asia? *(cont.)*

You can tell where things on the Earth are in two ways:

- You can give their exact or absolute location using latitude and longitude expressed in degrees (minutes and seconds).

- You can tell where they are in relation to other things.

Fill out the missing information to give the exact location of where you live:

house number	street name	apartment number
city	state/country	zip code

Now, use information from a map or globe to complete this description of the exact location of Asia.

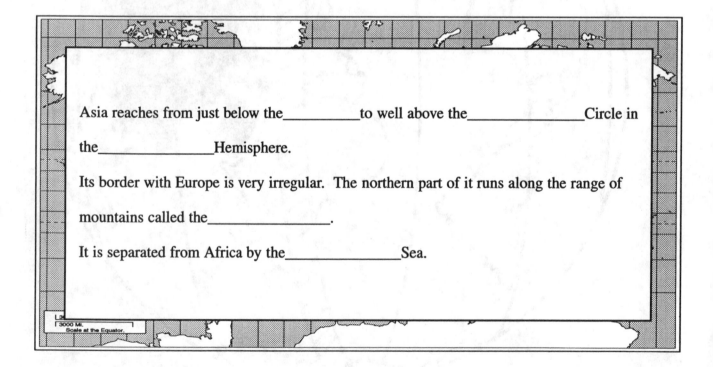

Asia reaches from just below the_____to well above the_____Circle in

the_____Hemisphere.

Its border with Europe is very irregular. The northern part of it runs along the range of

mountains called the_____.

It is separated from Africa by the_____Sea.

3000 Mi.
Scale at the Equator.

Where on Earth Is Asia? *(cont.)*

You can tell where things on the Earth are in two ways:

• You can give their exact or absolute location using latitude and longitude expressed in degrees (minutes and seconds).

• You can tell where they are in relation to other things.

Fill out the missing information to give the location of where you live in relation to other things:

I live
between_____and_____

near_____

and across
from_____.

Now, use information from a map or globe to complete this description of the relative location of Asia.

The continent of Asia is bordered on the north by the_____Ocean, on the

east by the_____Ocean, and on the south by the_____Ocean.

The northern part of Asia is connected to_____and the southern part is

separated from_____by the Red Sea.

3000 Mi.
Scale at the Equator.

Where in Asia Is_____?

Use information from a globe or map, an atlas, an encyclopedia, and your geography book to write both the exact and relative locations of five of the countries on the continent of Asia. See the next page for the names of the countries to choose from.

1. _____

   _____

   _____

   _____

2. _____

   _____

   _____

3. _____

   _____

   _____

   _____

4. _____

   _____

   _____

   _____

5. _____

   _____

   _____

Countries of Asia

There are 50 countries of Asia listed below. Find them forwards, backwards, and diagonally in the word search below.

```
Q B P R P H I L I P P I N E S G E O R G I A T Y
N R A U Z B E K I S T A N E P A L U Q C W Z H J
A U K S A U D I A R A B I A R T A E N Y K E A R
L N I S Y R I A Y I U I R O P C L I Y P A R I B
M E S I S R A E L L N Q A T A R A E L R Z B L M
R I T A R M E N I A A D Q M S R M D F U A A A A
K J A P A N I R A N G S I H H E J K L S K I N C
C I N K Z X C V Y K B O M A N A D R O J H J D O
L N O U N I T E D A R A B E M I R A T E S A C X
V D R W Q W K E R T Y L Y H U I O P A L T N A G
T O T A K R L E B A N O N J U H C H I N A G M N
V N H I U F D S K Y R G Y Z S T A N W Z N X B K
E E K T U R K M E N I S T A N C A V A B N M O U
A S O Q W E R T T A J I K I S T A N N Y U I D S
B I R A F G H A N I S T A N M A L D I V E S I P
W A E M O N G O L I A X B A N G L A D E S H A W
F M A L A Y S I A S O U T H K O R E A A S D F G
G H O N G K O N G M Y A N M A R V I E T N A M T
X S I N G A P O R E A S D F G H T R E W Q Z X Y
Z Y X V W U T S R Q P O A B C D E F G H I J K L
```

Cross off the countries as you find them: Russia, Georgia, Armenia, Azerbaijan, Kazakhstan, Turkmenistan, Uzbekistan, Kyrgyzstan, Iraq, Tajikistan, Turkey, Cyprus, Lebanon, Syria, Israel, Jordan, Saudi Arabia, Kuwait, Bahrain, Qatar, United Arab Emirates, Oman, Yemen, Iran, Afghanistan, Pakistan, India, Nepal, Bhutan, China, Taiwan, Bangladesh, Maldives, Sri Lanka, Mongolia, Macau, Hong Kong, North Korea, South Korea, Japan, Myanmar, Thailand, Laos, Cambodia, Vietnam, Philippines, Malaysia, Singapore, Brunei, Indonesia

Countries of Asia

Use information from an atlas, an encyclopedia, your geography book, or any other reference book to write one interesting fact about each country. (Because there are so many countries on the continent of Asia, you may want your students to pick just a few countries to write about.)

1. Afghanistan _____

   _____

2. Armenia _____

   _____

3. Azerbaijan _____

   _____

4. Bahrain_____

   _____

5. Bangladesh_____

   _____

6. Bhutan _____

   _____

7. Brunei_____

   _____

8. Cambodia_____

   _____

9. China _____

   _____

10. Cyprus _____

    _____

11. Georgia_____

    _____

Countries of Asia *(cont.)*

12. Hong Kong _____

_____

13. India _____

_____

14. Indonesia _____

_____

15. Iran _____

_____

16. Iraq _____

_____

17. Israel _____

_____

18. Japan _____

_____

19. Jordan _____

_____

20. Kazakhstan _____

_____

21. Kuwait _____

_____

22. Kyrgyzstan _____

_____

23. Laos _____

_____

24. Lebanon _____

_____

Countries of Asia (cont.)

25. Macau _____

_____

26. Malaysia _____

_____

27. Maldives _____

_____

28. Mongolia _____

_____

29. Myanmar _____

_____

30. Nepal _____

_____

31. North Korea _____

_____

32. Oman _____

_____

33. Pakistan _____

_____

34. Philippines _____

_____

35. Qatar _____

_____

36. Russia _____

_____

37. Saudi Arabia _____

_____

380

Countries of Asia (cont.)

38. Singapore _____

_____

39. South Korea _____

_____

40. Sri Lanka _____

_____

41. Syria _____

_____

42. Taiwan _____

_____

43. Tajikistan _____

_____

44. Thailand _____

_____

45. Turkey _____

_____

46. Turkmenistan _____

_____

47. United Arab Emirates _____

_____

48. Uzbekistan _____

_____

49. Vietnam _____

_____

50. Yemen _____

_____

Look at the Map

Use the numbered list of Asian countries on pages 378–381 to label the map below. Write the number of each country on the map and use the list for a key.

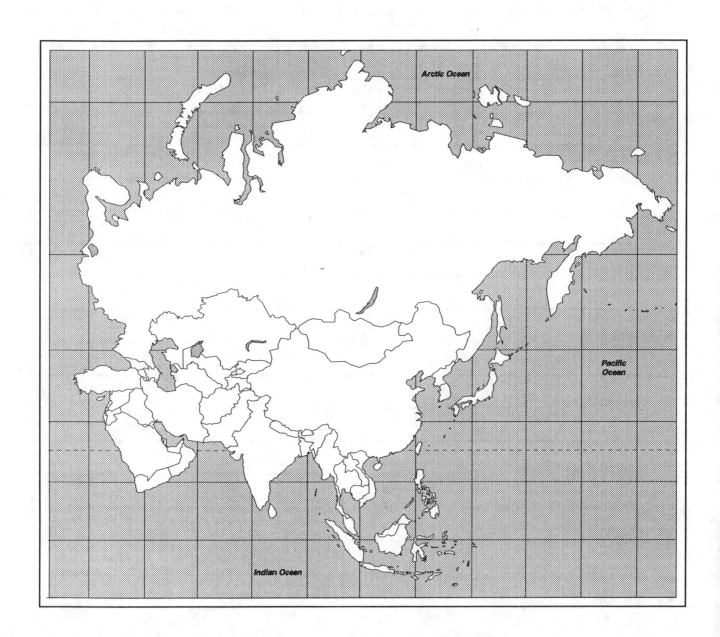

Physical Characteristics of Asia

Major Bodies of Water

Asia is bordered by the *Indian Ocean* to the south, the *Pacific Ocean* to the east, and the *Arctic Ocean* to the north. It is separated from Africa by the *Red Sea* and the *Suez Canal* and from North America by the *Bering Sea*.

Use reference sources to label these major bodies of water on the map of Asia.

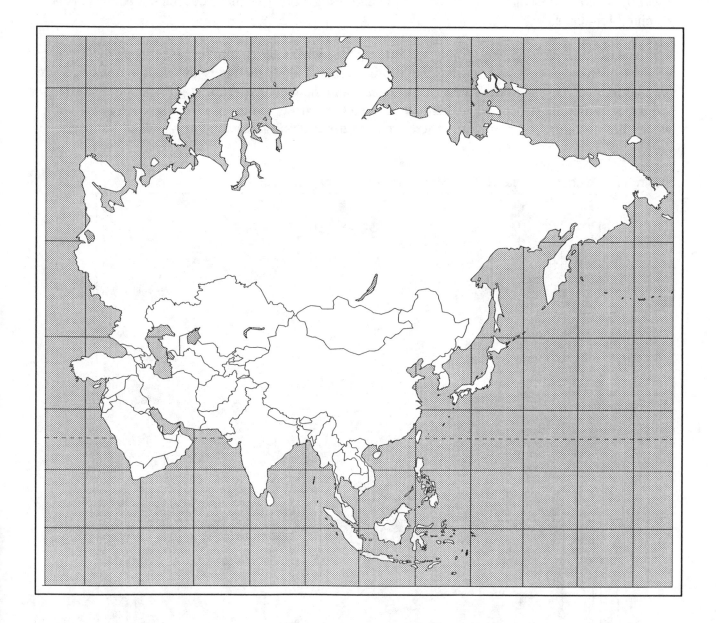

Physical Characteristics of Asia *(cont.)*

Landforms

Asia is the largest continent on Earth. It makes up almost a third of Earth's land surface and is populated by more than half of Earth's people.

Asia has great mountain ranges. The *Ural Mountains* divide it from Europe on the northwest. The *Himalaya Mountains,* the *Kunlun Mountains*, the *Tien Shan Mountains*, the *Altai Mountains*, and the *Hindu Kush* stretch in different directions from central Asia. The highest point on Earth, *Mount Everest,* is part of the Himalayan range and the high *Plateau of Tibet* lies between the Himalaya and Kunlun Mountains.

The land of Asia varies greatly. There are fertile plains where agriculture began between the Tigris and Euphrates Rivers in the area known as the Middle East and along the Indus and Yellow Rivers. There are interior deserts such as the *Takla Makan Desert* and the *Gobi Desert,* vast grasslands called *steppes, taiga* that border the steppes where hardy evergreen trees grow, and the *tundra,* the lands in the north where the subsoil is frozen all year. There are even tropical rain forests in the islands of Southeast Asia.

Use reference sources to label these landforms on the map of Asia.

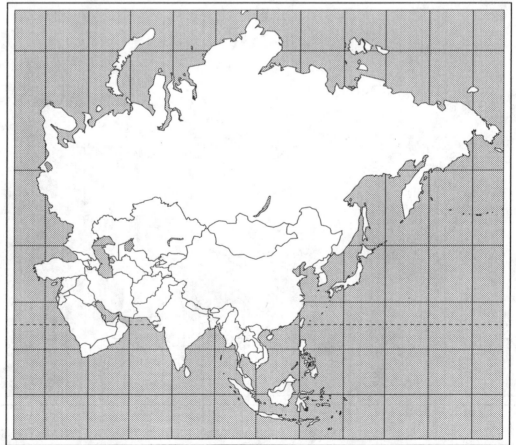

Physical Characteristics of Asia (cont.)

Other Bodies of Water

Asia has important seas, lakes, and rivers. *The Black Sea* and the *Caspian Sea* form part of its irregular border with Europe. Around the edges of the continent are found the *Arabian Sea, Bay of Bengal, South China Sea, Sea of Japan,* and *Sea of Okhotsk.*

The *Tigris* and *Euphrates Rivers* are two of the most historically important rivers in Asia. Three other important rivers are the *Indus, Ganges,* and *Brahmaputra.* They all rise in or near the Himalaya Mountains. China's most important rivers are the *Yellow River* and the *Yangtze River.* The *Mekong River* flows through Southeast Asia. The *Volga River* is Russia's most important river, but it flows through the part of Russia that lies in Europe and is actually Europe's longest river. The *Ob River* and the *Yenisey River* of Siberia flow northward and empty into the Arctic Ocean.

Use reference sources to draw in the rivers on the map on the next page. Then label the bodies of water with their numbers and use the list for a key.

1. Black Sea	10. Indus River
2. Caspian Sea	11. Ganges River
3. Arabian Sea	12. Brahmaputra River
4. Bay of Bengal	13. Yellow River
5. South China Sea	14. Yangtze River
6. Sea of Japan	15. Mekong River
7. Sea of Okhotsk	16. Ob River
8. Tigris River	17. Yenisey River
9. Euphrates River	

Bonus Questions!

What ancient civilization originated between the Tigris and Euphrates Rivers?

_____

What is the civilization famous for?

_____

What was the name of the country then? What is its name now?

_____

Physical Characteristics
of Asia *(cont.)*

Other Bodies of Water

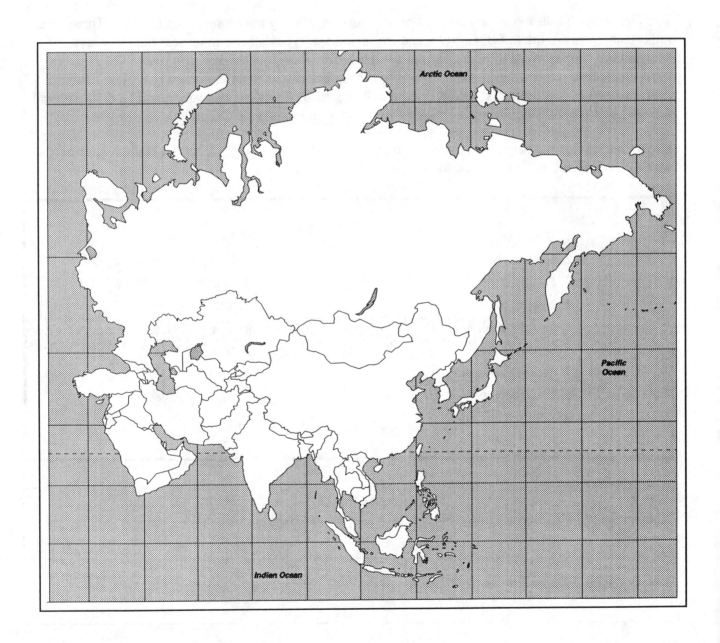

People in Asia

More than half of the people in the world live in Asia. Most of them cluster in the fertile river valleys and along the coasts. These places are among the most densely populated places on Earth. Many people have left farms in the country to live in the cities. They go to the cities in search of a better way of life and find themselves living in shanty towns and begging for food. There are great differences between the rich and the poor in Asia.

All of the world's major religions started in Asia, and all of them are practiced there today. Hinduism is the major religion of India where it originated around 3,500 years ago. Buddhism, which also began in India, is practiced in present day East and Southeast Asia. Judaism, Christianity, and Islam all began in the Middle East and are practiced there today, as well. All of these religions are reflected in the customs, lifestyles, and even governments of the people who practice them.

Hundreds of languages are spoken in Asia. Many different ethnic and cultural groups live there. The people are as different as their environments, which vary from desert to tropical rain forest to places where the ground is always frozen. This diversity of environments, cultures, languages, and religions has prevented the unification of Asia. The breakup of the former Soviet Union was caused at least in part by divisions based on ethnic differences.

European knowledge of and interest in Asia began in the 13th century when Marco Polo returned to his home to tell stories about his travels in Asia. As time went by, people traveled to the east for spices and other exotic goods. Columbus even discovered America while on his way to India. Asia still supplies the world with spices as well as with oil from the countries around the Persian Gulf.

Do some research about the big cities in Asia. Write the names of the five largest cities (by population) and the names of the countries in which they can be found.

City	Country

People in Asia *(cont.)*

Ethnic Groups

Pick an Asian ethnic group to learn about and answer the following questions. Some suggested groups are listed below. Use one of them or pick your own.

Arabs   **Sherpas**   **Ainu**   **Bedouins**   **Gypsies**

1. In which Asian environment does this group of people live?

   _____

2. Do they live the way their ancestors lived? If not, what changes have they made?

   _____

   _____

   _____

   _____

3. What are their homes like?

   _____

   _____

   _____

4. How do they earn a living? (What kind of work do they do?)

   _____

   _____

5. What religion do they practice?

   _____

   _____

6. Use the back of this page to tell about some of their customs.

Animals in Asia

Read the clues and unscramble the names of these Asian animals. Circle the names of the animals that are on the endangered species list.

1. _____   animals herded by the Lapps and associated with Santa Claus (indreere)

2. _____   an animal easily identified by its one hump (radmordey)

3. _____   a long-haired wild ox native to Tibet and central Asia (kay)

4. _____   an animal that is almost extinct because it is hunted for its horns (conshorier)

5. _____   a fierce snake killer; enemy of the king cobra (goonsemo)

6. _____   a black and white bear-like relative of the raccoon living in the mountains of western China (taing napad)

7. _____   an animal with a trunk and tusks; its ears are smaller than those of its African cousin (phalteen)

8. _____   an animal easily identified by its two humps (trinabac mecal)

9. _____   an animal that is reputed to commit mass suicide by running headlong off cliffs (minglem)

10. _____   an Indonesian lizard that can grow to be 10 feet (3 m) long; the largest lizard in the world (moodoK grando)

11. _____   a wild goat with large, backward-curving horns (exib)

12. _____   a large, ferocious member of the cat family (clabk pordale)

13. _____   a small, slender, long-armed ape of India, China, and Southeast Asia (bobing)

14. _____   an ape with shaggy reddish-brown hair, very long arms, and a hairless face; found only in the jungles of Borneo and Sumatra (troanguan)

15. _____   a sheep-like animal with black curly hair (lukarak)

People Depend on the Environment

Make a list of Asia's natural resources.

_____

_____

_____

_____

_____

Then create a symbol to go with each natural resource and make a key. Using your newly created symbols, show these resources on the map of Asia on the next page.

Resource Key

People Depend on the Environment *(cont.)*

Resource Map

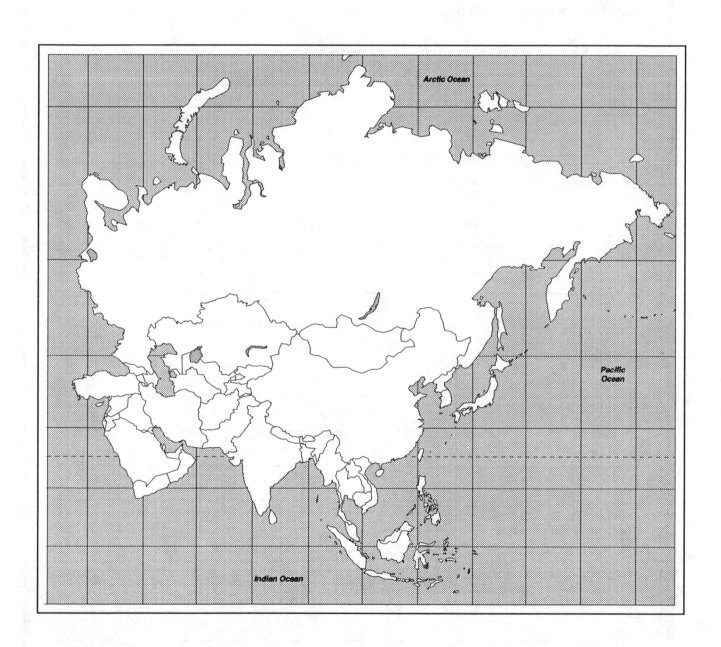

People Adapt to and Change the Environment

People adapt to and change the environment in many ways. Think of some possible solutions that may solve these environmental problems:

Very dry conditions for farming:

_____

_____

_____

Hills too steep for crops:

_____

_____

_____

Areas that flood:

_____

_____

_____

Housing in hot climates:

_____

_____

_____

_____

People Adapt to and Change the Environment *(cont.)*

People adapt to and change the environment in many ways. Think of some possible solutions that may solve these environmental problems:

Housing in cold climates:

_____

_____

_____

_____

Clothing in hot climates:

_____

_____

_____

_____

Clothing in cold climates:

_____

_____

_____

_____

Transportation in mountainous or hilly areas:

_____

_____

_____

_____

Technology Impacts the Environment

Resources are things valued and used by people. Natural resources are resources that occur in nature, such as minerals in the Earth, trees, water, and air.

The way people feel about and use natural resources is affected by the technology that is available to them. The availability of technology is affected by wealth or the lack of it. Since there is a big difference between the rich and the poor in Asia, there are big differences in the way technology is used.

Research how the everyday uses of technology in Asia might vary according to economic status.

Uses	Type of Technology	
	Rich	Poor
Cooking		
Heating		
Transportation		
Building Houses		

Technology Impacts the Environment *(cont.)*

Uses	Type of Technology	
	Rich	Poor
Building roads		
Farming		
Making clothes		
Getting an education		
Getting clean water		
Disposing of waste		

Movement Demonstrates Interdependence

Why do human activities require movement? _____

_____

_____

Do the people in your family go places?_____Choose two people and answer the following questions:

	Person #1	Person #2
Who?		
When?		
Where?		
How far?		
How often?		
Why?		
Mode of transportation?		

Movement Demonstrates Interdependence *(cont.)*

Use reference sources to figure the distances between these Asian cities.

Ankara/Baghdad _____

New Delhi/Bombay _____

New Delhi/Calcutta _____

Calcutta/Madras _____

Hong Kong/Shanghai _____

Manila/Seoul _____

Tokyo/Osaka _____

Hanoi/Ho Chi Minh City _____

Taipei/Kuala Lumpur _____

Omsk/Yakutsk _____

Beirut/Tehran _____

Jerusalem/Manila _____

Movement Involves Linkages

List several ways people travel from place to place in the rural parts of Asia.

_____

_____

_____

_____

_____

List several ways people travel from place to place in the urban areas of Asia.

_____

_____

_____

_____

_____

Bonus Question!

Why haven't freeways been built to link the cities in Asia?

_____

_____

_____

_____

_____

_____

Movement Involves Linkages *(cont.)*

How will people travel around Asia in the future?

Design your own future method of transportation. Explain it and then draw a picture of it below.

This Is How My Future Transportation Will Work:

This Is How My Future Transportation Will Look:

Movement Includes People, Ideas, and Products

People go places for business and for pleasure. Going places for pleasure is called touring.

_____

_____

_____

_____

Where have you gone for pleasure?

_____

_____

_____

Where would you like to go?

_____

_____

_____

Ideas can travel too. List some of the different ways ideas travel from place to place.

_____

_____

_____

Products also travel. What are some of the ways products travel?

_____

_____

_____

_____

Movement Includes People, Ideas, and Products *(cont.)*

Think about a place you would like to visit in Asia. Design a cover for a travel brochure about that place. Sketch your design below. Write a description of the place that will make other people want to travel there too.

Southeast Asia

Animals Across the Curriculum

A region is a portion of the Earth's surface that has characteristics unlike any other. Southeast Asia is a region. It includes the countries that used to be referred to as Indochina—Myanmar (formerly Burma), Thailand (formerly Siam), Laos, Cambodia, and Vietnam—as well as the scattered island countries of the Philippines, Malaysia, Singapore, Brunei, and Indonesia. These countries are hot all year round and very humid. They contain some of the world's most interesting rain forests. Although these rain forests are threatened by civilization, rare and unusual trees still grow there, providing beautiful woods and exotic spices.

Many unusual animals live in the rain forests of Southeast Asia, including apes such as the gibbon and orangutan and monkeys such as the rhesus monkey. There are lemurs and tarsiers which are sometimes confused with monkeys. There are very special animals such as the Malay tapir, the Java peacock, and the Komodo dragon. There are also animals in some parts of the region that have been domesticated and are used to carry heavy things. These include the water buffalo and elephant.

1. The Orangutan

Be ready to report on the orangutan. Find out where this animal lives, what it eats, and what its name means. Write down other facts that you think are interesting.

_____

_____

_____

_____

_____

2. The Java Peacock

Write a poem about the Java peacock. This beautiful bird looks like something out of a fairy tale. Try to see a video tape or read an illustrated book about this bird before you write your poem. Write your title here and use another piece of paper for your poem.

_____

_____

_____

_____

_____

Southeast Asia *(cont.)*

Animals Across the Curriculum *(cont.)*

3. Put the names of the italicized animals on page 402 in ABC order and tell how many syllables in each of the names.

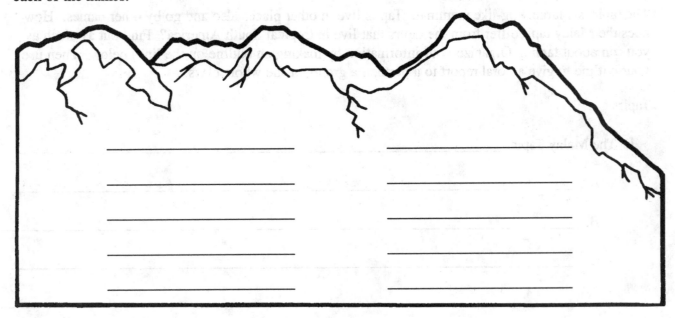

_____   _____

_____   _____

_____   _____

_____   _____

4. Monkeys and Apes

Compare and contrast these two kinds of animals. How are they alike? How are they different? How can you tell them apart? What else can you find out?

_____

_____

_____

_____

_____

_____

_____

_____

_____

_____

Southeast Asia *(cont.)*

Animals Across the Curriculum *(cont.)*

5. The Malay Tapir

The tapir is a large, hog-like mammal. Tapirs live in other places also and go by other names. How does the Malay tapir differ from the tapirs that live in tropical South America? Find out as much as you can about tapirs. Organize your information by making an outline on the lines below. Then use your outline to give an oral report to a partner, a group, or the whole class.

Tapirs

   I. The Malay Tapir_____

        A. _____

        B. _____

        C. _____

          _____

  II. The South American Tapir_____

        A. _____

        B. _____

        C. _____

          _____

          _____

 III. _____

        A. _____

        B. _____

        C. _____

          _____

          _____

Southeast Asia *(cont.)*

Animals Across the Curriculum *(cont.)*

6. The Tarsier

How many kinds of tarsiers live in the rain forests of Southeast Asia? What do they look like?

_____

_____

7. A Bar Graph

The countries of Southeast Asia have differing amounts of rain forest. Make a bar graph to compare the rain forest area of these countries in square miles (km2). Keep track of your facts here as you do your research.

Country		Square Miles (km²) of Rain Forest
Myanmar (formerly Burma)		
Thailand (formerly Siam)		
Laos		
Cambodia		
Vietnam		
Philippines		
Malaysia		
Singapore		
Brunei		
Indonesia		

The Middle East

The Middle East is the name given to a group of countries in western Asia. Some of these countries either border on or are near the Mediterranean Sea, extending to the east to include Iran. Others are on the Arabian peninsula which is separated from Africa by the Gulf of Aqaba and the Red Sea. This region is very much like North Africa. In fact, Egypt, which lies just west of the Red Sea in Africa, is usually included in any discussion of the Middle East. The land itself is hot and dry. The few trees that grow there are along the shores of the Mediterranean Sea, in fertile river valleys, or in desert oases. The Middle East is a region so different from Southeast Asia that it might be in another world instead of at the other side of the same continent.

Find information about this area in reference books and answer these questions.

1. What is the only city in the world that occupies land on two continents?

   _____

2. Which Middle Eastern country is an island nation?

   _____

3. What is the capital of Lebanon?

   _____

4. Which modern Middle Eastern country was created in 1948?

   _____

5. In which Middle Eastern country is Mecca located?

   _____

6. Why is Mecca important to people all over the world?

   _____

   _____

The Middle East *(cont.)*

7. Name four Middle Eastern countries that border on the Mediterranean Sea.

_____

_____

_____

_____

8. Which Middle Eastern country invaded its neighbor, Kuwait, in 1990, starting the Persian Gulf War?

_____

_____

9. What is Israel's most important river?

_____

_____

10. How has the discovery and production of oil affected the countries of the Middle East?

_____

_____

_____

_____

The Middle East *(cont.)*

Match each country with its capital city.

Iran	Cairo
Egypt	Ankara
Turkey	Tehran
Cyprus	Beirut
Lebanon	Nicosia
Syria	Damascus
Iraq	Amman
Israel	Baghdad
Jordan	Jerusalem
Saudi Arabia	Kuwait City
Kuwait	Riyadh
Bahrain	Abu Dubai
Qatar	Doha
United Arab Emirates	Manama
Oman	Sana
Yemen	Muscat

Asian Fact Game

This game can be played in different ways:

Game 1—You can use a Jeopardy format. Students love this, and they can set it up all by themselves or with just a little help. Run the answer cards on one color of paper and the question cards on another color for easy sorting.

Game 2—You can make a card game like rummy. All the cards should be run on one color for this. Shuffle the cards and deal five to each player. Put the leftovers facedown or in the middle of the table. Players draw from the stack and discard in another stack. The object of the game is to lay down pairs by matching questions and answers. You can make it more complicated by allowing students to challenge one another's matched pairs if they think the matches are incorrect. Have students keep track of the rules they make and write game directions.

Fact Game Cards

It is the highest point in Asia.	What is Mt. Everest?
It has the largest area of any country in Asia.	What is Russia? (Russian Federation)
It has the most people of any country in Asia.	What is China?

Asian Fact Game *(cont.)*

Fact Game Cards *(cont.)*

It is the largest continent.	What is Asia?
It is the longest river in Asia.	What is the Yangtze?
It is the largest desert in Asia.	What is the Gobi Desert?
It is the lowest point in Asia.	What is the Dead Sea?
A pair of these animals from China toured the big zoos of the United States.	What are giant pandas?
It has the most people of any city in Asia.	What is Tokyo?

Fact Game Cards (cont.)

It is the largest lake in the world.	What is the Caspian Sea?
It is a nomadic Arab of the desert.	What is a Bedouin?
It is Islam's holiest shrine.	What is the Kaaba?
It is the country whose population is second in size only to China's.	What is India?
It is the capital of China.	What is Beijing?
This colony of the United Kingdom will become part of China in 1997.	What is Hong Kong?

Asian Fact Game *(cont.)*

Fact Game Cards *(cont.)*

It is the world's leading producer of natural rubber.	What is Malaysia?
This tiny country located off the tip of the Malay Peninsula is made up of 58 islands.	What is Singapore?
It is the major food crop in many Asian countries.	What is rice?
This river in India is thought to be sacred by the Hindus.	What is the Ganges?
This is a collective farm in Israel.	What is a kibbutz?
The giant panda of China eats only this plant.	What is bamboo?

     412

Asian Fact Game *(cont.)*

Fact Game Cards *(cont.)*

Let your students make their own question-and-answer fact cards. Students usually like to make extra hard ones in hopes of stumping each other, so have them write the book and page number where the information can be found on the question card.

	Book:_____ Page: _____
	Book:_____ Page: _____
	Book:_____ Page: _____
	Book:_____ Page: _____
	Book:_____ Page: _____

The Geography Center

Putting the Center Together

You can set up your Geography Center in a corner of your classroom and make it as simple or as elaborate as you want. The center should have a map, a globe, and an atlas. (Several maps, a couple of globes, and multiple copies of the atlas would be even better.) A table and chairs will facilitate group activities and discussions. A supply of writing and drawing materials will also come in handy. A bookcase, shelf, or window sill can be utilized for storing reference books. The more reference books you can provide, the better the assigned projects will be. If you have access to a TV, VCR, and tapes, you can show movies about the places you are studying. There are many tapes of this variety available, and the visual learners in your class will really appreciate this. Cushions for sitting on the floor to read or view tapes add a cozy touch.

Making the Center Work

You can make the Geography Center part of your instructional day by scheduling groups to do center work. Change the materials daily or weekly or provide a set of task cards at the beginning of the unit and expect each student to work through them individually or as part of a group. (See pages 415–417.)

Use Portfolios

Have students make portfolios and store them in containers in an accessible area of your center. Try using the inexpensive but sturdy plastic crates that are available at local hardware stores. Make students responsible for their own progress by having them file their own work, both completed work and work in progress. Have students create attractive covers for their portfolios so the accumulated work can be attractively displayed at your school's open house.

Deck the Walls

Encourage artwork, creative writing, and exploratory math to go along with your geography unit and spread it throughout the curriculum. Display these products on a bulletin board in your Geography Center. Have students mount and post their own work. They can cut out letters and create colorful captions for the board.

Have another bulletin board reserved for posting newspaper and magazine articles dealing with the continent you are studying. Encourage your students to bring in these articles, share them, and discuss their meaning and importance.

The Geography Center *(cont.)*

Task Cards

Task Card #3

What is the highest mountain peak on the continent?

How tall is it?

In which country is it found?

Task Card #4

What is the largest country on the continent?

What countries or bodies of water border it?

What is its capital city?

Task Card #1

What is the longest river on the continent?

How long is it?

Through which country or countries does it flow?

Task Card #2

What is the most important mountain range on the continent?

How long is it?

In which country or countries are these mountains found?

The Geography Center (cont.)

Task Cards (cont.)

Task Card #7

What animals are associated with the continent?

In what country or countries do they live?

Are they in any danger in today's civilization?

Task Card #8

What variations in climate are found on the continent?

What variations in weather are found on the continent?

Can people live in all parts of the continent?

Task Card #5

What is the smallest country on the continent?

What countries or bodies of water border it?

What is its capital city?

Task Card #6

What is the largest lake on the continent?

In which country or countries is it found?

Which river is associated with it?

The Geography Center *(cont.)*

Task Card Response

Leave a stack of these task card response forms in the geography center for students to use.

Name _____ Date_____

Task Card #_____

Question #1

_____

_____

_____

_____

Question #2

_____

_____

_____

_____

Question #3

_____

_____

_____

_____

Bonus

I also learned_____

_____

_____

_____

The Culminating Activity: Making a Book

Method

You and your students can go about bookmaking in many different ways. Here are some suggestions:

- The book can be your students' showcase portfolios.

- Students can review and reflect upon the work they have accumulated in their portfolios, select the most representative samples or the pieces they like best, and put these things together in book form.

- The book can be a showcase portfolio based on the teacher's criteria.

- Have students select work from their portfolios based on a list you develop.

- The book can be comprised of new material that sums up the unit.

- Have students complete various assignments meant specifically for inclusion in their books, showing their grasp of the material. (See pages 419–429.)

Contents

In most cases you will probably want your students to include maps, facts about both physical and political geography, research about animals, people, and resources. They can review or report on any books they have read about the continent, and they can write about what they have learned and how it has affected the way they view the world.

Cover

You can specify and provide the design for the cover so that all of the books will be uniform, or you can encourage your students to design a cover that is representative of the continent. A collage of pictures cut from magazines and travel brochures is an option that works well.

Be sure to laminate the finished covers so the books can be used as part of your classroom library or Geography Center reference shelf. Your students may also want to share their books with students in other classes.

Exciting ideas for binding and publishing follow on pages 430–432.

The Culminating Activity:
Making a Book *(cont.)*

Trace an outline map of the continent. Transfer information about its physical features from all of the maps you have made. You might want to use different colors to create a key.

Name _____Date_____

Map of Physical Features

The Culminating Activity: Making a Book *(cont.)*

Use the information you have already gathered or do some new research to complete this page.

Name _____Date_____

Facts About Physical Features

Area: _____

_____

Highest Point: _____

_____

Lowest Point: _____

_____

Largest Island:_____

_____

Longest River:_____

_____

Largest Lake: _____

_____

Tallest Waterfall:_____

_____

Largest Desert: _____

_____

Longest Reef: _____

_____

The Culminating Activity:
Making a Book *(cont.)*

Trace an outline map of the continent. Transfer information about its political features from all of the maps you have made. You might want to use a numbered list to create a key.

Name _____ Date_____

Map of Political Features

The Culminating Activity: Making a Book (cont.)

Use the information you have already gathered or do some new research to complete this page.

Name _____ Date_____

Facts About Political Features

Population: _____

Largest County (by area): _____

Largest County (by population):_____

Smallest County (by area): _____

Smallest County (by population):_____

Largest Metropolitan Area (by population):_____

_____

_____

_____

_____

_____

Newest County/Countries_____

_____

_____

_____

_____

_____

The Culminating Activity: Making a Book *(cont.)*

Use the information you have already gathered or do some new research to complete this page.

Name _____ Date_____

The People

The people of this continent belong to these ethnic groups:

_____

_____

_____

They speak these languages:

_____

_____

_____

They live in these different environments:

_____

_____

_____

_____

Their ways of life have changed or are changing:

_____

_____

_____

_____

_____

The Culminating Activity: Making a Book *(cont.)*

Pick the city on the continent that is most interesting to you. Use the information you have already gathered or do some new research to complete this page.

Name _____ Date_____

The city of_____.

This city is in _____

Area: _____

Population: _____

_____

Language(s): _____

_____

Ethnic Groups: _____

_____

Religious Groups: _____

_____

Famous Natural Features: _____

_____

_____

Famous Constructed Features: _____

_____

_____

_____

_____

The Culminating Activity:
Making a Book (cont.)

Use the information you have already gathered or do some new research to complete this page.

Name _____Date_____

The Animals

The best known animals of this continent are _____

_____

_____

The animals of this continent are important because_____

_____

_____

The animals that still live in their natural habitats are _____

_____

_____

The animals that are on the endangered list are_____

_____

_____

_____

They are on the endangered list because _____

_____

_____

_____

_____

The Culminating Activity:
Making a Book *(cont.)*

Keep track of the books you read about the continent on this log.

Name _____Date_____

Book Log

Title: _____   Fiction: _____

Author: _____   Nonfiction: _____

Illustrator: _____   Rating:_____

Title: _____   Fiction: _____

Author: _____   Nonfiction: _____

Illustrator: _____   Rating:_____

Title: _____   Fiction: _____

Author: _____   Nonfiction: _____

Illustrator: _____   Rating:_____

Title: _____   Fiction: _____

Author: _____   Nonfiction: _____

Illustrator: _____   Rating:_____

The Culminating Activity: Making a Book *(cont.)*

Use copies of this form to review your favorite nonfiction books about the continent you have been studying.

Name _____Date_____

Book Review/Nonfiction

Title: _____

Author: _____

Illustrator: _____

Summary: _____

_____

_____

_____

_____

_____

Reasons I liked or did not like this book:_____

_____

_____

_____

_____

_____

_____

Bonus!

If you liked this book and think other people should read it, you can do one of two things. (1) Write a paragraph or two telling how a nonfiction book can help you understand a continent or a country and post it on the bulletin board in the Geography Center. (2) Make a poster advertising the book and post it on the bulletin board in the Geography Center.

The Culminating Activity: Making a Book *(cont.)*

Use copies of this form to review your favorite fiction books about the continent you have been studying.

Name_____Date_____

Book Review/Fiction

Title: _____

Author: _____

Illustrator: _____

Summary: _____

_____

_____

_____

_____

_____

Reasons I liked or did not like this book:_____

_____

_____

_____

_____

_____

_____

Bonus!

If you liked this book and think other people should read it, you can do one of two things. (1) Write a paragraph or two telling how a fiction book can help you understand a continent or a country and post it on the bulletin board in the Geography Center. (2) Make a poster advertising the book and post it on the bulletin board in the Geography Center.

The Culminating Activity:
Making a Book *(cont.)*

Write a reflective essay in which you discuss the ways that studying geography has given you a better understanding of the world and the people in it.

Name _____ Date_____

Title:_____

_____

_____

_____

_____

_____

_____

_____

_____

_____

_____

_____

_____

_____

_____

_____

_____

_____

_____

_____

_____

_____

The Culminating Activity: Making a Book *(cont.)*

Book Binding Ideas

1. Stack all the pages of the book in a neat pile.

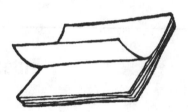

2. Place a blank sheet of paper on the top and bottom of the pages.

3. Leaving approximately 1/2" (1.25 cm) border, staple or sew all of the pages together on the left side.

4. Place two pieces of lightweight cardboard side by side. (Cereal boxes work well.) Each piece should be 1/2 to 1" (1.25 to 2.5 cm) larger than the size of the pages in the book.

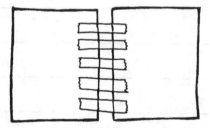

5. Leaving approximately 1" (2.5 cm) between them, tape the cardboard pieces together.

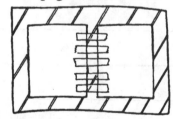

6. Put the cardboard on top of your covering material (e.g., fabric, wallpaper, contact paper, or wrapping paper). Glue the cardboard and covering material together, leaving a 1 to 1 1/2" (2.5 to 3.25 cm) material border.

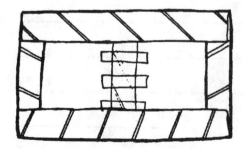

7. Fold up the edges of material over the cardboard and glue in place.

8. Glue the blank pages to the inside of the cardboard covers. Your book is ready to read and share.

The Culminating Activity: Making a Book *(cont.)*

Pop-Up Books

1. Fold a 8 1/2" x 11" (22 cm x 28 cm) piece of paper in half crosswise.

2. Measure and mark 2 3/4" (7 cm) from each side along the fold. Cut 2 3/4" (7 cm) slits at the marks.

3. Push cut area inside-out and crease to form the pop-up section.

4. Draw, color, and cut out the object to get "popped-up."

5. Glue it onto the pop-up section.

6. Glue two pages back to back, making sure the pop-up section is free.

7. Glue additional pages together, making as many pages (including pop-up pages) as you like. Be sure to include a free sheet on both the front and back so that those pages can be glued to a cover.

8. Glue a cover over the entire book.

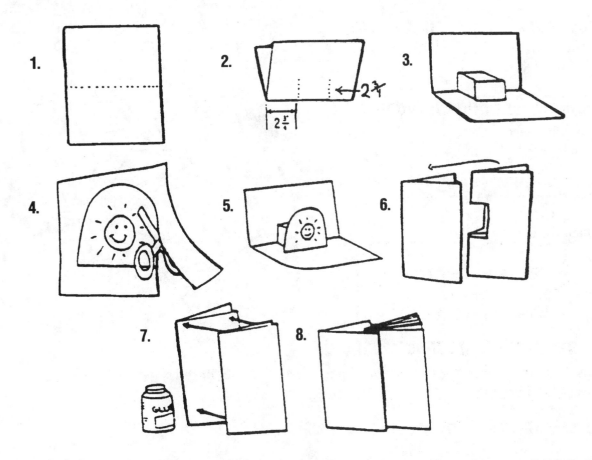

The Culminating Activity: Making a Book *(cont.)*

Real Markets for Student Writing

Student writing can be sent to the following addresses. Check your professional journals for more sources.

Children's Playmate (ages 5–8)

P.O. Box 567B
Indianapolis, Indiana 46206

Cricket (ages 6–12)

Cricket League
P.O. Box 300
Peru, Illinois 61354

Ebony Jr! (ages 6–12)

820 S. Michigan Avenue
Chicago, Illinois 60605

Flying Pencil Press (ages 8–14)

P.O. Box 7667
Elgin, Illinois 60121

Highlights for Children (ages 2–11)

803 Church Street
Honesdale, Pennsylvania 18431

Jack and Jill (ages 8–12)

P.O. Box 567B
Indianapolis, Indiana 46206

Stone Soup (ages 5–14)

P.O. Box 83
Santa Cruz, California 95063

National Written and Illustrated by...

(This is an awards contest for students in all grade levels. Write for rules and guidelines.)
Landmark Editions, Inc.
P.O. Box 4469
Kansas City, Missouri 64127

Software Review

Software: *PC Globe 5.0* (Broderbund)

Hardware: 640K IBM PC with hard drive

Grade Level: Intermediate

Summary: *PC Globe* provides your students with an up-to-date world atlas, which can be accessed through your classroom computer. In it they will find detailed maps (world & country), demographic, as well as political and cultural information on 208 countries world wide. Some of the more specific information that is contained on these countries include population data, language usage, political leaders, economic data, import and export data, etc. Also included are country maps showing major cities, topography, and important geographical sites. Not only does *PC Globe* provide all of the above information, but it also includes a flag of each country, along with its national anthem.

Students can use this resource to help them locate accurate information when doing country reports, participating in debates, giving presentations, etc. Graphics and text can be downloaded onto other programs for future use, and a teacher guide is included with the materials.

Bibliography

Afghanistan in Pictures. Lerner, 1989.

Ashby, Gwyneth. *A Family in South Korea.* Childrens, 1992.

Asia. Marshall Cavendish, 1990.

Asian Cultural Center for Unesco. *Folk Tales from Asia for Children Everywhere:* Book Three. Weatherhill, 1976.

Bennett, Gay. *A Family in Sri Lanka.* Lerner, 1985.

Brown, Marion. *Singapore.* Childrens, 1989.

China in Pictures. Lerner, 1989.

Chisman, Arthur B. *Shen of the Sea.* Dutton, 1968.

Climo, Shirley. *The Korean Cinderella.* Harper, 1993.

Coblence, Jean-Michel. *Asian Civilizations.* Silver, 1988.

Cole, Wendy. *Vietnam.* Chelsea, 1989.

Corwin, Judith Hoffman. *Asian Crafts.* Watts, 1992.

Crossland, Bert. *Where on Earth Are We?* Book Links, 1994.

Demi, adapt. *A Chinese Zoo: Fables and Proverbs.* Harcourt, 1987.

Dickinson, Mary B. (Ed.). *National Geographic Picture Atlas of Our World.* National Geographic Society, 1993.

Gabel, Susan. *Where the Sun Kisses the Sea.* Perspectives, 1989.

Geographic Education National Implementation Project. Guidelines, 1987.

Gordon, Susan. *Asian Indians.* Watts, 1990.

Greene, Carol. *Japan.* Childrens, 1983.

India in Pictures. Lerner, 1983.

Lord, Bette Bao. *In the Year of the Boar and Jackie Robinson.* Harper, 1984.

Mirpuri, Gouri. *Indonesia.* Marshall Cavendish, 1990.

Orihura, Kei. *Thailand.* Stevens, 1988.

Sabin, Louis. *Asia.* Troll, 1985.

Schlein, Miriam. *The Year of the Panda.* Harper, 1990.

Seros, Kathleen. *Sun and Moon: Fairy Tales from Korea.* Hollym, 1983.

Staam, Claus. *Three Strong Women: A Tall Tale from Japan.* Viking, 1990.

Tan, Amy. *The Moon Lady.* Macmillan, 1992.

Turner, Ann. *Through Moon and Stars and Night Skies.* Harper, 1990.

Uchida, Yoshiko. *Magic Listening Cap.* Creative Arts, 1987.

Vander Els, Betty. *The Bombers' Moon.* Farrar, 1992.

Vuong, Lynette Dyer. *The Brocaded Slipper and Other Vietnamese Tales.* Harper, 1982.

Wartski, Maureen Crane. *A Boat to Nowhere.* NAL, 1981.

Withington, William. *Southeast Asia.* Gateway, 1988.

Wright, David. *Malaysia.* Childrens, 1988.

Zimmerman, Robert. *Sri Lanka.* Childrens, 1992.

Bibliography *(cont.)*

Technology

Broderbund. ***MacGlobe & PC Globe.*** Available from Learning Services, (800)877-9378. disk

Broderbund. ***Where in the World Is Carmen Sandiego?*** Available from Troll, (800)526-5289. CD-ROM and disk

Bureau of Electronic Publishing Inc. ***World Fact Book.*** Available from Educational Resources, (800)624-2926. CD-ROM

CLEARVUE. ***The Earth, the Oceans, and Plants & Animals:*** Interactive, curriculum oriented CD-ROMs. Available from Educational Resources, (800)624-2926. CD-ROM

DeLorme Publishing. ***Global Explorer.*** Available from DeLorme Publishing, 1995. CD-ROM

Impressions. ***My First World Atlas.*** Available from Educational Resources, (800)624-2926.

Lawrence. ***Nigel's World Adventures in World Geography.*** Available from Educational Resources, (800)624-2926. CD-ROM and disk

Magic Quest. ***Time Treks and Earth Treks.*** Available from Educational Resources, (800)624-2926. disk

MECC. ***World GeoGraph.*** Available from Educational Resources, (800)624-2926. disk

Mindscape. ***World Atlas.*** Available from Educational Resources, (800)624-2926. disk

National Geographic. ***STV: World Geography.*** Available from National Geographic Educational Technology, (800)328-2936. videodisc

Newton Technology. ***GEOvista Tutor.*** Available from William K. Bradford, (800)421-2009. disk

Orange Cherry. ***China: Home of the Dragon and Time Traveler.*** Available from Educational Resources, (800)624-2926. CD-ROM

Partnership Plus. ***Vol. 3: World Hot Spots.*** Available from Educational Resources, (800)624-2926. disk

Pride in Learning. ***Global Issues.*** Available from Educational Resources, (800)624-2926. disk

Queue. ***Adventures of Sinbad, Aladdin, and Ali Baba and Ancient Egypt & the Middle East.*** Available from Learning Services, (800)877-3278. CD-ROM

Queue. ***Atlas Explorer.*** Available from Educational Resources, (800)624-2926. disk

Sanctuary Woods. ***Ecology Treks.*** Available from Learning Services, (800)624-2926. software and videodisc

Software Toolworks. ***World Atlas.*** Available from Learning Services, (800)877-9378. CD-ROM and disk

SVE. ***Geography on Laserdisc.*** Available from Learning Services, (800)877-9378. laserdisc.

Voyager. ***First Emperor of China.*** Available from Educational Resources, (800)624-2926. CD-ROM

Answer Key

Page 377

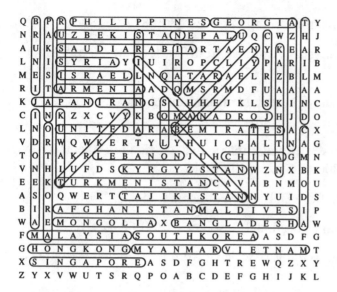

Page 389

1. reindeer
2. dromedary
3. yak
4. rhinoceros
5. mongoose
6. giant panda
7. elephant
8. Bactrian camel
9. lemming
10. Komodo dragon
11. ibex
12. black leopard
13. gibbon
14 orangutan
15. karakul

Pages 406–407

1. Istanbul, Turkey
2. Cyprus
3. Beirut
4. Israel
5. Saudi Arabia
6. All Muslims are required to make one pilgrimage to Mecca.
7. Israel, Lebanon, Syria, Turkey
8. Iraq
9. The Jordan River
10. (answers will vary)

Page 408

Iran—Tehran

Egypt—Cairo

Turkey—Ankara

Cyprus—Nicosia

Lebanon—Beirut

Syria—Damascus

Iraq—Baghdad

Israel—Jerusalem

Jordan—Amman

Saudi Arabia—Riyadh

Kuwait—Kuwait City

Bahrain—Manama

Qatar—Doha

United Arab Emirates—Abu Dubai

Oman—Muscat

Yemen—Sana

Europe

Table of Contents

Introduction *(cont.)*

Europe

This book was designed to present an overview of the geography of the continent of Europe. It is divided into five sections to match the themes of the Geographic Education National Implementation Project (GENIP), an educational project backed by the nation's most prestigious geographers.

Each section contains a selection of teaching pages, maps, activities, interesting facts, review questions, and puzzles or games. A plan for using the material to construct a geography center is also included, as well as ideas for putting together a book as a culminating activity.

You will also find a glossary of the specialized vocabulary used by geographers. This will make it easier for your students to talk about the world they live in.

A Word or Two About Maps

Projections

The landforms shown on maps and globes do not look exactly alike. This is because it is just as hard to "peel" a globe and flatten the Earth's "skin" out into a map as it is to peel an orange and flatten out its skin to make a smooth, even surface. Even if you can get the skin off the orange in one piece, the top and bottom edges must be broken and spread out.

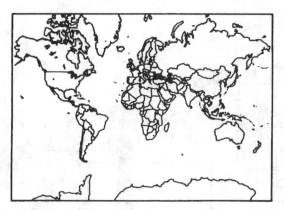

Different map makers (cartographers) have had different ideas about how to do this and have made different "projections." A projection is the way in which the map maker has chosen to flatten out the Earth's surface to make a flat map. Sometimes the map maker allows the breaks in the Earth's surface to show.

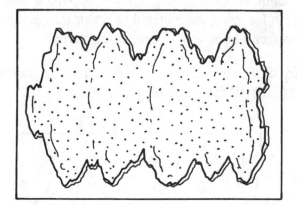

Sometimes the map maker stretches the Earth's "skin." This makes the countries near the poles look much bigger than they really are.

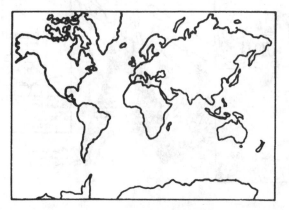

A Word or Two About Maps *(cont.)*

Projections *(cont.)*

Use your reference materials to find out the names of other common map projections and list them below. Research the advantages and disadvantages of each map projection you list and write them down below.

Map Projection	Advantages	Disadvantages

A Word or Two About Maps *(cont.)*

The Compass Rose

The compass rose is a small drawing that shows direction on a map. Most maps show north at the top and south at the bottom, west on the left and east on the right.

Look at maps to find some different styles of compass roses and then design your own. You can shrink your drawing and make multiple copies to use on the maps you make, color, or label.

Where on Earth Is Europe?

- Europe is smaller than all of the continents except Australia.

- Together with Asia, which is four times its size, Europe makes up the huge landmass sometimes called Eurasia.

- No part of Europe is very far from an arm of the ocean, giving it the most irregular and indented coastline of all of the continents.

- Europe is bordered by the Arctic Ocean on the north, the Atlantic Ocean on the west, and the Mediterranean Sea on the south.

Use these clues to find Europe on this map. Color it blue.

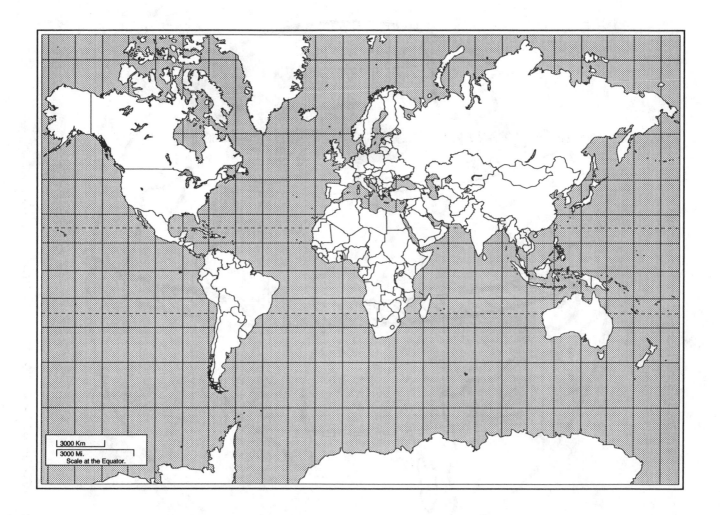

3000 Km
3000 Mi.
Scale at the Equator.

Where on Earth Is Europe? *(cont.)*

If you think of the Earth as a ball (a sphere or globe), you can draw a line around the middle (the equator) and separate the two halves into the top half (Northern Hemisphere) and the bottom half (Southern Hemisphere). Now you can talk about something as being in the Northern or Southern Hemisphere.

More lines are drawn around the Earth parallel to the equator and evenly spaced from the equator to the North and South Poles. They are called parallels or lines of latitude. They are numbered in degrees, starting with 0° at the equator and usually spaced at 15° intervals, ending with 90° N at the North Pole and 90° S at the South Pole.

(Geographers further divide their degrees into minutes and seconds so they can be very precise in locating the position of anything on the Earth's surface.)

If you divide the Earth into its Northern and Southern Hemispheres, Europe lies entirely in the_____Hemisphere.

Where on Earth Is Europe? *(cont.)*

You can also draw lines north and south around the Earth. These lines are called meridians or lines of longitude. They are usually shown 15° apart at the equator, but they all come together at the North and South Poles. (They also can be further divided into minutes and seconds, just like the parallels.)

The line that runs through Greenwich, England, is called the prime meridian (0°). Longitude is the distance east or west of the prime meridian. The line directly opposite the prime meridian is at 180° and is called the date line. If you are still thinking of the Earth as a ball (a sphere or globe), you can separate the two halves into the Western Hemisphere and the Eastern Hemisphere. (This is usually done along the meridians of 20° W and 160° E so all of Africa is in one hemisphere.)

If you divide the Earth into its Western and Eastern Hemisphere, Europe lies entirely in the_____Hemisphere.

Where on Earth Is Europe? *(cont.)*

You can tell where things on the Earth are in two ways:

- You can give their exact or absolute location using latitude and longitude expressed in degrees (minutes and seconds).

- You can tell where they are in relation to other things.

Fill out the missing information to give the exact location of where you live:

house number	street name	apartment number
city	state/country	zip code

Now, use information from a map or globe to complete this description of the exact location of Europe.

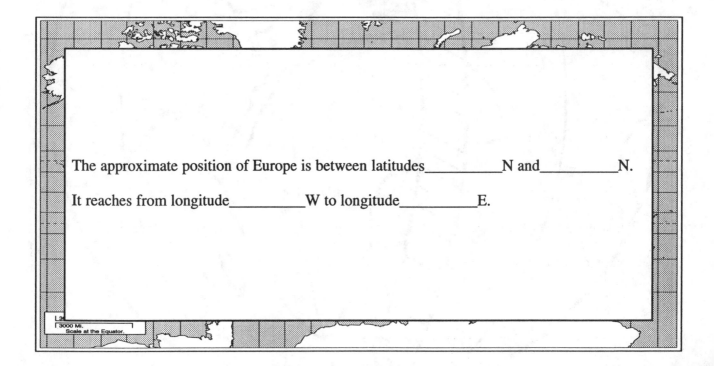

The approximate position of Europe is between latitudes_____N and_____N.

It reaches from longitude_____W to longitude_____E.

Where on Earth Is Europe? *(cont.)*

You can tell where things on the Earth are in two ways:

You can give their exact or absolute location using latitude and longitude expressed in degrees (minutes and seconds).

You can tell where they are in relation to other things.

Fill out the missing information to give the location of where you live in relation to other things:

I live
between_____and_____

near_____

and across
from_____.

Now, use information from a map or globe to complete this description of the relative location of Europe.

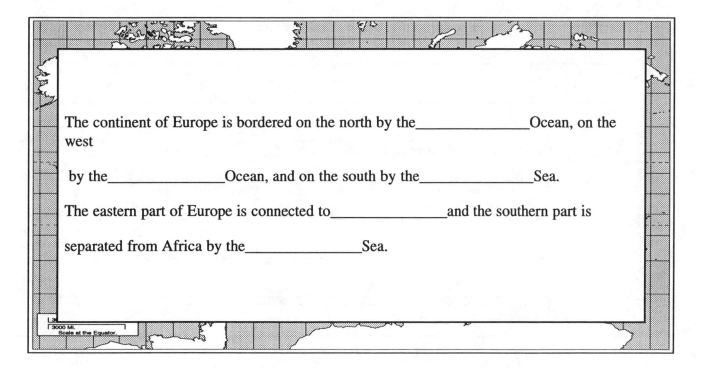

The continent of Europe is bordered on the north by the_____Ocean, on the west

 by the_____Ocean, and on the south by the_____Sea.

The eastern part of Europe is connected to_____and the southern part is

separated from Africa by the_____Sea.

Where in Europe Is_____?

Use information from a globe or map, an atlas, an encyclopedia, and your geography book to write both the exact and relative locations of five of the countries on the continent of Europe. See the next page for the names of the countries to choose from.

1. _____

   _____

   _____

   _____

2. _____

   _____

   _____

3. _____

   _____

   _____

   _____

4. _____

   _____

   _____

5. _____

   _____

   _____

   _____

Countries of Europe

There are 44 countries of Europe listed below. Find them forwards, backwards, and diagonally in the word search below.

```
A B B U L G A R I A F G E R M A N Y Q I W N L A
C D P O L A N D E R I T B E L A R U S T I V I B
E F L E S T O N I A N A S D F G M G H A J A E C
G H A M O N A C O S L O V A K I A O P L G T C D
I J T H Z O I C E L A N D X C V L S B Y L I H E
K L V U S R I A W E N G R T Y U T L R P U C T F
M N I N R W T A N D O R R A A A A O O X A E G
O P A G M A E S A N M A R I N O V V M R E N N H
Q R L A P Y L D I U D E N M A R K I A T M C S I
S T I R O I A U E Y T H T R E W Q A N U B I T J
U V T Y A S N D F N G H E F H G J K I G O T E K
W X H M O L D O V A Q W E R R R T G A A U Y I L
Y Z U K R A I N E D F G H A Z E L T R L R O N M
A B A G I B R A L T A R A N S E G H J K G R T N
C D N E T H E R L A N D S C B C G Q W E R T A O
E F I C R O A T I A X C V E B E N O M Q W E U P
G H A L B A N I A A S D F G H J K L V U Y T S Q
I J A S D F G H C Z E C H R E P U B L I C R T R
K L M A C E D O N I A P O I U Y T R E W N W R S
M N S W I T Z E R L A N D S D F G H J K L I I T
O P U N I T E D K I N G D O M S L O V E N I A U
```

Cross off the countries as you find them: Iceland, Norway, Denmark, Sweden, Finland, Estonia, Latvia, Spain, Lithuania, Ireland, United Kingdom, Netherlands, Belgium, Greece, Luxembourg, Germany, Poland, Czech Republic, Slovakia, Belarus, Malta, Ukraine, Moldova, Portugal, Andorra, Gibraltar, France, San Marino, Switzerland, Liechtenstein, Monaco, Italy, Vatican City, Albania, Herzegovina, Austria, Hungary, Slovenia, Croatia, Bosnia, Romania, Macedonia, Yugoslavia, Bulgaria

Countries of Europe *(cont.)*

Use information from an atlas, an encyclopedia, your geography book, or any other reference book to write one interesting fact about each country. (**Teacher Note:** Because there are so many countries on the continent of Europe, you may want your students to pick just a few countries to write about.)

Bonus Question Number One!

What happened in 1991 that increased the number of countries on the continent of Europe? _____

_____

1. Albania_____

   _____

2. Andorra _____

   _____

3. Austria _____

   _____

4. Belarus _____

   _____

5. Belgium _____

   _____

6. Bosnia _____

   _____

7. Bulgaria _____

   _____

8. Croatia _____

   _____

9. Czech Republic _____

   _____

Countries of Europe *(cont.)*

10. Denmark_____

_____

11. Estonia _____

_____

12. Finland _____

_____

13. France_____

_____

14. Germany_____

_____

15. Gibraltar_____

_____

16. Greece _____

_____

17. Herzegovina _____

_____

18. Hungary _____

_____

19. Iceland _____

_____

20. Ireland _____

_____

21. Italy _____

_____

22. Latvia _____

_____

23. Liechtenstein _____

_____

Countries of Europe *(cont.)*

24. Lithuania _____

_____

25. Luxembourg _____

_____

26. Macedonia _____

_____

27. Malta _____

_____

28. Moldova _____

_____

29. Monaco _____

_____

30. Netherlands _____

_____

31. Norway _____

_____

32. Poland _____

_____

33. Portugal _____

_____

34. Romania _____

_____

35. San Marino _____

_____

36. Slovakia _____

_____

Countries of Europe *(cont.)*

37. Slovenia _____

_____

38. Spain _____

_____

39. Sweden_____

_____

40. Switzerland _____

_____

41. Ukraine_____

_____

42. United Kingdom _____

_____

43. Vatican City _____

_____

44. Yugoslavia _____

_____

Bonus Question Number Two!

What are some of the results of the changes in Europe that began in 1991?

_____

_____

_____

_____

Look at the Map

Use the numbered list of European countries on pages 450–453 to label the map below. Write the number of each country on the map and use the list for a key.

Physical Characteristics of Europe

Major Bodies of Water

Europe is bordered by the *Arctic Ocean* to the north, the *Atlantic Ocean* to the west, and the *Mediterranean Sea* and the *Black Sea* to the south. *The Caspian Sea* on the southeast corner of the European continent makes up part of its border with Asia.

Use reference sources to label these major bodies of water on the map of Europe.

250 Km
250 Mi.

Physical Characteristics of Europe *(cont.)*

Landforms

Europe is the second smallest continent. Only Australia is smaller. Although Europe is divided into more than 40 countries, its area is only slightly greater than that of the United States. (Part of Russia is in Europe, but since most of its land is in Asia, we are not counting it as a European country.) During different periods of history, Europeans have controlled large areas of the Earth, and as a result, evidence of European influence can be found all over the world.

Europe has many different environments. In the far north there is frozen tundra. In the south there are big mountain ranges such as the Alps, *Pyrenees*, *Apennines*, *Balkans*, *Dinaric Alps*, *Carpathians*, and *Caucasus*. In addition, the *Ural Mountains*, which run north and south through Russia, form the border between Europe and Asia. The *Northern European Plain* stretches across Europe north of the Alps from the Pyrenees to the Urals. The Mediterranean countries, those bordering that sea, are generally warm and pleasant. Europe also has a number of island countries.

Use reference sources to label these landforms on the map of Europe.

Physical Characteristics of Europe *(cont.)*

Other Bodies of Water

Although Europe is a small continent, its coastline is very long because of its irregular shape. There are many peninsulas that extend into the oceans and seas and many inlets that allow the oceans and seas to reach into the continent. Europe has several important seas. The *Black Sea* and the *Caspian Sea* form part of its irregular border with Asia. The *Mediterranean Sea* separates it from Africa. The *Baltic Sea* separates Norway and Sweden from the rest of Europe to the south. Around the edge of the continent are found the *Barents Sea*, the *Norwegian Sea*, and the *North Sea*.

Europe has many rivers. Some of the most important are the *Loire,* the *Rhine,* the *Tagus*, the *Danube*, the *Dniester*, the *Dnieper*, and the *Volga*. The Volga River is actually in Russia, but it flows through the part of Russia that lies in Europe and is, as a result, Europe's longest river.

Use reference sources to draw in the rivers and seas on the map on the next page. Then label the bodies of water with their numbers and use the list for a key.

1. Black Sea	8. Loire River
2. Caspian Sea	9. Rhine River
3. Mediterranean Sea	10. Tagus River
4. Baltic Sea	11. Danube River
5. Barents Sea	12. Dniester River
6. Norwegian Sea	13. Dnieper River
7. North Sea	14. Volga River

Bonus Question!

Why do you think most of Europe's important cities are located on rivers?

_____

_____

_____

_____

_____

Physical Characteristic
of Europe *(cont.)*

Other Bodies of Water

People in Europe

Although it is small in area, Europe is home to more people than live on the continent of Africa. Most of them live in the warmer Mediterranean countries and on the Northern European Plain. These places have moderate temperatures, year-round rain, and fertile soil. Farms in these areas are very productive which is fortunate, since more and more food will be needed as more immigrants settle in Europe.

The continent of Europe is divided into many small countries. The people speak different languages, use different types of money, and have different customs, religions, and types of government. The countries of Europe have a long history of war. European civilization began with ancient Greece and Rome, and for centuries, one country after another has tried to control and unite the area with little success. Now, some of the countries of Europe are trying to agree on rules that will at least make travel and trade easier.

Europeans were the first to discover, explore, and settle North and South America. They believed they were supposed to convert the native people to Christianity and that this gave them the right to take the lands they discovered. They were also interested in gold.

Do some research about the big cities in Europe. Write the names of ten of the largest cities (by population), the names of the countries in which they can be found, and the names of the rivers they are on. If they are not situated on rivers, write "no river."

City	Country	River

People in Europe *(cont.)*

Cave Art

People know a great deal about prehistoric humans in Europe because of the well-preserved art that has been found in many European caves. Do some research to find out about European cave art. How was it discovered? Where? When? What do scientists say about it?

Write a short report about cave art on the lines below. Use the space at the bottom of the page for an illustration.

_____

_____

_____

_____

_____

_____

_____

Landmarks in Europe

Read the clues and unscramble the names of some European landmarks.

1. _____ When you see this clock in the Parliament clock tower, you know you are in London, England. (Gib Neb)

2. _____ When you see this towering structure, you know you are in Paris, France. (Fliefe Worte)

3. _____ When you see this tipped building, you know you are in Pisa, Italy. (Glinane Trowe)

4. _____ When you see this huge church, you know you are in Vatican City. (Ts. Treep's)

5. _____ When you see the gondolas on these waterways, you know you are in Venice, Italy. (slacan)

6. _____ When you see one of these towers rising from a field of tulips, you know you are in the Netherlands. (slidminlw)

7. _____ When you see the ruins of this ancient arena, you know you are in Rome, Italy. (Molocsuse)

8. _____ When you see the ruins of this temple built to honor the goddess Athena, you know you are in Athens, Greece. (Tharnenop)

9. _____ When you see this museum and the treasures it houses, you know you are in Paris, France. (Vrolue)

10. _____ When you see this Moorish palace, you know you are near Granada, Spain. (Habramal)

People Depend on the Environment

Make a list of Europe's natural resources.

_____

_____

_____

_____

_____

Then, create a symbol to go with each natural resource and make a key. Using your newly created symbols, show these resources on the map of Europe on the next page.

Resource Key

People Depend on the Environment *(cont.)*

Resource Map

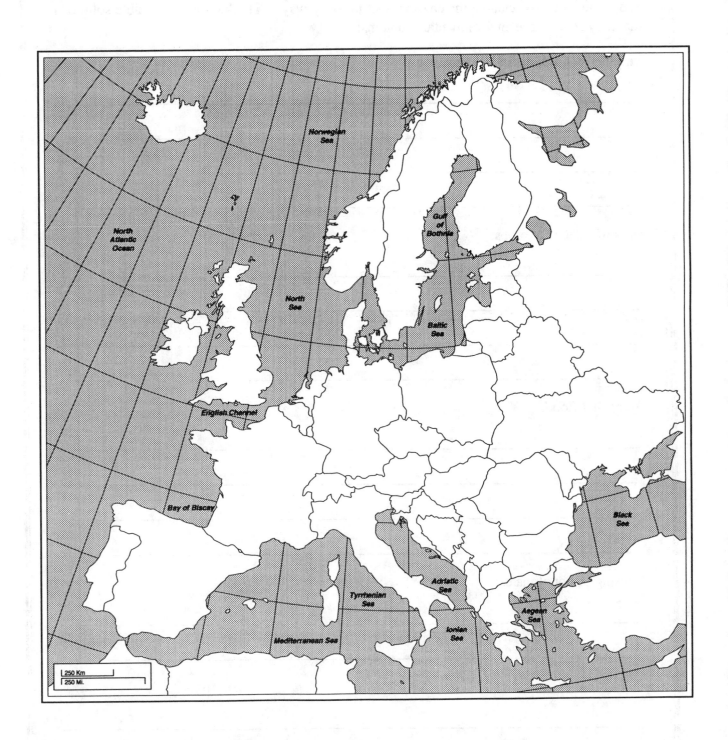

People Adapt to and Change the Environment

People adapt to and change the environment in many ways. Think of some possible solutions that may solve these environmental problems:

Very dry conditions for farming:

_____

_____

_____

_____

Hills too steep for crops:

_____

_____

_____

_____

Areas that flood:

_____

_____

_____

_____

Housing in hot climates:

_____

_____

_____

_____

People Adapt to and Change the Environment *(cont.)*

People adapt to and change the environment in many ways. Think of some possible solutions that may solve these environmental problems:

Housing in cold climates:

_____

_____

_____

_____

Clothing in hot climates:

_____

_____

_____

_____

Clothing in cold climates:

_____

_____

_____

_____

Transportation in mountainous or hilly areas:

_____

_____

_____

Technology Impacts the Environment

Resources are things that are valued and used by people. Natural resources are the resources that occur in nature, such as minerals in the Earth, trees, water, and air. The way people feel about and use resources changes not only as new technologies are developed but also as old technologies may begin to have a bad effect on the environment. In Europe, people are trying to control smog and acid rain. These results of old technologies are destroying buildings and statues, as well as the beautiful trees in places like the Black Forest.

Research how the use of natural resources has already changed in Europe and how it may change in the future.

Type of Resource	Past	Present	Future
Fuel for heating			
Fuel for ships			
Fuel for trains			
Fuel for cars			

Technology Impacts the Environment *(cont.)*

Type of Resource	Past	Present	Future
Materials for building			
Materials for containers			
Propellant for spray cans			
Material for paper			
Treatment of the air			
Use of water			

Movement Demonstrates Interdependence

Why does human activity require movement? _____

_____

_____

Do the people in your family go places?_____Choose two people and answer the following questions:

	Person #1	Person #2
Who?		
When?		
Where?		
How far?		
How often?		
Why?		
Mode of transportation?		

Movement Demonstrates
Interdependence *(cont.)*

Use reference sources to figure the distances between these European cities.

Lisbon/Rome _____

Paris/Berlin _____

Madrid/Athens _____

Warsaw/Prague _____

Oslo/Helsinki _____

Amsterdam/Vienna _____

Sophia/Minsk _____

Sarajevo/London _____

Riga/Brussels _____

Oslo/Stockholm _____

Dublin/Bern _____

Budapest/Zagreb _____

Athens 2970km.

Berlin 3190km

Rome 2900km.

Sarajevo 1900km

Movement Involves Linkages

List some of the ways people traveled in the past from place to place in Europe.

_____

_____

_____

_____

_____

List some of the ways people travel today from place to place in Europe.

_____

_____

_____

_____

_____

_____

Bonus Question!

Why have transportation methods changed over time in Europe?

_____

_____

_____

_____

_____

_____

Movement Involves Linkages *(cont.)*

How will people travel around Europe in the future?

_____

_____

_____

_____

Design your own future method of transportation. Explain it and then draw a picture of it below.

_____

_____

_____

_____

This Is How My Future Transportation Will Work:

_____

_____

_____

_____

This Is How My Future Transportation Will Look:

Movement Includes People, Ideas, and Products

People go places for business and for pleasure. Going somewhere for pleasure is called touring.

Where have you gone for pleasure?

_____

_____

_____

_____

Where would you like to go?

_____

_____

_____

_____

Ideas can travel too. List some of the different ways ideas travel from place to place.

_____

_____

_____

_____

Products also travel. What are some of the ways products travel?

_____

_____

_____

_____

Movement Includes People, Ideas, and Products *(cont.)*

Think about one of the places in Europe where you would like to travel for pleasure. Design a cover for a travel brochure about that place. Sketch your design below. Write a description of the place that will make other people want to travel there too.

_____

_____

_____

_____

The Mediterranean Coast

Plants and Animals Across the Curriculum

A region is a portion of the Earth's surface that has characteristics unlike any other. The Mediterranean coast of Europe is a region. The climate is warm and pleasant. Trees such as the *cork tree, umbrella pine tree, olive tree*, and *chestnut tree* grow there. Grapes are raised there. In many ways it is very much like Southern California.

All of Europe's wildlife has been greatly reduced by civilization and the Mediterranean coast is no exception. Wild animals cannot survive very long in civilized areas, and many of them now live only in zoos and animal preserves. Animals that were once more common in the Mediterranean area are the *Pyrenean ibex, Etruscan shrew, Greek tortoise, nightingale*, and *egret*, a bird prized for its beautiful feathers.

1. The Cork Tree

Many people have heard about cork trees because they have read the book *Ferdinand the Bull*. Be ready to report on this interesting tree. Find out where it grows, how people harvest the cork, and what it is used for. Write down any other facts that you think are interesting.

_____

_____

_____

_____

_____

_____

_____

_____

_____

2. The Nightingale

Write a poem about the nightingale. This bird's beautiful song has inspired many stories. Try to see a video tape or hear a recording of its song before you write your poem. Write your title here and use another piece of paper for your poem.

_____

The Mediterranean Coast *(cont.)*

Plants and Animals Across the Curriculum

3. Put the names of the italicized plants and animals on page 474 in ABC order and tell how many syllables are in each one.

_____   _____

_____   _____

_____   _____

_____   _____

_____   _____

4. The Etruscan Shrew

See what you can find out about this animal. What does it look like? Where does it live? Does it still live in the wild? Where did it get its name?

_____

_____

_____

_____

_____

_____

_____

_____

_____

The Mediterranean Coast *(cont.)*

Plants and Animals Across the Curriculum *(cont.)*

5. The Umbrella Pine

The umbrella pine is shaped like an umbrella. Find out some facts about this tree. Then write a legend about it. Call your legend "How the Umbrella Pine Got Its Shape."

_____

_____

_____

_____

_____

_____

_____

_____

_____

_____

_____

_____

_____

_____

_____

_____

_____

_____

_____

_____

_____

_____

_____

The Mediterranean Coast *(cont.)*

Plants and Animals Across the Curriculum *(cont.)*

6. The Egret

This beautiful bird almost became extinct earlier in the 20th century. Why was it hunted? What was done about it? See what you can find out.

_____

_____

_____

_____

_____

_____

_____

7. A Bar Graph

Make a bar graph comparing the Mediterranean coast of Europe with Southern California. Keep track of your facts here as you do your research.

	Mediterranean Coast	Southern California
Average high temperature		
Average low temperature		
Average rainfall		
Exports of wine		
Exports of olive oil		

Nordic Europe

Nordic Europe is the name given to the Scandinavian countries of Norway, Sweden, Denmark, Finland, and Iceland. These countries all share cultural similarities. Lapland, which is the traditional homeland of people called the Sami, crosses the boundaries of Norway, Sweden, and Finland above the Arctic Circle. Find these nations in reference books and answer these questions.

1. What natural process heats the hot springs in Iceland?

   _____

2. Which of these countries includes almost 500 islands?

   _____

3. What country is associated with the Nobel Prizes?

   _____

4. What is the national sport of Finland?

   _____

5. Sweden and Finland both have two official languages. What are they?

   _____

   _____

6. Which three of the countries are kingdoms?

   _____

   _____

   _____

Nordic Europe *(cont.)*

7. In which country do farmers specialize in the production and export of dairy products?

   _____

8. Which country has two self-governing possessions in the North Atlantic? What are the names of these possessions?

   _____

   _____

   _____

9. What famous statue overlooks Copenhagen's harbor?

   _____

10. What is Finland's greatest natural resource?

   _____

11. What are the narrow, steep-sided inlets of the sea on Norway's coasts called?

   _____

12. Which country uses geothermal energy for its heating needs?

   _____

Nordic Europe *(cont.)*

13. What is the capital city of each Nordic country?

    Iceland _____

    Norway _____

    Denmark _____

    Sweden _____

    Finland _____

14. What kind of money is used in each Nordic country?

    Iceland _____

    Norway _____

    Denmark _____

    Sweden _____

    Finland _____

15. What are the area and population of each Nordic country?

    Iceland _____

    Norway _____

    Denmark _____

    Sweden _____

    Finland _____

European Fact Game

This game can be played in different ways:

Game 1—You can use a Jeopardy format. Students love this, and they can set it up all by themselves or with just a little help. Run the answer cards on one color of paper and the question cards on another color for easy sorting.

Game 2—You can make a card game like rummy. All the cards should be run on one color for this. Shuffle the cards and deal five to each player. Put the leftovers facedown or in the middle of the table. Players draw from the stack and discard in another stack. The object of the game is to lay down pairs by matching questions and answers. You can make it more complicated by allowing students to challenge one another's matched pairs if they think the matches are incorrect. Have students keep track of the rules they make and write game directions.

Fact Game Cards

It is the highest point in Europe.	What is Mt. Elbrus?
It has the largest area of any country in Europe.	What is European Russia?
It has the greatest population of any country in Europe.	What is European Russia?

European Fact Game (cont.)

Fact Game Cards (cont.)

It is the second smallest continent.	What is Europe?
It is the longest river in Europe.	What is the Volga?
It is the smallest country in Europe.	What is Vatican City?
It is the lowest point in Europe.	What is the Caspian Sea?
This European bison now lives only on game reserves.	What is the wisent?
It has the highest population of any city in Europe.	What is Paris?

Fact Game Cards *(cont.)*

It is the smallest of the Baltic countries.	What is Estonia?
Its capital is Riga.	What is Latvia?
It is a city near the mouth of the Thames.	What is London?
It is the European country whose population is second in size only to European Russia's.	What is Germany?
It is the capital of Germany.	What is Berlin?
Its name means "the lowlands."	What is Netherlands?

European Fact Game (cont.)

Fact Game Cards (cont.)

This country began as a castle built on a cliff in 963.	What is Luxembourg?
This tiny country voted to end feudalism in June, 1993.	What is Andorra?
The East and West parts of this country were reunited in 1990.	What is Germany?
This German city is famous for its beer gardens and 16-day Oktoberfest.	What is Munich?
This country divided itself into the Czech Republic and Slovakia.	What was Czechoslovakia?
This country established colonies around the world in the 15th and 16th centuries.	What is Portugal?

484

European Fact Game *(cont.)*

Fact Game Cards *(cont.)*

Let your students make their own question-and-answer fact cards. Students usually like to make extra hard ones in hopes of stumping each other, so have them write the book and page number where the information can be found on the question card.

	Book:_____ Page: _____
	Book:_____ Page: _____
	Book:_____ Page: _____
	Book:_____ Page: _____
	Book:_____ Page: _____

The Geography Center

Putting the Center Together

You can set up your Geography Center in a corner of your classroom and make it as simple or as elaborate as you want. The center should have a map, a globe, and an atlas. (Several maps, a couple of globes, and multiple copies of the atlas would be even better.) A table and chairs will facilitate group activities and discussions. A supply of writing and drawing materials will also come in handy. A bookcase, shelf, or window sill can be utilized for storing reference books. The more reference books you can provide, the better the assigned projects will be. If you have access to a TV, VCR, and tapes, you can show movies about the places you are studying. There are many tapes of this variety available, and the visual learners in your class will really appreciate this. Cushions for sitting on the floor to read or view tapes add a cozy touch.

Making the Center Work

You can make the Geography Center part of your instructional day by scheduling groups to do center work. Change the materials daily or weekly or provide a set of task cards at the beginning of the unit and expect each student to work through them individually or as part of a group. (See pages 487–489.)

Use Portfolios

Have students make portfolios and store them in containers in an accessible area of your center. Try using the inexpensive but sturdy plastic crates that are available at local hardware stores. Make students responsible for their own progress by having them file their own work, both completed work and work in progress. Have students create attractive covers for their portfolios so the accumulated work can be attractively displayed at your school's open house.

Deck the Walls

Encourage artwork, creative writing, and exploratory math to go along with your geography unit and spread it throughout the curriculum. Display these products on a bulletin board in your Geography Center. Have students mount and post their own work. They can cut out letters and create colorful captions for the board.

Have another bulletin board reserved for posting newspaper and magazine articles dealing with the continent you are studying. Encourage your students to bring in these articles, share them, and discuss their meaning and importance.

Task Cards

Task Card #1

What is the longest river on the continent?

How long is it?

Through which country or countries does it flow?

Task Card #3

What is the highest mountain peak on the continent?

How tall is it?

In which country is it found?

Task Card #2

What is the most important mountain range on the continent?

How long is it?

In which country or countries are these mountains found?

Task Card #4

What is the largest country on the continent?

What countries or bodies of water border it?

What is its capital city?

The Geography Center *(cont.)*

Task Cards *(cont.)*

Task Card #5

What is the smallest country on the continent?

What countries or bodies of water border it?

What is its capital city?

Task Card #6

What is the largest lake on the continent?

In which country or countries is it found?

Which river is associated with it?

Task Card #7

What animals are associated with the continent?

In what country or countries do they live?

Are they in any danger in today's civilization?

Task Card #8

What variations in climate are found on the continent?

What variations in weather are found on the continent?

Can people live in all parts of the continent?

The Geography Center *(cont.)*

Task Card Response

Leave a stack of these task card response forms in the geography center for students to use.

Name _____ Date _____

Task Card #_____

Question #1

_____

_____

_____

_____

Question #2

_____

_____

_____

_____

Question #3

_____

_____

_____

_____

Bonus

I also learned_____

_____

_____

_____

The Culminating Activity: Making a Book

Method

You and your students can go about bookmaking in many different ways. Here are some suggestions:

- The book can be your students' showcase portfolios.

- Students can review and reflect upon the work they have accumulated in their portfolios, select the most representative samples or the pieces they like best, and put these things together in book form.

- The book can be a showcase portfolio based on the teacher's criteria.

- Have students select work from their portfolios based on a list you develop.

- The book can be comprised of new material that sums up the unit.

- Have students complete various assignments meant specifically for inclusion in their books, showing their grasp of the material. (See pages 491–501.)

Contents

In most cases you will probably want your students to include maps, facts about both physical and political geography, research about animals, people, and resources. They can review or report on any books they have read about the continent, and they can write about what they have learned and how it has affected the way they view the world.

Cover

You can specify and provide the design for the cover so that all of the books will be uniform, or you can encourage your students to design a cover that is representative of the continent. A collage of pictures cut from magazines and travel brochures is an option that works well.

Be sure to laminate the finished covers so the books can be used as part of your classroom library or Geography Center reference shelf. Your students may also want to share their books with students in other classes.

Exciting ideas for binding and publishing follow on pages 502–504.

The Culminating Activity:
Making a Book *(cont.)*

Trace an outline map of the continent. Transfer information about its physical features from all of the maps you have made. You might want to use different colors to create a key.

Name _____Date_____

Map of Physical Features

The Culminating Activity: Making a Book *(cont.)*

Use the information you have already gathered or do some new research to complete this page.

Name _____ Date_____

Facts About Physical Features

Area: _____

_____

Highest Point: _____

_____

Lowest Point: _____

_____

Largest Island:_____

_____

Longest River:_____

_____

Largest Lake: _____

_____

Tallest Waterfall:_____

_____

Largest Desert: _____

_____

Longest Reef: _____

_____

The Culminating Activity: Making a Book *(cont.)*

Trace an outline map of the continent. Transfer information about its political features from all of the maps you have made. You might want to use a numbered list to create a key.

Name _____Date_____

Map of Political Features

The Culminating Activity: Making a Book *(cont.)*

Use the information you have already gathered or do some new research to complete this page.

Name _____ Date_____

Facts About Political Features

Population: _____

Largest Country or Countries (by area):_____

Largest Country or Countries (by population): _____

Smallest Country or Countries (by area):_____

Smallest Country or Countries (by population): _____

Largest Metropolitan Area (by population):_____

_____

_____

_____

_____

_____

Newest Country/Countries:_____

_____

_____

_____

_____

_____

_____

The Culminating Activity: Making a Book *(cont.)*

Use the information you have already gathered or do some new research to complete this page.

Name _____ Date_____

The People

The people of this continent belong to these ethnic groups:

_____

_____

_____

They speak these languages:

_____

_____

_____

They live in these different environments:

_____

_____

_____

_____

Their ways of life have changed or are changing:

_____

_____

_____

_____

_____

The Culminating Activity: Making a Book *(cont.)*

Pick the city on the continent that is most interesting to you. Use the information you have already gathered or do some new research to complete this page.

Name _____ Date _____

The city of_____.

This city is in _____

Area: _____

Population: _____

_____

Language(s): _____

_____

Ethnic Groups: _____

_____

Religious Groups: _____

_____

Famous Natural Features: _____

_____

_____

Famous Constructed Features: _____

_____

_____

_____

_____

_____

The Culminating Activity: Making a Book (cont.)

Use the information you have already gathered or do some new research to complete this page.

Name _____ Date_____

The Animals

The best known animals of this continent are _____

_____

_____

The animals of this continent are important because _____

_____

_____

The animals that still live in their natural habitats are _____

_____

_____

The animals that are on the endangered list are _____

_____

_____

_____

They are on the endangered list because _____

_____

_____

_____

_____

The Culminating Activity: Making a Book *(cont.)*

Keep track of the books you read about the continent on this log.

Name _____ Date _____

Book Log

Title: _____   Fiction: _____

Author: _____   Nonfiction: _____

Illustrator: _____   Rating: _____

Title: _____   Fiction: _____

Author: _____   Nonfiction: _____

Illustrator: _____   Rating: _____

Title: _____   Fiction: _____

Author: _____   Nonfiction: _____

Illustrator: _____   Rating: _____

Title: _____   Fiction: _____

Author: _____   Nonfiction: _____

Illustrator: _____   Rating: _____

The Culminating Activity: Making a Book *(cont.)*

Use copies of this form to review your favorite nonfiction books about the continent you have been studying.

Name _____ Date_____

Book Review/Nonfiction

Title: _____

Author: _____

Illustrator: _____

Summary: _____

_____

_____

_____

_____

_____

Reasons I liked or did not like this book:_____

_____

_____

_____

_____

_____

_____

_____

Bonus!

If you liked this book and think other people should read it, you can do one of two things. (1) Write a paragraph or two telling how a nonfiction book can help you understand a continent or a country and post it on the bulletin board in the Geography Center. (2) Make a poster advertising the book and post it on the bulletin board in the Geography Center.

The Culminating Activity:
Making a Book *(cont.)*

Use copies of this form to review your favorite fiction books about the continent you have been studying.

Name _____ Date_____

Book Review/Fiction

Title: _____

Author: _____

Illustrator: _____

Summary: _____

_____

_____

_____

_____

_____

Reasons I liked or did not like this book:_____

_____

_____

_____

_____

_____

_____

Bonus!

If you liked this book and think other people should read it, you can do one of two things. (1) Write a paragraph or two telling how a fiction book can help you understand a continent or a country and post it on the bulletin board in the Geography Center. (2) Make a poster advertising the book and post it on the bulletin board in the Geography Center.

The Culminating Activity: Making a Book *(cont.)*

Write a reflective essay in which you discuss the ways that studying geography has given you a better understanding of the world and the people in it.

Name _____Date_____

Title:_____

_____

_____

_____

_____

_____

_____

_____

_____

_____

_____

_____

_____

_____

_____

_____

_____

_____

_____

The Culminating Activity:
Making a Book (cont.)

Book Binding Ideas

1. Stack all the pages of the book in a neat pile.

2. Place a blank sheet of paper on the top and bottom of the pages.

3. Leaving approximately 1/2" (1.25 cm) border, staple or sew all of the pages together on the left side.

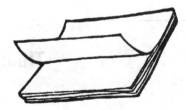

4. Place two pieces of lightweight cardboard side by side. (Cereal boxes work well.) Each piece should be 1/2 to 1" (1.25 to 2.5 cm) larger than the size of the pages in the book.

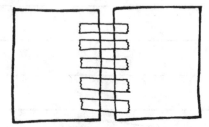

5. Leaving approximately 1" (2.5 cm) between them, tape the cardboard pieces together.

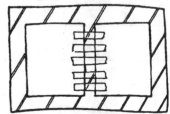

6. Put the cardboard on top of your covering material (e.g., fabric, wallpaper, contact paper, or wrapping paper). Glue the cardboard and covering material together, leaving a 1 to 1 1/2" (2.5 to 3.25 cm) material border.

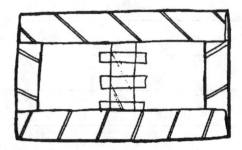

7. Fold up the edges of material over the cardboard and glue in place.

8. Glue the blank pages to the inside of the cardboard covers. Your book is ready to read and share.

The Culminating Activity: Making a Book *(cont.)*

Pop-Up Books

1. Fold a 8 1/2" x 11" (22 cm x 28 cm) piece of paper in half crosswise.

2. Measure and mark 2 3/4" (7 cm) from each side along the fold. Cut 2 3/4" (7 cm) slits at the marks.

3. Push cut area inside-out and crease to form the pop-up section.

4. Draw, color, and cut out the object to get "popped-up."

5. Glue it onto the pop-up section.

6. Glue two pages back to back, making sure the pop-up section is free.

7. Glue additional pages together, making as many pages (including pop-up pages) as you like. Be sure to include a free sheet on both the front and back so that those pages can be glued to a cover.

8. Glue a cover over the entire book.

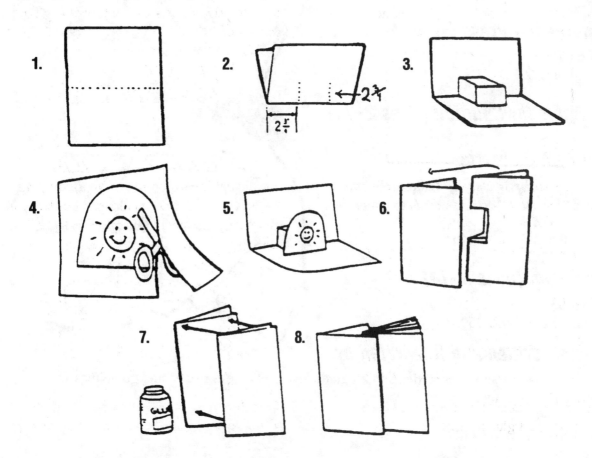

The Culminating Activity: Making a Book *(cont.)*

Real Markets for Student Writing

Student writing can be sent to the following addresses. Check your professional journals for more sources.

Children's Playmate (ages 5–8)

P.O. Box 567B
Indianapolis, Indiana 46206

Cricket (ages 6–12)

Cricket League
P.O. Box 300
Peru, Illinois 61354

Ebony Jr! (ages 6–12)

820 S. Michigan Avenue
Chicago, Illinois 60605

Flying Pencil Press (ages 8–14)

P.O. Box 7667
Elgin, Illinois 60121

Highlights for Children (ages 2–11)

803 Church Street
Honesdale, Pennsylvania 18431

Jack and Jill (ages 8–12)

P.O. Box 567B
Indianapolis, Indiana 46206

Stone Soup (ages 5–14)

P.O. Box 83
Santa Cruz, California 95063

National Written and Illustrated by...

(This is an awards contest for students in all grade levels. Write for rules and guidelines.)
Landmark Editions, Inc.
P.O. Box 4469
Kansas City, Missouri 64127

Software Review

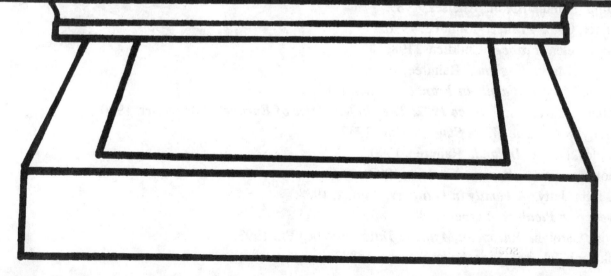

Software: *Swamp Gas Visits Europe* (Inline Software)

Hardware: Macintosh or Windows

Grade Level: Intermediate

Summary: The name Swamp Gas was given to unidentifiable cloud formations by the U.S. Air Force in the 1950s during their UFO investigations. *Swamp Gas Visits Europe* is a geography program where your students become the extraterrestrial "Swamp Gas" and fly around in their space craft to different locations in Europe. During each mission they search for specific cities and landmarks throughout Europe by answering questions about what they are looking for. When they successfully complete a mission, they are rewarded with the opportunity to play one of three different arcade games: Andromedroids, Fungus Patrol, or Quasar Rain.

This program has up-to-date information on Europe, provides multi-colored maps, and has generous on-screen help.

Bibliography

Allen, Peter. *The Origins of World War II.* Watts, 1992.

Atkinson, Ian. *The Viking Ships.* Cambridge Pr, 1979.

Bains, Rae. *Europe.* Troll, 1985.

Barker, Peter. *Eastern Europe.* Silver Burdett, 1979.

Biel, Timothy. *The Black Death.* Lucent Books, 1990.

Cairns, Trevor. *Europe Rules the World.* Cambridge Pr., 1981.

Caran, Betty. *Romania.* Childrens, 1988.

Crossland, Bert. *Where on Earth Are We?* Book Links, 1994.

Cross, Esther and Wilbur Cross. *Portugal.* Childrens, 1986.

Dickinson, Mary B. (Ed.). *National Geographic Picture Atlas of Our World.* National Geographic Society, 1993.

DuBois, Jill. *Greece.* Marshall Cavendish, 1992.

Dunnan, Nancy. *One Europe.* Millbrook, 1992.

Ecke, Worlfgang. *The Face at the Window.* Prentice Hall, 1979.

Europe at the Time of Greece & Rome. Raintree Steck-V, 1988.

Finland in Pictures. Lerner, 1991.

Flint, David. *The Baltic States: Estonia, Latvia, Lithuania.* Millbook, 1992.

Fradin, Dennis B. *The Netherlands.* Childrens, 1983.

Garett, Dan. *Germany.* Raintree, 1992.

Greene, Carol. *Austria.* Childrens, 1986.

Hargrove, Jim. *Germany.* Childrens, 1992.

Harris, Jonathan. *The Land and People of France.* Harper, 1989.

Horejs, Vit. *Twelve Iron Sandals: And Other Czechoslovak Tales.* Prentice Hall, 1985.

Hubley, Penny, and John Hubley. *A Family in Italy.* Lerner, 1987.

James, Ian. *Inside Italy.* Watts, 1988.

Kuniczak, W.S. *The Glass Mountain: Twenty-Six Ancient Polish Folktales and Fables.* Hippocrene, 1992.

Mayer, Marianna. *The Prince and the Princess: A Bohemian Fairy Tale.* Bantam, 1989.

Miller, Arthur. *Spain.* Chelsea, 1989.

Milner, Cate. *France.* Raintree, 1990.

Moss, Peter. *France.* Childrens, 1986.

Peplow, Mary. *England.* Raintree, 1990.

Regan, Mary. *A Family in France.* Lerner, 1985.

Roberts, Elizabeth. *Europe 1992: The United States of Europe?* Gloucester, 1990.

Seredy, Kate. *The White Stag.* Viking, 1937.

Shipley, Debra. *Ireland.* Raintree, 1990.

Sookram, Brian. *France.* Chelsea, 1990.

St. John, Jetty. *A Family in Hungary.* Lerner, 1988.

Sweden in Pictures. Lerner, 1990.

Swift, Carolyn. *European Myths & Tales.* Poolbeg Pr., 1993.

Yokatani, Takako. *Yugoslavia.* Stevens, 1988.

Bibliography *(cont.)*

Technology

Broderbund. ***MacGlobe & PC Globe.*** Available from Learning Services, (800)877-9378. disk

Broderbund. ***Where in the World Is Carmen Sandiego?*** Available from Troll, (800)526-5289. CD-ROM and disk

Bureau of Electronic Publishing Inc. ***World Fact Book.*** Available from Educational Resources, (800)624-2926. CD-ROM

CLEARVUE. ***The Earth, the Oceans, and Plants & Animals:*** Available from Educational Resources, (800)624-2926. CD-ROM

DeLorme Publishing. ***Global Explorer.*** Available from DeLorme Publishing, 1995. CD-ROM

Entrex. ***Europe: September 1, 1939.*** Available from Educational Resources, (800)624-2926 CD-ROM and disk

Impressions. ***My First World Atlas.*** Available from Educational Resources, (800)624-2926. disk

Inline Software/Focus Enhancements. ***Swamp Gas Visits Europe.*** Available from MacMall, (800)222-2808. disk

Lawrence. ***Nigel's World Adventures in World Geography.*** Available from Educational Resources, (800)624-2926. CD-ROM and disk

Magic Quest. ***Time Treks and Earth Treks.*** Available from Educational Resources, (800)624-2926. disk and CD-ROM

MECC. ***World GeoGraph.*** Available from Educational Resources, (800)624-2926. disk

Mindscape. ***World Atlas.*** Available from Educational Resources, (800)624-2926. disk

National Geographic. ***STV: World Geography.*** Available from National Geographic Educational Technology, (800)328-2936. videodisc

Newton Technology. ***GEOvista Tutor.*** Available from William K. Bradford, (800)421-2009. disk

Orange Cherry. ***Time Traveler.*** Available from Educational Resources, (800)624-2926. CD-ROM

Partnership Plus. ***Vol. 3: World Hot Spots.*** Educational Resources, (800)624-2926. disk

Pride in Learning. ***Global Issues.*** Available from Educational Resources, (800)624-2926. disk

Queue. ***Atlas Explorer.*** Available from Educational Resources, (800)624-2926. disk

Sanctuary Woods. ***Ecology Treks.*** Available from Learning Services, (800)624-2926. software and videodisc

Software Toolworks. ***World Atlas.*** Available from Learning Services, (800)877-9378. CD-ROM and disk

Answer Key

Page 449

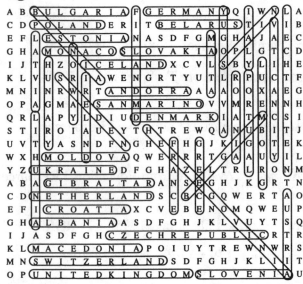

Page 461

1. Big Ben
2. Eiffel Tower
3. Leaning Tower
4. St. Peter's
5. canals
6. windmills
7. Colosseum
8. Parthenon
9. Louvre
10. Alhambra

Pages 478–480

1. volcanic action
2. Denmark
3. Sweden
4. cross-country skiing
5. Swedish and Finnish
6. Norway, Denmark, and Sweden
7. Denmark
8. Denmark. Greenland and the Faroe Islands
9. The Little Mermaid
10. forests of spruce, pine, and birch
11. fjords
12. Iceland

13. Iceland–Reykjavik
    Norway–Oslo
    Denmark–Copenhagen
    Sweden–Stockholm
    Finland–Helsinki

14. Iceland–Icelandic krona
    Norway–Norwegian krone
    Denmark–Danish krone
    Sweden–Swedish krona
    Finland–Finish markka

15. Iceland–39,791 sq. mi. (103,059 km^2)–260,000
    Norway–125,182 sq. mi. (324,221 km^2)–4,276,000
    Denmark–16,638 sq. mi. (43,092 km^2)–5,168,000
    Sweden–173,732 sq. mi. (449,966 km^2)–8,669,000
    Finland–130,558 sq. mi. (338,145 km^2)–5,028,000

Glossary

A absolute location—See exact location.
altiplano—a high plateau or valley between higher mountains; particularly the high plain where the Andes divide in Peru and Bolivia
altitude—the height of land above the level of the sea
Antarctic Circle—an imaginary circle parallel to the equator and 23 degrees 30' from the South Pole.
aquifer—an underground reservoir of water contained within a porous rock layer
archipelago—a group or chain of islands
Arctic Circle—an imaginary circle parallel to the equator and 23 degrees 30' from the North Pole.
atoll—a ring of coral islands encircling a lagoon
axis—an imaginary line that runs through the center of the Earth from the North Pole to the South Pole

B basin—an area of land that is surrounded by higher land
bay—a body of water having land on at least two sides
boundary—a line on a map that separates one country from another

C canal—a waterway dug across land for ships to go through
canyon—a deep valley with steep sides
cape—a piece of land that extends into a river, lake, or ocean
cardinal directions—the four main points of the compass: north, south, east, and west
cargo—a load of products carried from one place to another
cartographer—a map maker
channel—a waterway between two land masses; also, the part of a river that is deepest and carries the most water
climate—the kind of weather a region has over a long period of time
communication—the sending out of ideas and information; the means by which people do this
compass rose—the drawing that shows the directions of north, south, east, and west on a map
conservation—preserving valuable resources
continent—one of the seven main land masses on the earth's surface: North America, South America, Europe, Asia, Africa, Australia, and Antarctica
continental divide—the geographic area that separates the direction in which water currents flow
continental shelf—the shallow, gently sloping sea floor that surrounds each continent
country—the territory of a nation, marked by a boundary that separates it from other nations
current—a fast-moving stream of water in the ocean

D degree—one 360th part of the circumference of a circle; used as a unit of measurement
delta—an area of silt, sand, and gravel deposited at the mouth of a river
deposit—a large area of mineral deep in the Earth
desert—a very dry area of land covered with rocks and/or sand
distance scale—a measuring line on a map that helps to figure out the distance from one place to another
dormant volcano—a temporarily inactive volcano
drought—a long period without rain

E economic activity—a way that people use their resources to live
ecosystem—a system formed by the interaction of living organisms with each other and with their environment

Glossary *(cont.)*

environment—the surroundings in which everything lives

equator—the imaginary line that circles the middle of the earth, halfway between the North Pole and the South Pole

erosion—the wearing away of land by the elements (ice, sun, water, and wind)

escarpment—a cliff separating two nearly flat land surfaces that lie at different levels

estuary—the widening mouth of a river where it meets the sea; tides ebb and flow within this area

exact location—the location of a point which can be given in latitude and longitude, also called absolute location

extinct volcano—a totally inactive volcano

F

fertile—good for growing plants and crops

fjord—a narrow, steep-sided ocean inlet that reaches far into a coastline

forest—a large area covered with trees and undergrowth

frontier—land that is mostly unsettled

G

geothermal power—energy from heat within the Earth

geyser—a hot spring that shoots water and steam into the air

glacier—a large, thick, slow moving mass of ice

globe—a round model of the Earth

gorge—a deep, narrow passage between mountains

grassland—a wide area covered with grass and an occasional tree

grid—a series of evenly spaced lines used to locate places on a map

grove—a large field of trees

growing season—the period of time in which the weather is warm enough for crops to grow

gulf—an area of sea that is partly surrounded by land

H

harbor—a body of water sheltered by natural or artificial barriers and deep enough to moor ships

hemisphere—half of a sphere; on a globe, a hemisphere represents one half of the Earth

highland—an area of hills or mountains

humid—moist or damp

hurricane—a fierce storm of wind and rain

hydroelectric power—electric energy produced by water power

I

iceberg—a huge chunk of ice floating in the sea

ice sheet—a broad, thick layer of glacial ice that covers a wide area

irrigation—supplying water to dry land through pipes, ditches, or canals

island—a piece of land entirely surrounded by water

isthmus—a narrow strip of land that connects two larger landmasses and has water on both sides

---

J

jungle—a hot, humid area of land which is overgrown with trees and other plants

---

K

key—the section that explains the symbols used on a map

L

lagoon—a shallow body of water opening to the sea, protected by a sandbar or coral reef

lake—a body of water completely surrounded by land

landform—a shape of land, such as a mountain, valley, or plateau

landforms map—a map that uses colors to show the height and shape of the land; also called a contour map

---

Glossary (cont.)

landlocked country—a country surrounded by land without access to the sea
landmark—an important thing or place that stands out from everything around it
latitude line—an east-west line drawn parallel to the equator on a globe
lava—hot, liquid rock
location—the position of a point on the surface of the earth; can be exact or relative
longitude line—a north-south line drawn from pole to pole on a globe
lowland—a low, flat area of land

M

manufacturing—making finished goods from raw materials
map—a drawing of all or part of the earth's surface showing where things are located
meridian—any of the lines of longitude running north and south on a globe or map and representing a great circle of the earth that passes through the poles
mesa—a broad, flat-topped landform with steep sides found in arid or semiarid regions
mineral—a natural occurring substance found on the earth
mining—the process of taking mineral deposits from the earth
moisture—water or other liquids in the air or on the ground; wetness
monsoon—a wind that produces wet and dry seasons in southern and eastern Asia
moor—an open expanse of rolling land covered with grass or other low vegetation
moraine—an accumulation of debris carried and deposited by a glacier
mountain—a large mass of land that rises high above the surrounding land
mountain range—a group or series of mountains
mouth—the place where a river empties into a larger body of water

N

natural gas—a light mineral often used for fuel; usually found near petroleum
natural resource—something occurring in nature that people need or want
North Pole—the point located at the most northern place on a globe

O

oasis—a place in the desert where water from underground springs allows plants to grow
ocean—a large body of salt water that covers much of the earth's surface
ore—a mixture of rock, soil, and minerals
outback—the remote backcountry of Australia

P

parallel—any of the imaginary lines parallel to the equator and representing degrees of latitude on the Earth's surface
peninsula—a body of land almost completely surrounded by water
petroleum—an oily liquid mineral
place—an area having characteristics that define them and make them different from other areas
plain—a low, flat land area
plateau—an area of flat land higher than the land around it
pollution—damage to air, water, or land by smoke, dust, or chemicals
population—all of the people who live in a particular place
population density—the number of people living in each square mile or kilometer of an area
port—a place where ships can load
prairie—a large area of flat land covered with tall, thick grass
preservation—keeping things safe from damage or destruction
prime meridian (Greenwich Meridian)—the special longitude line that is the starting point for measuring all the other lines of longitude
projection—a way of transferring the features of the Earth as represented on a globe to a flat piece of paper (map); the resulting style of map

Glossary *(cont.)*

rain forest—dense forest mostly composed of broadleaved evergreens found in wet tropical regions

ravine—a narrow valley with steep sides

raw material—a material in its natural state, used for making finished goods

reef—a narrow ridge of rock, sand, or coral just above or below the surface of the water

region—an area having distinctive characteristics that make it different from the surrounding areas

relative location—the location of a point on the earth's surface in relation to other points

reservoir—a lake or pond where water is stored for future use

resource—a supply of valuable or useful things such as water, coal, soil, forests, or air; see natural resource

revolution—the movement of the Earth in orbit around the sun; one complete revolution equals a year

river—a large stream of water flowing in a channel

rotation—the movement of the earth turning on its axis; one complete rotation equals 24 hours

rural—away from cities and close to farms

savanna—a tropical grassland with scattered trees

scale—the ratio of map distance to actual distance on the Earth's surface

sea—a large body of salt water

sound—a long, broad ocean inlet usually parallel to the coast, or a long stretch of water separating an island from the mainland

South Pole—the point located at the most southern place on a globe

state—the strongest governing body, subordinate to a national government. (Not to be confused with the nation-state.)

steppe—a grassland in the temperate zone where limited rainfall prevents tree growth

strait—a narrow waterway that connects two seas

swamp—a lowland area covered with shallow water and dense vegetation

symbol—something that stands for a real thing

temperature—the measure of how hot or cold a place is

territory—a region that is owned or controlled by another country or political unit.

time zone—one of 24 areas or zones of the Earth in which the time is one hour earlier than in the zone to its east

tributary—a river or stream that flows into a larger body of water

transportation—the way in which people or goods travel or are moved from one place to another

Tropic of Cancer—the parallel of latitude that lies 23 degrees 27' north of the equator

Tropic of Capricorn—the parallel of latitude that lies 23 degrees 27' south of the equator

tundra—a wide, treeless arctic plain where few plants or animals live because of frozen subsoil called permafrost

urban sea—the city and its surrounding built-up area

valley—a long, low area between hills or mountains

volcano—an opening in the earth's surface through which hot liquid rock (magma) and other materials are forced out

weather—the condition of the air at a certain time or place
